# THE AMERICAN MUSICAL
### by Tom Vallance

*Above : Gene Kelly*

# THE AMERICAN MUSICAL

## by TOM VALLANCE

CASTLE BOOKS — NEW YORK

# Acknowledgements

I would like to thank the many people without whose generous assistance this book would not have been possible. The major film companies—Columbia, M-G-M, Paramount, Twentieth Century-Fox, United Artists, Universal and Warners—were all helpful with information and stills, and I would offer special thanks to Jo Wimshurst (Fox), Carole Fleming and Edward Patman (M-G-M), who were of particular assistance. The facilities and staff of the British Film Institute and the Westminster Library were of immeasurable help, while for various forms of assistance I am grateful to Peter Armitage, Jamie Bloy, Alec Bregonzi, John and Barbara Cutts, Bernard Hrusa, Neil Stevens, Michael Sutton and Geoffrey Wheatley. Particular thanks go to Douglas McVay for correcting portions of the manuscript and offering invaluable suggestions for its improvement. Finally, I would like to dedicate this book to my sister Jean, who first introduced me to the world of the Hollywood movie.

COVER STILLS
Front: Cyd Charisse and Fred Astaire in *The Band Wagon*
(courtesy of M-G-M)
Back: (top) Marilyn Monroe in *Bus Stop*
(below) the "Dancing" number from *Hello Dolly!*
(both courtesy of 20th Century-Fox)

This Edition Published by Arrangement
With A. S. Barnes & Co., Inc.

Printed in the United States of America

# Introduction

THE MUSICAL is a form that has always been the particular property of Hollywood. The first talkie was a musical and throughout the years most of the major studios have relied heavily on the form—Warners got out of the red in the early Thirties with Al Jolson and the Busby Berkeley extravaganzas; RKO became an important company with Astaire and Rogers; Deanna Durbin helped save Universal from bankruptcy; during the war years Fox relied on Grable and Paramount on Crosby to satisfy an escapism-seeking public, while in the Forties the word M-G-M and "musical" became almost synonymous.

This book is a guide to the artists who gave Hollywood supremacy in the form of the musical. It lists their musical credits with a small amount of biographical material and comment. Though complete objectivity is probably impossible, I have generally tried to keep any controversial views in check and have given what are mainly widely-held judgements and opinions on the artists involved.

Only musicals are covered by the book, and filmographies include only films in this *genre*. I have, though, tried to include for all major artists any film in which song or musical content was important, however small. Comedies, Westerns and dramas in which song or dance played an important part are included, and distinguished by the abbreviations shown in the Key. Singing cowboys, who proliferated in second-features during the late Thirties, have been omitted as they are really part of another *genre* entirely. Similarly comics are omitted unless their musical contributions were particularly strong. (e.g. Bob Hope and Dean Martin are in, Jerry Lewis and Abbott & Costello out). Non-musicals are sometimes mentioned in the text and occasionally (in the case of theme songs) in filmographies. These are described as such and not included in the Index.

Song titles are listed under both composers and stars, in the latter case when the song concerned has become particularly associated with the star. It has not been possible for space reasons to list all songs composed for a film under the composer, but notable songs have been included. When song listings are preceded by the abbreviation 'inc.' it means that only part of a score is listed—song titles listed without this comprise the entire work of the composer concerned for that particular film. Only songs composed directly for the screen are listed, unless otherwise stated. Thus no titles are listed after Berlin's *This Is the Army*, for example, as the score was originally written for the stage.

If a film is a re-make of another musical, the information is listed in the filmography of the director. If the director is not in the book, then the information will be listed under the film's major star. When a star has appeared in a re-make of his own film, then this is mentioned in his filmography.

This sort of retrospective guide is bound to be largely nostalgic, but perhaps even more so in the case of the musical, for no form has been harder hit by the economic and distribution problems faced by Hollywood since the early Fifties. For this reason many filmographies seem to come to a dead halt around this period and rather than repeat the comment "career hampered by lack of musical production," I have left it unsaid. But should the reader wonder what suddenly happened to Cyd Charisse,

*"Prehistoric Man" : Frank Sinatra, Ann Miller and Jules Munshin in ON THE TOWN*

Ann Miller, Vera-Ellen and others, the answer is that Hollywood just wasn't providing parts for them any more.

THE NUMBERING of entries is for the Index, which starts on page 156. Films are listed in order of release, the year of release being listed in the Index.

Commas separate film titles, except in cases of particularly long periods between musicals, in which case they are separated by a semi-colon.

The film's original title is listed first—if it was changed for British release this title is given afterwards, with a stroke between, e.g. *Damn Yankees/What Lola Wants.*

Most abbreviations used will be self-explanatory (Dir. for *directed,* etc.) but less familiar ones are as follows: cs = comedy with songs, ds = drama with songs, ws = Western with songs, MD = Musical Director (conductor), orch. = orchestrated, ch. = choreographed, comp. = composed, intro. = introduced, st. = story, sc. = screenplay. The abbreviation Co. used with any of these means that the work was done in collaboration.

6

**1 ABBOTT, GEORGE** (1889–    ). Stage director and librettist noted for breathless pace and tempo. Occasional films.

Films as dir: *Why Bring That Up?; Too Many Girls.* Co-prod., co-dir. *The Pajama Game, Damn Yankees/What Lola Wants.*

**2 ADAMSON, HAROLD** (1906–    ). Lyricist who worked mainly with Jimmy McHugh (q.v.). Wrote poetry at college, contributed to Harvard revues.

Films: *Dancing Lady* (inc. "Everything I Have Is Yours"), *Bottoms Up, Strictly Dynamite, Palooka, Kid Millions, Folies Bergere, Reckless, A Perfect Gentleman, Here Comes the Band, The Great Ziegfeld, Banjo on My Knee* (ds), *When Love Is Young, Hitting a New High, Breezing Home, You're a Sweetheart, Top of the Town* (inc. "Where Are You?"), *Merry-go-round of 1938, Youth Takes a Fling, Road to Reno, Mad about Music* (inc. "I Love to Whistle"), *That Certain Age, Hold That Ghost* ("Aurora"), *Around the World, Hit Parade of 1943, Higher and Higher* (inc. "I Couldn't Sleep a Wink Last Night"), *Four Jills in a Jeep, Something for the Boys, Nob Hill, Doll Face/Come Back to Me, Bring on the Girls, Do You Love Me?, Calendar Girl, Hit Parade of 1947, Smash Up/A Woman Destroyed* (ds), *If You Knew Susie, A Date with Judy* ("It's a Most Unusual Day"), *His Kind of Woman* (ds, "You'll Know"), *Gentlemen Prefer Blondes* ("When Love Goes Wrong," "Ain't There Anyone Here for Love?").

**3 ALEXANDER, ROD** (1920–    ). Choreographer, former dancer. In chorus 1938, formed own dance company 1958, supervised script, lyrics and choreographed first Japanese Western-style musical *Asphalt Girl* 1964. Danced in *The Heat's On/Tropicana, Ziegfeld Follies, Tars and Spars, Down to Earth.* Ch. *Carousel, The Best Things in Life Are Free.*

**4 ALLYSON, JUNE** (1917–    ). RN: Ella Geisman. Favourite girl next door of the Forties whose fresh personality and huskily individual voice made her a top attraction. Born in Bronx, learned dancing by watching Astaire–Rogers films. Made 2-reelers in 1937; became Broadway chorus girl. Understudied Betty Hutton (q.v.) in *Panama Hattie,* chosen by George Abbott (q.v.) for a lead in *Best Foot Forward* and signed by M-G-M to repeat role in film version. Often the wallflower who won hero at the end. Although an actress of ability, found transition to mature roles difficult, becoming typecast as understanding wife. Now does television and theatre.

Films: *Best Foot Forward, Girl Crazy* (sang and danced "Treat Me Rough" with Mickey Rooney q.v.), *Thousands Cheer, Meet the People, Two Girls and a Sailor* (first star part), *Music for Millions, Her Highness and the Bellboy* (ds), *Two Sisters from Boston, Till the Clouds Roll By, Good News, Words and Music* (her "Thou Swell" with the Blackburn Twins stands up today as best sequence in the film), *Remains to Be Seen* (cs), *The Glenn Miller Story* (her last completely effective role), *The Opposite Sex, You Can't Run away from It.*

**5 ALTON, JOHN** (1901–    ). Hungarian-born photographer who wrote, photographed and directed many Spanish pictures besides working in Hollywood. Won Oscar for ballet in *An American in Paris.*

Films: *Melody for Three, Johnny Doughboy, Atlantic City, Lake Placid Serenade, Grounds for Marriage, An*

*"Thou Swell": June Allyson and the Blackburn Twins in WORDS AND MUSIC*

*American in Paris* (ballet only), *Designing Woman* (cs).

**6 ALTON, ROBERT** (1903–1957). RN: Robert Alton Hart. Choreographer of some of the film musical's most memorable routines. Though his *ensemble* work has sometimes dated, his work with couples is unsurpassed. Staged Astaire–Bremer sequences in *Ziegfeld Follies* and was equally successful with Astaire and Vera-Ellen *(Belle of New York)*, Vera-Ellen and Donald O'Connor *(Call Me Madam)*, O'Connor and Debbie Reynolds *(I Love Melvin)*, and the Champions *(Show Boat)*. Also worked well with Judy Garland (q.v.) and later staged her act at the Palace. Studied with Mikhail Mordkin and started as dancer, turning choreographer for Broadway musicals inc. *Anything Goes, Hellzapoppin* and *Pal Joey*. First Hollywood film 1935, later worked at M-G-M, occasionally directing.

*Robert Alton with Vera-Ellen*
*on the set of WHITE CHRISTMAS*

Films: Ch. *Strike Me Pink, Two Faced Woman* (cs, also danced as Garbo's partner), *You'll Never Get Rich, Ziegfeld Follies, Till the Clouds Roll By, The Pirate, Easter Parade, The Kissing Bandit, Words and Music* (except "Slaughter on Tenth Avenue"), *The Barkleys of Broadway, In the Good Old Summertime, Annie Get Your Gun, Pagan Love Song* (also dir.), *Show Boat* (51), *The Belle of New York, I Love Melvin, Call Me Madam, There's No Business like Show Business, White Christmas, The Girl Rush* (also assoc. prod.), *The Country Girl* (ds).

**7  AMECHE, DON** (1908–    ). RN: Dominic Amici. Stolid actor-singer who left law school to become radio actor. Signed by Fox in 1936, and remained one of studio's staples for many years. Frequently stars on Broadway.

Films: *Ramona, One in a Million, You Can't Have Everything, In Old Chicago* (ds), *Alexander's Ragtime Band, Josette, Three Musketeers, Hollywood Cavalcade, Swanee River* (as composer Stephen Foster), *Lillian Russell, Down Argentine Way, That Night in Rio, Moon over Miami, Kiss the Boys Goodbye, Something to Shout About, Greenwich Village, Slightly French.*

**8  ANDERSON, Eddie "Rochester"** (1905–    ). Negro comedian with rolling eyes and gravel voice who also sings and dances. Started in vaudeville and night clubs. Long associated with comedian Jack Benny in radio, TV and films.

Films: *Thanks for the Memory, Buck Benny Rides Again, Birth of the Blues, Kiss the Boys Goodbye, Star Spangled Rhythm, Tales of Manhattan* (ds), *Cabin in the Sky* (as Little Joe, his best film role), *Stormy Weather, What's Buzzin' Cousin?, Broadway Rhythm, I Love a Band-leader.*

**9  ANDREWS, JULIE** (1934–    ). RN: Julia Welles. British singing star, an older successor to Deanna Durbin (q.v.), whose film roles are invariably sweet but saved from cloying by actress's skill. Former child singer and part of vaudeville act with parents. Not considered for film version of *My Fair Lady*, in which she had originated part of Eliza, she went on to win an Oscar for first film role.

Films: *Mary Poppins* (début), *The Sound of Music, Hawaii* (ds), *Thoroughly Modern Millie, Star!* (also known as *Those Were the Happy Times*), *Darling Lili.*

**10  ANDREWS SISTERS, THE. Patti** (1920–    ), **Maxene** (1918–    ),

9

*Julie Andrews in DARLING LILI*

**La Verne** (1915–1967). Close-harmony group of such popularity during the Forties that several B pictures were built around their talents.

Films: *Argentine Nights, Buck Privates/ Rookies, In the Navy, Hold That Ghost, Give Out Sisters* (intro. "Pennsylvania Polka"), *Private Buckaroo, What's Cooking?, How's about It?* (in which they sang their 1939 hit "Beer Barrel Polka" with new lyrics as "Here Comes the Navy"), *Always a Bridesmaid, Moonlight and Cactus, Follow the Boys* (44), *Swingtime Johnny* (intro. "Boogie Woogie Bugle Boy"), *Hollywood Canteen* (intro. "Don't Fence Me In"), *Make Mine Music* (voices only), *Melody Time* (voices only), *Road to Rio* (intro. "You Don't Have to Know the Language").

10

## 11  ANIMATION IN THE MUSICAL.

The name of WALT DISNEY dominates the history of musical cartoons in America. His "Silly Symphony" shorts in the early Thirties, setting all the action to music, led in 1933 to a colour cartoon short, *The Three Little Pigs*, with its hit tune "Who's Afraid of the Big Bad Wolf?" Its tremendous success spurred Disney to think of feature-length cartoons and in 1937, after years of work, came *Snow White and the Seven Dwarfs*, the biggest musical success of its year. Frank Churchill, the composer who with Ann Ronell had written the hit from *Three Little Pigs,* collaborated with Larry Morey for the score which included "Heigh Ho, Heigh Ho," "Someday My Prince Will Come" and "Whistle While You Work." Leigh Harline and Ned Washington supplied the songs for Disney's next, *Pinocchio,* including "Got No Strings," "Hi Diddle-dee-dee" and the 1940 Oscar-winner "When You Wish upon a Star." New ground was again broken by *Fantasia,* setting a series of episodes to classical music, recorded by Leopold Stokowski in stereophonic sound and filmed in a wide-screen process. Churchill and Washington collaborated on songs for *Dumbo,* the hit being "When I See an Elephant Fly," and Churchill did the songs for *The Reluctant Dragon,* which mingled live action with cartoons. The endearing and moving *Bambi,* five years in the making, had a delightful score by Churchill and Morey, including "Little April Shower," "Love Is a Song" and a splendid background score by Churchill and Ed Plumb. Disney's next, *Saludos Amigos* was an ambitious blending of live action with animation. It featured Aurora Miranda, sister of Carmen (q.v.), and included Latin-American favourites "Brazil" and "Tico Tico." *The Three Caballeros* had the title

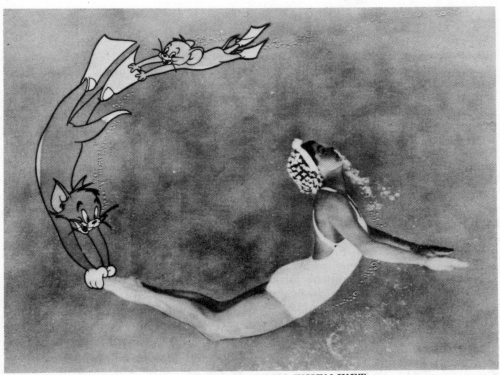

*Tom and Jerry with Esther Williams in DANGEROUS WHEN WET*

characters, one of whom was Donald Duck, touring South America in another mixture of live action and animation, while *Make Mine Music* was a collection of ten short cartoons, attempting to do for popular music what *Fantasia* did for classical. Charles Wolcott and Ray Gilbert composed the popular "Two Silhouettes." *Song of the South,* which linked the Uncle Remus stories about Brer Rabbit and his friends with live action in which James Baskett played the story-teller had that year's Oscar-winning song "Zip-a-dee-doo-dah," but is now considered so racially patronising that it is withheld from re-issue. *Fun and Fancy Free* and *Melody Time* were both collections of musical shorts similar to *Make Mine Music,* while *Ichabod and Mr. Toad* combined just two stories, "The Legend of Sleepy Hollow," narrated and

sung by Bing Crosby (q.v.), and "The Wind in the Willows," narrated by Basil Rathbone. In 1950 Disney produced his first full-length entirely animated cartoon since *Bambi* to concentrate on one story, Cinderella, its score by Mack David, Al Hoffman and Jerry Livingston including "A Dream Is a Wish Your Heart Makes" and "Bibbidi-bobbidi-boo." The same team wrote the amusing "A Very Merry Un-birthday" for *Alice in Wonderland,* though most of that film's score was by Bob Hilliard and Sammy Fain (q.v.). Fain and Sammy Cahn (q.v.) wrote the songs for *Peter Pan.* Disney's first cartoon in CinemaScope, *The Lady and the Tramp,* revealed a growing sophistication in the drawing and had an amusing score by Sonny Burke and Peggy Lee (q.v.) including "He's a Tramp" and "The Siamese Cat Song." *The Sleeping Beauty,*

11

one of the most expensive cartoon films of all time, fared disappointingly with critics and public but *101 Dalmatians,* with its score by George Bruns, was a complete success. A mis-guided re-make of *Babes in Toyland* (61) mingled cartoon sequences with live action, but with *The Sword in the Stone* Disney went back to complete animation. Cartoon characters danced with live ones again in *Mary Poppins,* as Julie Andrews and Dick Van Dyke (qq.v.) sang "Jolly Holiday" with a collection of farm animals. Disney's last cartoon was *The Jungle Book,* with a score by the Sherman brothers (q.v.) and based on the Kipling stories. Few producers have tried to emulate Disney with full-length cartoon musicals, but notable exceptions were DAVE and MAX FLEISCHER, creators of Popeye, who produced *Gulliver's Travels,* with its hit song "It's a Hap-Hap-Happy Day" composed by Sammy Timberg, Winston Sharples and Al J. Neiburg, and *Mr. Bug Goes to Town/Hoppity Goes to Town,* with its score by Frank Loesser and Hoagy Carmichael (qq.v.). UPA, creators of Mr. Magoo, put him into the full-length *1001 Arabian Nights* and combined the voice of Judy Garland (q.v.) with the music of Harold Arlen (q.v.) in *Gay Purr-ee,* while Charles Schulz's "Peanuts" strip was brought to the screen by LEE MENDELSON and BILL MELENDEZ in *A Boy Named Charlie Brown,* with songs by Rod McKuen. Interpolated cartoon sequences are more frequent, dating back to *Hollywood Party* in 1934, but the blending of live action with cartoons, even in the best of Disney, is generally unsatisfying, leaving an impression of giving the best of neither world, the unfocused stare of the live characters and the trick photography involved destroying to some extent the feeling of spontaneity and freshness.

Most successful of such sequences is the celebrated dance routine by Gene Kelly (q.v.) and Jerry the mouse in *Anchors Aweigh.* Kelly danced with cartoons again in *Invitation to the Dance,* while Jerry popped up with his partner Tom the cat to share a dream sequence under water with Esther Williams (q.v.) in *Dangerous when Wet. The Girl Next Door* featured a cartoonist as its hero, a good enough excuse to involve its star Dan Dailey (q.v.) with some UPA characters in a dance sequence. The "Put on a Happy Face" number in *Bye Bye Birdie* was, perhaps, typical of these attempts, the addition of animation diminishing the impact of what might have been a pleasing dance routine by Dick Van Dyke (q.v.) and Janet Leigh (q.v.).

**12 ANN-MARGRET** (1941–     ). RN: Ann Margret Olson. Torrid Swedish-born dancer-actress, former radio and band singer.

Films: *Pocketful of Miracles* (cs, début), *State Fair* (62), *Bye Bye Birdie, Viva Las Vegas/Love in Las Vegas, The Pleasure Seekers* (cs), *Made in Paris* (cs), *The Swinger* (cs).

**13 ARLEN, HAROLD** (1905–     ). Prolific composer of Broadway and Hollywood scores. Was singer-pianist until a rehearsal vamp became "Get Happy" and changed course of his career.

Films: *Manhattan Parade, Take a Chance* ("It's only a Paper Moon"), *Let's Fall in Love, Strike Me Pink, The Singing Kid, Stage Struck, Gold Diggers of 1937, Artists and Models* (37), *Love Affair* (ds), *Babes in Arms* ("God's Country"), *At the Circus* (inc. "Lydia the Tattooed Lady"), *The Wizard of Oz* (1940 Oscar, "Over the Rainbow"), *Road to Zanzibar, Blues in the Night, Rio Rita* (42), *Cabin in the Sky* (inc. "Happiness is a Thing Called Joe," "Life's Full O'Consequence"), *Star Spangled Rhythm* (inc. "Hit the Road to Dreamland," "That Old Black Magic"), *The Sky's the Limit* (inc. "My Shining Hour," "One for My Baby"), *Here Come the Waves* (inc. "Accentuate the Positive," "Let's Take the Long Way Home"), *They Got Me Covered* (cs), *Up in Arms* (inc. "Now I Know"), *Kismet* (ds, 44), *Out of This World, Casbah, My Blue Heaven, The Petty Girl/Girl of the Year, Down among the Sheltering Palms, Mr. Imperium/You Belong to My Heart, The Farmer Takes a Wife* (inc. "Today I Love Everybody"), *A Star Is Born* (inc. "The Man That Got Away"), *The Country Girl* (ds), *Gay Purree, I Could Go On Singing* (Brit.).

**14 ARMSTRONG, LOUIS** (1900– ). Gravel-voiced Negro trumpeter, one of the greats of jazz, who has also shown the ability to handle a comic line. Born in New Orleans, made professional *début* with Kid Ory's band in 1917. His mopping handkerchief is a trademark. Has appeared sporadically in films since Thirties.

Films: *Pennies from Heaven, Artists and Models* (37), *Every Day's a Holiday, Doctor Rhythm, Going Places* (intro. "Jeepers Creepers"), *Cabin in the Sky, Jam Session, Atlantic City, Pillow to Post* (cs), *New Orleans, A Song Is Born, The Strip, Here Comes the Groom, Glory Alley, The Glenn Miller Story, High Society* (intro. "Now You Has Jazz" with Bing Crosby, q.v.), *Jazz on a Summer's Day, The Five Pennies* (inc. duet with Danny Kaye, q.v., "When the Saints Go Marching In"), *Paris Blues* (ds), *When the Boys Meet the Girls, A Man Called Adam* (ds), *Hello Dolly!*

**15 ARNAUD, LEO** (1904– ). French-born arranger, former symphony conductor and musical director in France and England before joining Fred Waring's band in U.S.A. 1936: to M-G-M as vocal coach, composer and music director, later free-lancing.

Films: Co-orchestrated: *Babes in Arms, Broadway Melody of 1940, Two Girls on Broadway, Lady Be Good, The Big Store, Babes on Broadway, Panama Hattie, Rio Rita* (42), *Ship Ahoy, For Me and My Gal, DuBarry Was a Lady, Best Foot Forward, Calendar Girl* (solo), *One Touch of Venus, Easter Parade, A Date with Judy, Three Little Words, Lovely to Look At, Rose Marie* (54), *Stars and Stripes Forever/Marching Along, Seven Brides for Seven Brothers*.

**16 ASTAIRE, FRED** (1899– ). RN: Frederick Austerlitz. Generally considered the greatest dancer the cinema has known. Has a distinctive style all his own—springy walk, crooked grin, oddly attractive singing voice allied to tremendous precision and skill of dancing. Started in vaudeville as dancing act with sister Adele, with whom starred in musical comedy inc. *Funny Face, Lady Be Good*. First screen test a disaster ("Can't sing. Can't act. Can dance a little.") Partnered Joan Crawford (q.v.) as guest star in *Dancing Lady*, then came *Flying Down to Rio* and start of partnership with Ginger Rogers (q.v.). Top composers wrote for their films and Astaire has probably introduced more great standards than any other film star, including Crosby (q.v.). Irving Berlin (also q.v.) once said, "I'd rather have Astaire sing my songs than anyone else." Throughout Thirties he expanded scope of screen choreography with virtuoso solos, dazzlingly romantic duets, miniature modern ballets leading to the surreal exoticism of *Ziegfeld Follies* and *Yolanda and the Thief* and creating atmosphere in which Gene Kelly (q.v.) took the film musical to new heights. Announced retirement with *Blue Skies*, but agreed to replace an indisposed Kelly in *Easter Parade*, which started another brilliant decade. Took first non-musical role 1959 *(On the Beach)*. Appears with great success on TV and is still active in films, though he has declared *Finian's Rainbow* his dancing swan-song. Oscar 1949 for "raising the standards of all musicals."

Films: *Dancing Lady* (début), *Flying down to Rio, The Gay Divorcee, Roberta, Top Hat, Follow the Fleet, Swing Time, Shall We Dance?, Damsel in Distress, Carefree, The Story of Vernon and Irene Castle, Broadway Melody of 1940, Second Chorus, You'll Never Get Rich, Holiday Inn, You Were Never Lovelier, The Sky's the Limit, Ziegfeld Follies, Yolanda and the Thief, Blue Skies, Easter Parade, The Barkleys of Broadway, Three Little Words, Let's Dance, Royal Wedding/ Wedding Bells, The Belle of New York, The Band Wagon, Daddy Long Legs, Funny Face, Silk Stockings, Paris When It Sizzles* (voice only, singing "That Face"); *Finian's Rainbow*.

**17  AUER, JOHN H.** (1906–    ). Hungarian-born director of several minor but pleasant musicals for RKO and Republic. Started by directing foreign versions of Universal films.

Films: *Frankie and Johnny* (35), *Outside of Paradise, Hit Parade of 1941, Moonlight Masquerade, Johnny Doughboy, Tahiti Honey, Music in Manhattan, Seven Days Ashore, Pan Americana, Beat the Band, Hit Parade of 1951*.

**18  AVALON, FRANKIE** (1939–    ). RN: Francis Avallone. Popular singer, a trumpet prodigy at nine, later a top recording star who made several 'teenage-slanted musicals.

Films: *The Alamo* (ws), *Beach Party, Muscle Beach Party, Bikini Beach, Beach Blanket Bingo, Jet Set, I'll Take Sweden* (cs), *Skidoo* (cs).

**19  BACON, LLOYD** (1889–1955). Director of the memorable *Forty-Second Street* and several lively backstage musicals of the Thirties with spirited putting-on-a-show atmosphere, wise-cracking chorines and Busby Berkeley (q.v.) numbers. Later musicals were generally routine and sometimes less. Was a stage actor (in Wilde's *Salome*) then acted in Chaplin shorts before graduating to directing in 1921. Worked with Sennett and at Universal before Warner contract.

Films: *The Singing Fool, Honky Tonk, Say It with Songs, So Long Letty, She Couldn't Say No, Fifty Million Frenchmen, Manhattan Parade, The Crooner, Forty-Second Street, Footlight Parade, Wonder Bar, In Caliente, Broadway Gondolier, Cain and Mabel, Gold Diggers of 1937, Sons O'Guns, Ever Since Eve, San Quentin* (ds), *Cowboy from Brooklyn, Navy Blues, Wake Up and Dream* (46),

*Pearl Bailey*

*I Wonder Who's Kissing Her Now?, You Were Meant for Me* (re-make of *Orchestra Wives*), *Give My Regards to Broadway, Call Me Mister, Golden Girl, The I Don't Care Girl, Walking My Baby Back Home, The French Line.*

**20 BAILEY, PEARL** (1918–   ). Negro singer and comedienne, more active in cabaret and theatre than films. Won contest when fifteen, toured as dancer.

Films: *Variety Girl* (début), *Isn't It Romantic?, Carmen Jones, That Certain Feeling* (cs), *St. Louis Blues* (58), *Porgy and Bess, All the Fine Young Cannibals* (ds).

**21 BAKER, KENNY** (1912–   ). Tenor with rather wooden style who played juvenile lead in several musicals.

Films: *King of Burlesque, Fifty-Second Street, Mr. Dodd Takes the Air, Turn off the Moon, The King and the Chorus Girl, Goldwyn Follies, The Mikado* (in G.B.), *Love on Toast, Radio City Revels, At the Circus, Hit Parade of 1941, Silver Skates, Stage Door Canteen, Doughboys in Ireland, The Harvey Girls, Calendar Girl.*

**22 BALL, LUCILLE** (1910–   ). Comedienne whose talents were rarely fully exploited by the cinema. Started as a Goldwyn Girl and spent several years in chorus before graduating to leading roles (notably in *The Big Street*). Though a hit in Broadway musical *Wildcat* (60), her singing voice in films was dubbed. Scored biggest success of career with TV series *I Love Lucy*. Has since made several film comedies, but concentrates on television.

Films: *Roman Scandals* (début), *Broadway Through a Keyhole, Hold That Girl* (cs), *Bottoms Up, Moulin Rouge, Kid Millions, Murder at the Vanities, Roberta, Top Hat, I Dream Too Much, That Girl from Paris, Follow the Fleet, The Joy of Living, Having a Wonderful Time, That's Right You're Wrong, Dance Girl Dance, Too Many Girls, Seven Days Leave, The Big Street* (ds), *Best Foot Forward, DuBarry Was a Lady, Thousands Cheer, Meet the People, Ziegfeld Follies, Easy to Wed* (one of her best roles), *In Hollywood* (guest), *Lover Come Back, Sorrowful Jones* (cs), *Fancy Pants* (cs), *Forever Darling* (cs).

*"Bring On the Beautiful Girls"* : Lucille Ball in ZIEGFELD FOLLIES

## 23  BALLET IN THE MUSICAL.

Classical ballet has, not surprisingly, been warily treated by Hollywood, but its influences have been felt since the early days of talkies. The long, patterned Busby Berkeley (q.v.) numbers, though they often contained little dancing, sometimes attempted to tell a story through song and dance ("Forty-Second Street," "Shanghai Lil," "Lullaby of Broadway"). The long set-pieces of Astaire and Rogers (qq.v.) were abstract extensions of this, while their "Let's Face the Music and Dance" in *Follow the Fleet*, with its tale of a shipboard thief, was a fore-runner of Astaire's more ambitious "This Heart of Mine" *(Ziegfeld Follies)* ten years later. Broadway, though, led the way when in *On Your Toes* (36) a complete ballet was interpolated into a conventional musical. The film version recreated choreographer George Balanchine's "Slaughter on Tenth Avenue," as well as the ballet "La Princesse Zénobia," both danced by Vera Zorina (q.v.). Balanchine had taken his own company, the American Ballet, to Hollywood for *The Goldwyn Follies* for which he created two ballets, an abstract "Water-Lily" number and a more ambitious routine in which a couple found themselves in a "Romeo and Juliet" situation—one family liked ballet, the other tap! Balanchine himself appeared in *I Was an Adventuress* with excerpts from *Swan Lake* using real swans. He also staged Zorina's "That Old Black Magic" for *Star Spangled Rhythm,* but his screen work can not be said to be as distinguished as his work in the theatre. Vera Zorina's movie career too was chequered, as was Moira Shearer's, though it was Britain's *The Red Shoes* that proved a cinema audience for ballet existed. Against a melodramatic story of career-versus-love it presented long sections of unadulterated classical ballet, including the title piece, and prompted a later film version of Offenbach's opera-ballet *The Tales of Hoffmann,* less successful commercially and artistically. Shearer danced in *The Story of Three Loves,* but meanwhile Leslie Caron (q.v.) had become the best hope of bringing ballet to the cinema. After the success of the ballet in *An American in Paris,* Caron danced some Roland Petit sequences in *The Glass Slipper* and *Daddy Long Legs* and played a ballet dancer in *Gaby,* but when musicals fell out of favour she hung up her dancing shoes. Roland Petit was also responsible for the pretentious ballet sequences in *Hans Christian Andersen,* in which he danced with his wife Zizi Jeanmaire, and Erik Bruhn. Petit also staged a ballet sequence in *Anything Goes* (56), also for Jeanmaire. Chaplin's *Limelight* included a complete ballet, "Death of Harlequin," featuring Melissa Hayden, but Gene Kelly's (q.v.) all-dance film *Invitation to the Dance* was not a success, and the best forms of cinema ballet continued to be the interpolated sequences best described as ambitious dance routines. *Ziegfeld Follies* had included two particularly successful examples, the beautiful "This Heart of Mine" and the baroque *tour-de-force* "Limehouse Blues," both danced by Astaire and Lucille Bremer (qq.v.). The "Atchison, Topeka and Santa Fe" number in *The Harvey Girls* was virtually a miniature ballet, though its centrepiece was Judy Garland's (q.v.) vocal, and the success of *An American in Paris* led to similar extended routines—the "Broadway Ballet" in *Singin' in the Rain* (Kelly and Cyd Charisse, qq.v.), the "Girl Hunt" ballet in *The Band Wagon* (Charisse again, with Astaire), while in *Meet Me in Las Vegas/Viva Las Vegas* Charisse was given two ballets by Eugene Loring (q.v.), a traditional "Sleeping Beauty" and a modern "Frankie and Johnny," the latter danced with John Brascia and similar to the earlier "Slaughter on Tenth Avenue" danced by Kelly and Vera-Ellen (q.v.) in *Words and Music*. Earlier in her career Charisse had displayed her ballet skill in *The Unfinished Dance*, in which a heroine-worshiping Margaret O'Brien (q.v.) released a trapdoor to cripple Charisse's rival in the middle of *Swan Lake*. The Broadway influence was again felt in the ballets for *On the Town*, *Oklahoma*, *Carousel*, Jerome Robbins's (q.v.) "Small House of Uncle Thomas" in *The King and I* and *West Side Story,* with its emphasis on dance to express mood, character and plot. Traditional ballet continued to be featured in small doses—Tamara Toumanova impersonated Pavlova doing "The Dying Swan" in *Tonight We Sing* (she had earlier acted, as well as danced, in the 1944 *Days of Glory*), Alicia Markova and Anton Dolin danced in *A Song for Miss Julie*, while the British *Honeymoon* featured Ludmilla Tcherina in two full-length ballets. All-ballet films, such as *Black Tights,* the Fonteyn–Nureyev *Romeo and Juliet* and the New York City Ballet's *A Midsummer Night's Dream* established the existence of a vast audience for ballet taken straight, but these films had (and will continue to have) special treatment and careful exploitation.

**24 BAND LEADERS.** From the start of talkies Hollywood realised the value of top dance bands on a marquee, and the first leaders to be starred in features were TED LEWIS *(Is Everybody Happy?)* and FRED WARING *(Syncopation)* both in 1929. The following year PAUL WHITEMAN starred as *King of Jazz* while most of the top bands of the day,

such as IRVING AARONSON, GUS ARNHEIM and RUDY VALLEE (q.v.) were busily making two-reelers. But it was with the advent of swing and the big-band era of the late Thirties that the studios began to consider the inclusion of at least one name band an essential ingredient of musicals. Though generally spotted for one or two guest numbers, occasionally an orchestra or its leader would play an important role in the plot. Most successful in this respect was the GLENN MILLER band, which had the advantage of two well-made features *Sun Valley Serenade* and *Orchestra Wives* in which Miller and his band were presented as likeable and believable characters rather than gum-chewing parodies.

Most prominent leader of the era was HARRY JAMES, who not only played several acting roles, but completed his film-star image by marrying pin-up queen Betty Grable (q.v.). James was featured in *Private Buckaroo*, *Syncopation* (42), *Springtime in the Rockies*, *Best Foot Forward*, *Two Girls and a Sailor* (doing a number with June Allyson, q.v., "Young Man with a Horn," which they re-created twelve years later in *The Opposite Sex*), *Bathing Beauty*, *If I'm Lucky*, *Carnegie Hall*, *I'll Get By*, *The Benny Goodman Story* and *The Big Beat*. He had his biggest acting role in *Do You Love Me?* James also played trumpet for Kirk Douglas on the soundtrack of *Young Man with a Horn/Young Man of Music* and can be seen in the 1937 movie *Hollywood Hotel* as part of the BENNY GOODMAN orchestra. Goodman, Glenn Miller's chief rival for dance band popularity, had his biggest acting role in *Sweet and Low Down* and duetted "Paduccah" with Carmen Miranda (q.v.) in *The Gang's All Here/The Girls He Left Behind*. He also featured in *The Big Broadcast of 1937*, *The Powers Girl*,

*Stage Door Canteen* (with vocalist Peggy Lee, q.v.), *A Song Is Born* and on the soundtrack of Disney's *Make Mine Music* (a sequence titled "All the Cats Join In").

ARTIE SHAW who, like Harry James, married a Hollywood glamour girl (Lana Turner), was in Turner's *Dancing Co-Ed* and starred with Fred Astaire (q.v.) in *Second Chorus*. TOMMY DORSEY was a popular film figure in *Las Vegas Nights* (with vocalist Frank Sinatra, q.v.), *Ship Ahoy, Presenting Lily Mars, Du Barry Was a Lady, Girl Crazy* (43), *Broadway Rhythm, Thrill of a Romance, A Song Is Born* and *Disc Jockey*. His brother JIMMY DORSEY featured prominently in *The Fleet's In* with his vocalists Bob Eberly and Helen O'Connell singing what was to become one of their most famous duets, "Tangerine." Jimmy was also in *Hollywood Canteen, Four Jills in a Jeep* and *The Music Man* (49).

BOB CROSBY was a frequent film star in his triple roles of band-leader, singer and actor. He was in *Pardon My Rhythm, Let's Make Music, Rookies on Parade, Sis Hopkins, Reveille with Beverley, Presenting Lily Mars, Thousands Cheer, Kansas City Kitty, The Singing Sheriff, Meet Miss Bobbysox, My Gal Loves Music, When You're Smiling* and *Two Tickets to Broadway*, in which he sang "Let's Make Comparisons" to a cardboard replica of brother Bing (q.v.).

Latin-American band-leader XAVIER CUGAT, who in 1930 had appeared in and composed tango music for *In Gay Madrid*, and who once hired Rita Hayworth (q.v.) as dancer with his band, was particularly favoured by M-G-M in the Forties. He was prominent (with his chihuahua) in *Two Girls and a Sailor, Bathing Beauty, Holiday in Mexico, No Leave No Love, This Time for Keeps, On an Island with You, A Date with Judy* and *Neptune's Daughter*, as well as making *You Were Never Lovelier, The Heat's On/Tropicana* and *Stage Door Canteen* for other studios.

Pianist-leader CARMEN CAVALLARO was featured in *Hollywood Canteen, Out of This World* and *The Time, the Place and the Girl* (46), while Cary Grant-lookalike RAY ANTHONY led his band in *This Could Be the Night* and *Daddy Long Legs*. FREDDY MARTIN was the first band-leader to make a hit out of the theme from Tchaikovsky's First Piano Concerto (this version was called "Tonight We Love") and he played it in *Mayor of 44th Street*. Martin was also in *Hit Parade of 1943* and *What's Buzzin' Cousin?*

KAY KYSER, who won radio fame by mixing novelty numbers and games, notably his College of Musical Knowledge, with dance music, starred in *That's Right You're Wrong, You'll Find Out, Playmates, Stage Door Canteen, Thousands Cheer* and *Swing Fever*, while the crazy band of SPIKE JONES and his City Slickers played their novelty numbers such as "Chlo-ee" and "Cocktails for Two" in *Thank Your Lucky Stars, Bring On the Girls, Ladies' Man* (47) and *Variety Girl*.

Of less commercial orchestras, WOODY HERMAN's was probably the most prolific in films, with *What's Cooking?, Wintertime, Hit Parade of 1943, Sensations of 1945, Earl Carroll's Vanities* and *New Orleans*. Herman also composed and played the music for George Pal's Puppetoon *Rhapsody in Wood*. COUNT BASIE made *Hit Parade of 1943, Top Man, Crazy House, Stage Door Canteen* and *Cinderfella*, while DUKE ELLINGTON made notable contributions to *Belle of the Nineties, Murder at the Vanities, The Hit Parade* (37) and *Cabin in the Sky*. CHARLIE BARNET, a leader who also liked to act when given the chance, played in *Sally Irene and Mary, Love and Hisses, Music in Manhattan, Make Believe Ballroom, A Song Is Born* and *The Big Beat.* JACK TEAGARDEN, besides joining Bing Crosby (q.v.) and Mary Martin (q.v.) for their memorable "Waiter and the Porter and the Upstairs Maid" number in *Birth of the Blues*, was featured with his orchestra in *Hi Good Lookin'* and *The Strip* as well as the Newport Jazz Festival documentary *Jazz on a Summer's Day.*

PAUL WHITEMAN, grand-daddy of dance-band leaders, was still around in the Forties with *Atlantic City* and the Gershwin biography *Rhapsody in Blue.* Drummer-leader GENE KRUPA had prominent roles in *Some Like It Hot* (39), *Ball of Fire* (cs), *George White's Scandals of 1945, Beat the Band* (in which he performed a solo drumming on hot-water pipes to the accompaniment of hissing steam), *Glamour Girl, The Glenn Miller Story* and *The Benny Goodman Story.*

Less prolific leaders included LES BROWN *(Seven Days Leave)*, CAB CALLOWAY *(Sensations of 1945)*, FRANKIE CARLE *(My Dream Is Yours, Footlight Varieties)*, TED FIORITO *(Out of This World)*, GLEN GRAY *(Jam Session)*, female band-leader INA RAY HUTTON *(Ever since Eve)*, GUY LOMBARDO *(Stage Door Canteen)*, RAY McKINLEY *(Hit Parade of 1943)*, RAY NOBLE (in Vera Hruba Ralston's ice film *Lake Placid Serenade)* and CHARLIE SPIVAK *(Pin Up Girl)*. Several band-leaders have had their stories told, and their music recreated, by Hollywood biographies: *The Fabulous Dorseys* (they played themselves), *The Benny Goodman Story* (Steve Allen), *The Gene Krupa Story* (Sal Mineo), *The Eddy Duchin Story* (Tyrone Power with Carmen Cavallaro providing piano on soundtrack) and *The Five Pennies* (Danny Kaye as Red Nichols). Apart from Duchin, the leaders themselves were able to provide music for these films, but again it was Glenn Miller who came off best, albeit posthumously (he was killed in an air crash in 1944) in *The Glenn Miller Story*, which is likely to remain not only the best film ever made about the dance band business, but the summation of a whole era of popular music.

**25 BARI, LYNN** (1916–    ). RN: Marjorie Bitzer. Former chorus-girl with a distinctive line in allure, type-cast by Fox as "the other woman" in a series of musicals and melodramas.

Films: *Dancing Lady* (début), *Stand Up and Cheer, You Can't Have Everything, Battle of Broadway, Moon over Her Shoulder, Lillian Russell, Sun Valley Serenade, Orchestra Wives, Hello Frisco Hello, Sweet and Low Down, Nocturne* (ds), *Margie, Sunny Side of the Street, I Dream of Jeanie, Has anybody Seen My Gal?*

**26 BARTON, CHARLES** (1902–    ). Director of variable low-budget films. From vaudeville became prop boy for Cruze and Wellman, then assistant director. Now in television.

Films: *Two Latins from Manhattan, Sing for Your Supper, Honolulu Lu, Sweetheart of the Fleet, Laugh Your Blues Away, Is Everybody Happy?* (43), *Reveille with Beverley, What's Buzzin' Cousin?, Lucky Legs, She Has What It Takes, Beautiful but Broke, Hey Rookie, Jam Session, Louisiana Hayride, Mexican Hayride, The Milkman* (cs), *Double Crossbones, Dance with Me Henry* (cs), *Swingin' Along.*

**27 BARTON, JAMES** (1890–1962). Ex-burlesque performer who later played lovable old-timer roles on Broadway *(Paint Your Wagon)* and in Hollywood.

Films: *Wabash Avenue, Daughter of Rosie O'Grady, Golden Girl, Here Comes the Groom.*

**28 BASSMAN, GEORGE.** Arranger, composer and conductor who spent twelve years as Musical Director at M-G-M. Started as pianist-arranger, joined Fletcher Henderson's orchestra and arranged for Duke Ellington, Tommy Dorsey, Benny Goodman, Andre Kostelanetz and others before working at M-G-M. Active in television. Orchestrated, with others unless stated.

Films: *Damsel in Distress, A Day at the Races, Everybody Sing* (solo), *The Wizard of Oz, Babes in Arms, Too Many Girls, Two Girls on Broadway, Go West* (solo), *Lady Be Good, The Big Store, Babes on Broadway, Panama Hattie, For Me and My Gal, DuBarry Was a Lady, Cabin in the Sky* (solo), *Best Foot Forward.* Cond. *In Hollywood.*

**29 BEAUMONT, HARRY** (1893–1966). Director of early talkies at M-G-M. After vaudeville experience, became writer and actor in silents, made experimental talkie in 1913.

Films: *Broadway Melody, Children of Pleasure, Lord Byron of Broadway/What Price Melody?* (co.), *Those Three French Girls, Dance Fools Dance, Maisie Goes to Reno/You Can't Do That to Me* (cs).

**30 BELITA** (1923– ). RN: Gladys Jepson-Turner. English skater and dancer. In French ice ballet when eleven, exhibition skater in U.S.A. before Hollywood.

Films: *Ice Capades* (début), *Silver Skates, Lady Let's Dance, Suspense* (ds), *Invitation to the Dance, Silk Stockings.*

**31 BERKELEY, BUSBY** (1895– ). RN: William Berkeley-Enos. Choreographer-director noted for his long, kaleidoscopic routines featuring bevies of chorus girls forming intricate patterns. Brought to Hollywood by Sam Goldwyn (q.v.) after staging dances for Broadway musicals. Not a trained dancer, he has admitted that his routines often contain little real dancing, the choreography being performed by the camera rather than the girls. Invented the monorail and pioneered massive crane and tracking shots that were features of his films. A leading musical influence in Thirties, most of which he spent with Warners.

Films: Ch. *Whoopee, Palmy Days* (also acted), *The Kid from Spain, Roman Scandals, Forty-Second Street, Gold Diggers of 1933* (also acted briefly), *Footlight Parade, Dames, Fashions of 1934, Wonder Bar, Stars over Broadway, In Caliente, Go into your Dance* (also co-dir.), *Bright Lights* (35, also dir.), *Gold Diggers of Broadway* (also dir.), *I Live for Love* (also dir.), *Stage Struck* (cs, also dir.), *Gold Diggers of 1937, Hollywood Hotel* (also dir.), *Varsity Show, The Singing Marine, Gold Diggers in Paris, Garden of the Moon* (also dir.), *Broadway Serenade, Babes in Arms* (also dir.), *Forty Little Mothers* (also dir.), *Strike up the Band* (also dir.), *Lady Be Good, Ziegfeld Girl, Babes on Broadway* (also dir.), *Born to Sing, For Me and My Gal* (also dir.), *Girl Crazy* (43), *The Gang's All Here/ The Girls He Left Behind* (also dir.), *Cinderella Jones* (also dir.), *Take Me out to the Ball Game/Everybody's Cheering* (also dir.), *Two Weeks with Love, Million Dollar Mermaid/The One-Piece Bathing Suit, Call Me Mister, Two Tickets to Broadway, Easy to Love, Small Town*

*Girl, Rose Marie* (54), *Billy Rose's Jumbo* (also second unit dir.).

**32 BERLIN, IRVING** (1888– ). RN: Israel Baline. America's most popular composer, who in 1911 revolutionised song-writing with "Alexander's Ragtime Band" and was a direct influence on Gershwin, Kern (qq.v.) and others. Born in a Siberian village and raised in New York tenement, to which family came as refugees. Started supporting family when eight, selling newspapers and singing songs for pennies. Worked as singing waiter and in 1907 had his first number published (lyrics only). In 1910 made stage *début* in Broadway revue and following year became partner in publishing firm. With ragtime hits his fame

was established and million-sellers followed in quick succession. Composed for Broadway (inc. *Ziegfeld Follies, Music Box Revues*), wrote successful army shows for both World Wars, and in 1946 the classic *Annie Get Your Gun*. His words and music have been used in films since the coming of sound. Al Jolson (q.v.) sang "Blue Skies" in *The Jazz Singer*, "Marie" was written for Goldwyn's (q.v.) Vilma Banky film *The Awakening* (28) and for Mary Pickford's *Coquette* he provided the lilting title song. Berlin had no musical training, and has

composed and played only in key of F sharp. His celebrated piano has a lever that enables it to change key mechanically. Most of his films have used Berlin standards in addition to those composed especially for the film.

Films: *The Cocoanuts* (cs), *Lady of the Pavements* (ds), *Hallelujah* (all-Negro musical for which he wrote "Swanee Shuffle" and one of most beautiful songs "Waiting at the End of the Road"), *Puttin' On the Ritz* (title tune for this Harry Richman vehicle was later used by Astaire (q.v.) in *Blue Skies*), *Mammy* (inc. "Let Me Sing and I'm Happy"), *Reaching for the Moon* (ds, title tune), *Top Hat* ("Cheek to Cheek," "Isn't This a Lovely Day To Be Caught in the Rain?" "No Strings," "The Piccolino," "Top Hat, White Tie and Tails"), *Follow the Fleet* (inc. "I'm Putting All My Eggs in One Basket," "Let's Face the Music and Dance," "Let Yourself Go"), *On the Avenue* (inc. "This Year's Kisses," "I've Got My Love To Keep Me Warm"), *Alexander's Ragtime Band* (inc. "Now It Can Be Told"), *Carefree* ("Change Partners," "I Used To Be Colour Blind," "The Yam"), *Second Fiddle* (inc. "Back to Back," "I Poured My Heart into a Song," "When Winter Comes"), *Louisiana Purchase, Holiday Inn* (inc. "Be Careful It's My Heart," "White Christmas"), *This Is the Army* (also assoc. prod. and acted), *Blue Skies* (inc. "You Keep Coming Back like a Song"), *Easter Parade* ("Better Luck Next Time," "Drum Crazy," "A Couple of Swells," "A Fella with an Umbrella," "Happy Easter," "It Only Happens when I Dance with You," "Stepping out with My Baby"), *Annie Get Your Gun* (a new song "Let's Go West Again" was recorded for the soundtrack by Judy Garland, q.v., but not used in Betty Hutton, also q.v., version), *Call Me Madam, There's No*

*Business like Show Business* ("A Man Chases a Girl"), *White Christmas* (inc. "The Best Things Happen While You're Dancing," "Count Your Blessings," "Choreography," "Love You Didn't Do Right By Me," "Sisters," "Snow"), *Sayonara* (ds, title tune).

**33 BERMAN, PANDRO S.** (1905– ). Producer of several Astaire–Rogers (q.v.) musicals. Son of Universal executive, started as assist. dir., editor, became chief editor RKO, producer 1931. Joined M-G-M in 1940.

Films: *The Gay Divorcee, Roberta, Top Hat, Swing Time, Shall We Dance?, Damsel in Distress, The Story of Vernon and Irene Castle, Love Affair* (ds), *Ziegfeld Girl, Rio Rita* (42), *The Picture of Dorian Gray* (ds), *Living in a Big Way.*

**34 BERNSTEIN, LEONARD** (1918– ). Composer, conductor and pianist, famous in both concert hall and Broadway theatre. Composed background score for *On the Waterfront* (non-musical) and two of his Broadway successes have been transferred to the screen, *On the Town* and *West Side Story.*

**BIOGRAPHIES.** See "Composers' Biographies," "Entertainers' Biographies."

**35 BLAINE, VIVIAN** (1921– ). RN: Vivienne Stapleton. Singer-actress, former band and night club singer given Fox contract in 1942. Made likeable impression during Forties, but failed to defeat the Fox tradition that allowed only one musical star to reign at a time. Scored greatest success later on Broadway as Adelaide in *Guys and Dolls.*

Films: *Jitterbugs, Greenwich Village, Something for the Boys, State Fair* (45, intro. "That's for Me"), *Nob Hill,*

*Doll Face/Come Back to Me, If I'm Lucky, Three Little Girls in Blue, Skirts Ahoy, Guys and Dolls, Public Pigeon No. 1* (cs).

**36 BLAIR, JANET** (1923– ). RN: Martha Jane Lafferty. Ex-band singer who became Columbia's second-string to Rita Hayworth (q.v.) during the Forties.

Films: *Blondie Goes to College* (cs), *Broadway* (42), *Something to Shout About* (intro. "You'd Be So Nice to Come Home To"), *Tonight and Every Night, Tars and Spars, The Fabulous Dorseys, Public Pigeon No 1* (cs), *The One and Only Genuine Original Family Band.*

**37 BLANE, RALPH** (1914– ). Lyricist who started as singer then vocal arranger for Broadway shows. After hit stage musical *Best Foot Forward* with Hugh Martin (q.v.), signed by M-G-M.

Films: *Best Foot Forward, Thousands Cheer* ("The Joint Is Really Jumping"), *Broadway Rhythm, Meet Me in St. Louis* (inc. "The Trolley Song," "The Boy Next Door," "Have Yourself a Merry Little Christmas"), *In Hollywood, Easy to Wed, No Leave No Love, Ziegfeld Follies* ("Love"), *Good News* (47, "Pass That Peace Pipe"), *Summer Holiday, One Sunday Afternoon* (music also), *My Dream Is Yours, My Blue Heaven, Skirts Ahoy* (inc. "What Good Is a Gal without a Guy?"), *Athena, The French Line, The Girl Most Likely, The Girl Rush* (54, inc. "An Occasional Man"), *Down among the Sheltering Palms.*

**38 BLONDELL, JOAN** (1909– ). RN: Rosebud Blondell. Bright wisecracking performer of the Thirties who later made as great a success as a character player.

Films: *Blonde Crazy, Big City Blues, Broadway Bad, Gold Diggers of 1933,*

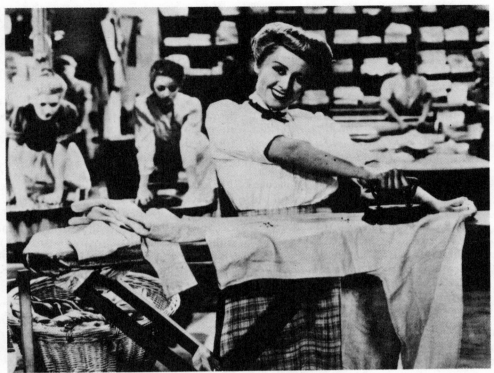

*"The Girl at the Ironing Board" : Joan Blondell in DAMES*

*Footlight Parade, Dames, Broadway Gondolier, We're in the Money* (cs), *Colleen, Gold Diggers of 1937, Sons O'Guns, The King and the Chorus Girl* (cs), *East Side of Heaven, Two Girls on Broadway; This Could Be the Night, The Opposite Sex.*

**39  BLYTH, ANN** (1928–   ). Sweet-voiced successor to Gloria Jean (q.v.) at Universal, who later broadened scope with dramatic roles and made a brave attempt to portray Helen Morgan (q.v.) with a dubbed singing voice. Former star on radio, spent three years with San Carlos Opera.

Films: *Chip Off the Old Block* (début), *Babes on Swing Street, The Merry Monahans, Bowery to Broadway, Killer McCoy* (ds), *Top O' The Morning, The Great Caruso, Rose Marie* (54), *The Student Prince, Kismet* (55), *The Helen Morgan Story/Both Ends of the Candle.*

**40  BOLES, JOHN** (1898–1969). Dashing singer-actor, a matinée-idol of the Thirties. Given first opportunity in silents by Gloria Swanson after she saw him on stage, but talkies made him a star.

Films: *Romance of the Underworld* (ds), *The Desert Song* (29), *Rio Rita* (29), *King of Jazz, Song of the West, Captain of the Guard, One Heavenly Night, Careless Lady, My Lips Betray, Child of Manhattan* (ds), *Bottoms Up, Music in the Air, Stand Up and Cheer, Beloved, I Believed in You* (ds), *Wild Gold, Curly Top, Red Heads on Parade, The Littlest Rebel, Rose of the Rancho, Romance in the Dark; Thousands Cheer.*

**41  BOLGER, RAY** (1903–   ). Loose-limbed dancer and comedian, in several Ziegfeld shows before Hollywood *début*. Memorable as the Scarecrow in *The Wizard of Oz*, but has remained a bigger name in theatre than in films.

Films: *The Great Ziegfeld* (début), *Rosalie, Sweethearts, The Wizard of Oz, Sunny* (41), *Four Jacks and a Jill, Stage Door Canteen, The Harvey Girls, Look for the Silver Lining, Make Mine Laughs, Where's Charley?* (recreating Broadway starring role in musical version of *Charley's Aunt* made in England), *April in Paris, Babes in Toyland* (61).

**42 BOONE, PAT** (1934– ). Pop singer whose film career foundered when he tried to change his all-American clean-cut image.

Films: *Bernadine* (début), *April Love, Mardi Gras, The Main Attraction* (ds, in G.B.), *State Fair* (61), *All Hands on Deck* (cs), *The Yellow Canary* (ds).

**43 BORZAGE, FRANK** (1893–1961). Director, former coalminer and Hollywood extra, whose musicals form only a small proportion of his output. Noted especially for romantic movies.

Films: *Song O' My Heart, Bad Girl, Flirtation Walk, Shipmates Forever, Desire* (ds), *Hearts Divided, The Vanishing Virginian* (ds), *Smilin' Through* (ds), *Seven Sweethearts, Stage Door Canteen, His Butler's Sister, Concerto/I've Always Loved You.*

**44 BOSWELL SISTERS, The (Connee, Vet, Martha**). Close-harmony group of the Thirties, stars of radio and recording. Connee later went solo.

Films: *The Big Broadcast, Moulin Rouge, Transatlantic Merry-go-round.* Connee only: *Artists and Models* (37), *Kiss the Boys Goodbye* (intro. "Sand in My Shoes"), *Syncopation* (42), *Swing Parade of 1946.*

**45 BRACKEN, EDDIE** (1920– ). Comedian specialising in well-meaning blunderers. On stage as child, given adult chance by George Abbott (q.v.) in Broadway's *Too Many Girls* and signed to repeat role in film. Paramount contract followed, and particular success in Sturges comedies.

Films: *Too Many Girls, Sweater Girl, The Fleet's In, Star Spangled Rhythm, Happy Go Lucky, Rainbow Island, Bring on the Girls, Out of This World* (a parody of Sinatra, q.v., in which Bracken was dubbed by Bing Crosby, also q.v.), *Duffy's Tavern, Ladies' Man* (47), *Summer Stock/If You Feel like Singing, Two Tickets to Broadway, About Face.*

**46 BRECHER, IRVING S.** (1914– ). Writer, former newspaper and radio reporter, in films since 1937.

Films: sc. *At the Circus, Go West.* Co-sc. *Best Foot Forward,* sc. *DuBarry Was a Lady,* co-sc. *Meet Me in St. Louis,* sc. *Yolanda and the Thief,* co-adapt. *Summer Holiday,* sc. *Somebody Loves Me* (also dir.), sc. *Bye Bye Birdie.*

**47 BREEN, BOBBY** (1927– ). Child singing star, male answer to Shirley Temple (q.v.). Enjoyed brief career in late Thirties.

Films: *Rainbow on the River, Let's Sing Again, Make a Wish, Breaking the Ice, Hawaii Calls, Fisherman's Wharf, Way down South, Johnny Doughboy.*

**48 BREMER, LUCILLE** (c. 1923- ). Dancer, former member of Rockettes at Radio City Music Hall, whose film career was distinguished, but brief.

Films: *Meet Me in St. Louis* (début), *Ziegfeld Follies, Yolanda and the Thief, Till the Clouds Roll By.*

24

**49 BRICE, FANNY** (1891–1951). RN: Fanny Borach. Comedienne discovered in an obscure burlesque house by Ziegfeld and starred in his 1910 Follies. In 1921 effectively changed pace singing "My Man," a song audiences associated with her own tragic romance.

Films: *My Man* (début including several songs associated with her— "Second Hand Rose," "I'd Rather Be Blue" and title song), *Be Yourself, The Great Ziegfeld* (as herself), *Everybody Sing, Ziegfeld Follies* (her sketch was cut from some release prints).

**50 BRISSON, CARL** (1895–1958). RN: Carl Pedersen. Danish-born matinée idol of early talkies. Started as boxer, formed dancing act with sister, toured Europe. London success in *The Merry Widow.*

Films: *Murder at the Vanities, All the King's Horses, Ship Café.*

**51 BRODSZKY, NICHOLAS** (1905– ). Composer who wrote several operettas in native Hungary before success in Hollywood.

Films: *The Toast of New Orleans* (inc. "Be My Love"), *Rich Young and Pretty* (inc. "We Never Talk Much," "Wonder Why"), *Because You're Mine, Small Town Girl, The Student Prince* ("Beloved"), *Ten Thousand Bedrooms, Let's Be Happy* (in G.B.).

**52 BROWN, LEW** (1893–1958). Russian-born lyricist, brought to U.S.A. as child, started writing songs while at school. Had written several hits ("Give Me the Moonlight," "Oh By Jingo") when he formed partnership with Ray Henderson and Buddy DeSylva (qq.v.) to become one of America's foremost song-writing teams. For their films see HENDERSON, RAY. Others with Lew Brown lyrics: *Carolina, Stand Up and Cheer, Loud Speaker, Now I'll Tell* (ds), *Change of Heart, The Music Goes Round, Strike Me Pink, New Faces of 1937, Tarnished Angel* (ds), *Swing Fever, Sing Dance and Plenty Hot/Melody Girl, Yokel Boy.*

**53 BROWN, NACIO HERB** (1896– 1964). Composer whose virtually entire output was for musical pictures. Was managing a real estate office and composing in spare time when Irving Thalberg asked him to collaborate with Arthur Freed (q.v.) on songs for M-G-M's first musical *Broadway Melody.* Spent most of his career with M-G-M.

Films: *Broadway Melody* (inc. "Wedding of the Painted Doll," "You Were Meant for Me"), *Marianne, Hollywood Revue* (inc. "Singing in the Rain"), *Untamed* (ds), *The Pagan* (ds, "Pagan Love Song"), *Lord Byron of Broadway/ What Price Melody?* (inc. "Should I?"), *Montana Moon* (ws), *The Barbarian* (ds), *Peg O' My Heart, Going Hollywood* (inc. "Temptation"), *Stage Mother, Take a Chance, Sadie McKee* (ds, inc. "All I Do Is Dream of You"), *Hollywood Party, Student Tour, Broadway Melody of 1936* (inc. "You Are My Lucky Star"), *A Night at the Opera* ("Alone"), *San Francisco* (ds, "Would You?"), *After the Thin Man* (cs), *Broadway Melody of 1937* (inc. "Broadway Rhythm"), *Thoroughbreds Don't Cry, Babes in Arms* ("Good Morning"), *Two Girls on Broadway, Ziegfeld Girl* ("You Stepped Out of a Dream"), *Wintertime, Greenwich Village, On an Island with You, The Kissing Bandit* (inc. "Love Is Where You Find It"), *Pagan Love Song, Singin' in the Rain* (this film used most of Brown and Freed's biggest hits from previous M-G-M musicals).

**54 BRUCE, VIRGINIA** (1910–   ).
Sophisticated actress-singer, usually
coolly self-assured. After crowd work in
early talkies, given role in *Why Bring
That Up?*

Other films: *Paramount on Parade,
The Love Parade, Safety in Numbers,
Here Comes the Band, Times Square Lady,
Metropolitan, Born to Dance* (intro. "I've
Got You under My Skin"), *When Love
Is Young, Let Freedom Ring, Society
Lawyer* (intro. "I'm in Love with the
Honourable Mr. So and So"), *Pardon
My Sarong, Brazil.*

**55 BUCHANAN, JACK** (1891–1957).
Debonair British singer-dancer also
popular in the U.S.A. Many British
silents and talkies.

Other films: *Show of Shows, Monte
Carlo, Paris, The Band Wagon.*

**56 BURKE, JOHNNY** (1908–1964).
Lyricist, once a pianist for Irving Berlin
(q.v.). Bing Crosby (q.v.) brought about
his long and successful collaboration with
James Van Heusen (q.v.). Lyrics include
"Moonlight Becomes You," "Swinging
on a Star," "It Could Happen to You,"
"His Rocking Horse Ran Away," "Like
Someone in Love," "Personality,"
"Aren't You Glad You're You?"
"Country Style," "But Beautiful," "You
Don't Have to Know the Language,"
"Busy Doing Nothing," "Life Is So
Peculiar." For their films see VAN
HEUSEN, JAMES.

Other films: *Murder at the Vanities,
Go West Young Man, Pennies from
Heaven, Double or Nothing, Doctor
Rhythm, Sing You Sinners, The Star
Maker* (inc. "An Apple for the Teacher"),
*East Side of Heaven, That's Right You're
Wrong* ("Scatterbrain"), *Road to Singa-
pore* (40, inc. "Too Romantic"), *If I had
My Way, Rhythm on the River* (inc. "I
Don't Want To Cry Any More").

**57 BUTLER, DAVID** (1894–   ).
Director of many lively musicals who
came to films from theatre stage managing
to become a star of silents. Directed Fox's
first big musical and several successes for
Shirley Temple and Doris Day (qq.v.).

Films: *Fox Movietone Follies, Sunny
Side Up, High Society Blues, Just Imagine,
A Connecticut Yankee* (31), *Delicious, My
Weakness, Bottoms Up, Bright Eyes, Have
a Heart, The Little Colonel, The Littlest
Rebel, Captain January, Pigskin Parade,
Ali Baba Goes to Town, You're a Sweet-
heart, Kentucky Moonshine, Straight
Place and Show/They're Off, East Side of
Heaven, That's Right You're Wrong, If I
Had My Way, You'll Find Out, Play-
mates, Road to Morocco, They Got Me
Covered* (cs), *Thank Your Lucky Stars,
The Princess and the Pirate* (cs), *Shine
On Harvest Moon, The Time the Place
and the Girl, Two Guys from Milwaukee/
Royal Flush, My Wild Irish Rose, Two
Guys from Texas, It's a Great Feeling,
Look for the Silver Lining, Tea for Two,*

*The Daughter of Rosie O'Grady, Lullaby of Broadway, Painting the Clouds with Sunshine* (re-make *Gold Diggers of 1933*), *Where's Charley?, April in Paris, By the Light of the Silvery Moon, Calamity Jane, Glory* (cs, also prod.), *The Right Approach*.

**58 BUZZELL, EDDIE** (1897–    ). Director-actor, former musical comedy star of Twenties.

Films: acted in *Little Johnny Jones*, many two-reelers. Dir. *Child of Manhattan* (ds), *The Girl Friend, Honolulu, At the Circus, Go West, Ship Ahoy, Best*

*"It Could Only Happen in Brooklyn"* : *James Cagney and Virginia Mayo in WEST POINT STORY/FINE AND DANDY*

Foot Forward, Easy to Wed, Song of the Thin Man (cs), Neptune's Daughter, Ain't Misbehavin' (also co-sc.).

**59 CAGNEY, JAMES** (1904–    ). Actor noted as a tough guy but equally distinctive in comedy or musicals, where his stiff but rhythmic dancing and rasping voice are indelible. Vaudeville dancer and female impersonator before his Hollywood *début* 1930.

Films: *Blonde Crazy, Footlight Parade, Something to Sing About, Torrid Zone* (ds), *Yankee Doodle Dandy* (1942 Oscar as George M. Cohan), *West Point Story/ Fine and Dandy, Starlift, The Seven Little Foys* (as Cohan again in guest song-and-dance with Bob Hope), *Love Me or Leave Me, Never Steal Anything Small*.

**60 CAHN, SAMMY** (1913–    ). Lyricist who has collaborated with Jule Styne (q.v.) and James Van Heusen (q.v.) on many film and stage scores. A New Yorker, he wrote parodies of popular songs as boy. First film work at Columbia with Saul Chaplin (q.v.) as composer.

Films: *Argentine Nights, Go West Young Lady, Rookies on Parade/Jamboree, Time Out for Rhythm, Sing for Your Supper, Johnny Doughboy, Blondie Goes to College* (cs), *Blondie's Blessed Event* (cs), *Honolulu Lu, Youth on Parade* (inc. "I've Heard That Song Before"), *Crazy House, Here Comes Elmer/Hitchhike to Happiness, Let's Face It, Red Head from Manhattan, Thumbs Up, Lady of Burlesque/Striptease Lady* (ds), *Carolina Blues, Ever Since Venus, Follow the Boys* (44, inc. "I'll Walk Alone"), *Jam Session, Knickerbocker Holiday, Janie* (cs), *Step Lively, Anchors Aweigh* (inc. "I Fall in Love Too Easily"), *Tonight and Every Night, The Stork Club, Tars and Spars, Sweetheart of Sigma Chi* (46, inc. "Five Minutes More"), *Cinderella Jones, The Kid from Brooklyn, Earl Carroll Sketch Book/Hats Off to Rhythm, Ladies' Man* (47), *It Happened in Brooklyn* (inc. "Time after Time"), *Glamour Girl, Romance on the High Seas/It's Magic, Two Guys from Texas, It's a Great Feeling, Always Leave Them Laughing, West Point Story/Fine and Dandy, Double Dynamite/It's Only Money, Rich Young and Pretty* (inc. "We Never Talk Much"), *Because You're Mine, She's Working Her Way through College, April in Paris* (inc. "That's What Makes Paris Paree"), *The Court Jester* (cs), *Three Coins in the Fountain* (ds, 54 Oscar title tune), *The Tender Trap* (cs, title tune), *Three Sailors and a Girl* (also prod.), *Peter Pan, Love Me or Leave Me, Meet Me in Las Vegas/Viva Las Vegas, Forever Darling* (cs), *You're Never Too Young* (cs), *Anything Goes* (56), *The Opposite Sex, Ten Thousand Bedrooms, Rock-a-bye Baby* (cs), *The Joker Is Wild* (ds, 1957 Oscar "All the Way"), *Paris Holiday* (cs), *Say One for Me, A Hole in the Head* (cs, 1959 Oscar "High Hopes"), *High Time* (inc. "The Second Time Around"), *Pocketful of Miracles* (cs), *Papa's Delicate Condition* (cs, 63 Oscar "Call Me Irresponsible"), *Robin and the Seven Hoods* (inc. "My Kind of Town"), *The Pleasure Seekers* (cs), *Thoroughly Modern Millie, Star!/Those Were the Happy Times* (title tune).

**61 CANOVA, JUDY** (1916–    ). Comedienne who sang, clowned and yodelled her way through several bright hill-billy musicals.

Films: *In Caliente, Going Highbrow, Artists and Models* (37), *Scatterbrain, Puddin' Head, Sis Hopkins, Sleepy Time Gal, True to the Army, Joan of Ozarks, Chatterbox, Sleepy Lagoon, Louisiana Hayride, Singin' in the Corn, Hit the Hay, Honeychile, Oklahoma Annie, Untamed Heiress*.

*Eddie Cantor with George Murphy and actress in KID MILLIONS*

**62 CANTOR, EDDIE** (1892–1964). RN: Isa Isskowitz. Comedian famous for his rolling eyes, clapping hands and good-natured delivery of *risqué* lyrics. Child vaudeville performer, Ziegfeld *début* in 1917, made several silents. Biggest screen successes were lavish Goldwyn (q.v.) productions of the Thirties.

Films: *Whoopee, Glorifying the American Girl, Palmy Days, The Kid from Spain* (intro. "What a Perfect Combination"), *Roman Scandals* (intro. "Keep Young and Beautiful"), *Kid Millions, Strike Me Pink, Ali Baba Goes to Town, Forty Little Mothers, Thank Your Lucky Stars, Hollywood Canteen, Show Business* (also st., prod.), *If You Knew Susie, The Eddie Cantor Story* (voice, and acted in prologue).

**63 CARMICHAEL, HOAGY** (1899– ). RN: Hoagland Howard Carmichael. Composer who has also sung and acted with effect in both musicals and dramas. Indiana-born, studied law till publication of his "Washboard Blues" induced him to take up songwriting.

"Stardust" and "Georgia on My Mind" preceded first film work.

Films: *Anything Goes* (36, "Moonburn"), *Every Day's a Holiday, College Swing/Swing Teacher Swing, Romance in the Dark* ("The Nearness of You"), *Sing You Sinners* ("Small Fry"), *A Song Is Born* (38 short introduced "Heart and Soul," used again in 48 full-length movie with Danny Kaye, q.v.), *Thanks for the Memory* ("Two Sleepy People"), *Mr. Bug Goes to Town/Hoppity Goes to Town, Road Show* (lyrics also), *True to Life* (inc. "Old Music Master"), *To Have and Have Not* (ds, "How Little We Know," also acted), *The Stork Club* (inc. "Doctor Lawyer and Indian Chief"), *Johnny Angel* (ds, "Memphis in June"), *Canyon Passage* (ws, inc. "Ole Buttermilk Sky," also acted), *The Best Years of Our Lives* (ds, also acted), *Night Song* (ds, also acted), *Johnny Holiday* (ds, also acted), *Young Man with a Horn/Young Man of Music* (acted only), *Here Comes the Groom* (1951 Oscar, "In the Cool Cool Cool of the Evening"), *Belles on Their Toes* (cs, also acted), *The Las Vegas Story* (ds, also acted), *Gentlemen Prefer Blondes*

*Leslie Caron and Gene Kelly in AN AMERICAN IN PARIS*

(inc. "When Love Goes Wrong"), *Those Redheads from Seattle*, *Timberjack* (ws, also acted), *Three for the Show* ("Down Boy").

**64  CARON, LESLIE** (1931–    ). French dancer who was with Roland Petit's Ballet des Champs-Elysées when discovered by Gene Kelly (q.v.) for *An American in Paris*. Later turned to straight roles with mixed success.

Films: *An American in Paris* (début), *Glory Alley* (ds), *Lili*, *The Story of Three Loves* (ds), *The Glass Slipper*, *Gaby* (ds), *Daddy Long Legs*, *Gigi*, *The Subterraneans* (ds).

*Fiesta* (47), *Hit Parade of 1951*, *The Farmer Takes a Wife*, *Geraldine*.

**65  CARROLL, JOHN** (c. 1907–    ). RN: Julian la Faye. Handsome moustached singer, and leading man of second features. Studied singing in Europe, made Hollywood *début* when RKO wanted an athlete who could sing.

Films: *Hi Gaucho* (début), *Go West, Sunny* (41), *Lady Be Good*, *Rio Rita* (42), *Hit Parade of 1943*, *Old Los Angeles*,

**66  CARROLL, NANCY** (1906–1965). RN: Anna La Hiff. Actress who could sing and dance with great charm. Signed for silents after success in stage revues, and just as big a success in talkies. Often teamed with Charles "Buddy" Rogers (q.v.).

Films: *Close Harmony*, *Dance of Life*, *Follow Through*, *Honey*, *Paramount on*

30

*Parade, Child of Manhattan* (ds), *Transatlantic Merry-go-round, After the Dance ; That Certain Age.*

**67 CARSON, JACK** (1910-1963). RN: John Elmer Carson. Reliable performer, often cast as the comic heel but capable of a strong performance when the material demanded. Was part of a vaudeville double-act before his Hollywood *début* in 1937, where after a series of walk-ons at RKO he landed his first good part in *Carefree.*

Films: *Having a Wonderful Time, Carefree, Destry Rides Again* (ws), *Love Thy Neighbour, Blues in the Night, Navy Blues, The Hard Way* (ds), *Hollywood Canteen, Thank Your Lucky Stars, Shine On Harvest Moon, One More Tomorrow* (ds), *The Time the Place and the Girl, Two Guys from Milwaukee/Royal Flush, Love and Learn, Two Guys from Texas, Romance on the High Seas/It's Magic, April Showers, My Dream Is Yours, It's a Great Feeling, Dangerous When Wet, Red Garters, A Star Is Born, Ain't Misbehavin'.*

*Jack Carson with Doris Day in ROMANCE ON THE HIGH SEAS/IT'S MAGIC*

**68 CASTLE, NICK** (1910–1968). Choreographer, former vaudeville dancer signed by Fox as dance director in Thirties. In later years active in television.

Films: ch. *One in a Million, Love and Hisses, Rebecca of Sunnybrook Farm, The Little Princess* (ds), *Swanee River, Down Argentine Way, Hellzapoppin, Mayor of 44th Street, Orchestra Wives, Stormy Weather, This Is the Army, Something for the Boys, Thrill of Brazil, Nancy Goes to Rio, Summer Stock/If You Feel like Singing, Rich Young and Pretty, The Strip, Royal Wedding/Wedding Bells, Skirts Ahoy, Everything I Have Is Yours* (w. Gower Champion, q.v.), *Here Come the Girls, Red Garters, The Seven Little Foys, Anything Goes* (56), *The Birds and the Bees, That Certain Feeling* (cs), *Bundle of Joy, State Fair* (62).

**69 CHAKIRIS, GEORGE** (1933– ). Dancer who made screen *début* as boy when, as singer with St. Luke Choristers, sang in *Song of Love.* Later had chorus roles, as George Kerris, in *White Christmas, The Girl Rush* (54), *Gentlemen Prefer Blondes* and *Meet Me in Las Vegas/Viva Las Vegas.* Success as Riff in London production of *West Side Story* led to Oscar-winning role of Bernardo in film. Subsequent career has disappointed, only musical being *Les Demoiselles de Rochefort/Young Girls of Rochefort* (French).

**70 CHAMPION, MARGE** (1923– ) and **GOWER** (1921– ). Dance team who performed several stunning routines in Fifties. Marge (RN: Marge Belcher) was daughter of ballet master, made professional *début* at thirteen. Model for Disney's Snow White and for the Blue Fairy in *Pinocchio.* As Marjorie Bell acted in *The Story of Vernon and Irene Castle.* Gower was half of vaudeville dance team that broke up at start of war. After service signed by M-G-M but given little work so formed partnership

31

*Marge and Gower Champion in GIVE A GIRL A BREAK*

with Marge (as "Gower and Bell") for night clubs and television. Also choreographed Broadway shows. A special spot in *Mr. Music* led to M-G-M contract. Gower now directs and choreographs Broadway musicals (inc. *Hello Dolly!*).

Films: Gower only: *Till the Clouds Roll By, Words and Music*. Together: *Mr. Music, Show Boat* (51), *Lovely to Look At, Everything I Have Is Yours* (Gower co-ch.), *Give a Girl a Break* (Gower co-ch.), *Jupiter's Darling, Three for the Show*. Gower also ch. *The Girl Most Likely*.

**71 CHANNING, CAROL** (1921–    ). Broadway's sensational star of *Hello*

Dolly!* has made only three films to date, and none has provided the opportunity for her fully to exploit her unusual talent.

Films: *The First Travelling Saleslady* (cs), *Thoroughly Modern Millie, Skidoo* (cs), *Archy and Mehitabel* (voice only).

**72 CHAPLIN, SAUL** (1912–    ). Composer and arranger at Columbia in Forties, then M-G-M. Lately a producer of big-budget roadshow musicals. Former writer of vaudeville material.

Films: comp. *Argentine Nights, Rookies on Parade/Jamboree, Go West Young Lady, Time Out for Rhythm, Sing for Your Supper, Blondie Goes to College* (cs), *Blondie's Blessed Event* (cs), *Honolulu Lu,*

*Red Head from Manhattan, Crazy House, Cowboy Canteen* (ws), *Ever Since Venus, Kansas City Kitty, Louisiana Hayride, She's a Sweetheart, Meet Me on Broadway, Two Blondes and a Redhead, The Countess of Monte Cristo, Summer Stock/ If You feel like Singing* ("You Wonderful You"), *Everything I Have Is Yours, Merry Andrew.* Orch. *The Jolson Story* (voc. arr.), *Summer Stock/If You feel like Singing, An American in Paris* (1951 Oscar), *Lovely to Look At, Give a Girl a Break, Kiss Me Kate, Jupiter's Darling, Interrupted Melody, High Society, Seven Brides for Seven Brothers* (1954 Oscar), *West Side Story* (1961 Oscar), *I Could Go On Singing* (Brit.). Assoc. Prod. *Les Girls, Merry Andrew, Can Can, West Side Story, I Could Go On Singing* (in G.B.), *The Sound of Music.* Prod. *Star!* (also known as *Those Were the Happy Times*).

## 73 CHARISSE, CYD (1923– ).

RN: Tula Finklea. Long-legged dancer-actress whose personality takes on an added vibrance when she dances. Attended Hollywood Professional School, danced with Ballet Russe. Seemed doomed to colourless secondary roles till her stunning dance with Gene Kelly (q.v.) in *Singin' in the Rain* brought

*Maurice Chevalier*

stardom. Apart from guest role in *The Silencers* (non-musical), recent dancing has been in night clubs and television. Married to Tony Martin (q.v.).

Films: *Something to Shout About* (début, as Lily Norwood), *Thousands Cheer, Ziegfeld Follies, The Harvey Girls, Till the Clouds Roll By, Fiesta* (47), *The Unfinished Dance, On an Island with You, Words and Music, The Kissing Bandit, Mark of the Renegade* (ds), *Singin' in the Rain, Sombrero, The Band Wagon, Easy to Love, Deep in My Heart, Brigadoon, It's Always Fair Weather, Meet Me in Las Vegas/Viva Las Vegas, Silk Stockings, Party Girl* (ds), *Black Tights* (French).

## 74 CHEVALIER, MAURICE (1887–

). French singer-actor who oozes Gallic charm. Was café entertainer when Mistinguette made him her dancing partner. In British and French films as well as many in Hollywood.

Films: *Innocents of Paris* (Hollywood début), *The Love Parade, The Big Pond* (intro. "You Brought a New Kind of Love To Me"), *Playboy of Paris, Paramount on Parade, The Smiling Lieutenant, Love Me Tonight* (intro. "Isn't It Romantic?" "Mimi"), *One Hour with You, The Way to Love, A Bedtime Story, The Merry Widow* (34), *Folies Bergere/The Man from the Folies Bergere; Gigi* (intro. "I'm Glad I'm Not Young Any More," "Thank Heaven for Little Girls"), *Black Tights* (narrator), *Can Can, Pepe, In Search of the Castaways* (cs), *I'd Rather Be Rich* (cs).

## 75 CLARK, PETULA (1932– ).

British singer-actress, former child vaudeville performer who made several British films inc. *London Town/My Heart Goes Crazy.* Adult success as pop singer led to starring roles in *Finian's Rainbow, Goodbye Mr. Chips* (Brit.).

**76 CLINE, EDWARD F.** (1892–1961). Director, formerly one of original Keystone Kops in Mack Sennett comedies. Turned out many low-budget films for Universal.

Films: *Million Dollar Legs, Breaking the Ice, Hawaii Calls, My Little Chickadee* (cs), *Never Give a Sucker an Even Break/What a Man!* (cs), *Give Out Sisters, Private Buckaroo, What's Cooking?, Crazy House, He's My Guy, Ghost Catchers, Hat Check Honey, Night Club Girl, Moonlight and Cactus, Slightly Terrific, Swingtime Johnny, See My Lawyer, Penthouse Rhythm*.

**77 CLOONEY, ROSEMARY** (1928– ). Former band vocalist who became top recording star, signed by Paramount. An attractive singer, but career in films failed to gather momentum.

Films: *The Stars Are Singing* (début), *Here Come the Girls, Red Garters, White Christmas, Deep in My Heart*.

**78 COLE, JACK** (1914– ). Choreographer and dancer whose later work, in which hand movements were more prominent than footwork, was particularly favoured by Marilyn Monroe (q.v.). Danced on Broadway and in ballet, formed own dance group 1937. Organised dance workshop at Columbia 1944–48. Pupils included Rod Alexander (q.v.), Carol Haney (q.v.) and later Gwen Verdon (q.v.).

Films: As dancer: *Moon over Miami*. Ch. *Cover Girl* (one number), *Eadie Was a Lady, Tonight and Every Night* (also danced), *Tars and Spars, Gilda* (ds), *Thrill of Brazil, The Jolson Story, Down to Earth; On the Riviera, Meet Me after the Show, The Merry Widow* (52), *The I Don't Care Girl, The Farmer Takes a Wife, Gentlemen Prefer Blondes, River of No Return* (ds), *Three for the Show,*

*Gentlemen Marry Brunettes, Kismet* (55, also danced), *Designing Woman* (cs, also acted), *Les Girls, Some Like It Hot* (cs, 59), *Let's Make Love*.

**79 COLUMBO, RUSS** (1908–1934). RN: Ruggerio de Rudolpho Columbo. Popular crooner, chief rival to Bing Crosby (q.v.) in Thirties. Former child violin prodigy who played in silent studios.

Films: *The Wolf Song, The Street Girl, Wonder of Women* (ds), *Dynamite* (ds), *Hell Bound* (ds, also comp. "Is It Love?"), *Broadway through a Keyhole, Moulin Rouge, Wake Up and Dream* (34).

**80 COMDEN, BETTY** (1916– ) and **GREEN, ADOLPH.** Writers of some of Broadway and Hollywood's wittiest stories, screenplays and lyrics. Former writer-performers in group called "The Revuers" playing night clubs, graduated to Broadway with *On*

*the Town*. Particularly happy when dealing with New York and show business.

Films: sc. *Good News* (47, also lyrics "The French Lesson"), sc., lyrics *On the Town*, st., sc. *The Barkleys of Broadway*, st., sc. *Singin' in the Rain* (also lyrics "Moses"), st., sc. *The Band Wagon*, st., sc., lyrics *It's always Fair Weather*, st., sc., lyrics *Bells Are Ringing,* sc., lyrics *What a Way to Go* (cs).

**81 COMO, PERRY** (1912–    ). Singer, former barber, noted for relaxed style. Brief film career, but seemed more at ease in later television series.

Films: *Something for the Boys* (début), *Doll Face/Come Back to Me, If I'm Lucky, Words and Music.*

**82 COMPOSERS ON THE SCREEN.** The lavish story of Viennese waltz king Johann Strauss, played by Fernand Gravet in *The Great Waltz* (1938) was the first of Hollywood's composer-biographies, but the first American composer to have his life told on screen was, aptly enough, the country's first prolific popular songwriter, Stephen Collins Foster. Never having been justly rewarded with financial success or artistic recognition during his short and tragic lifetime (1826–1864), the composer of "Old Folks at Home," "Oh Sussanna," "De Camptown Races," "Old Kentucky Home" and "Beautiful Dreamer" was given Hollywood's tribute in 1939 when played by Don Ameche (q.v.) in *Swanee River,* many of Foster's songs being sung by Al Jolson (q.v.). A later film, *I Dream of Jeanie,* featured Bill Shirley as Foster and concentrated on his early life and romance with his boyhood sweetheart Jane McDowell, later his wife, for whom he wrote the song which gave the film its title.

Foster, influenced by the Negro spirituals and songs he heard as a boy, realised his ambition to create truly American popular music, starting a tradition that reached its popular and artistic peak in the Twenties and Thirties. During this magnificent period, five composers were often bracketted together, considered supreme masters of their craft—Irving Berlin, George Gershwin, Jerome Kern, Cole Porter and Richard Rodgers, working with lyricist Lorenz Hart (qq.v.). Of these only Berlin has never been celebrated by a Hollywood biography, having firmly refused to allow one during his lifetime. (He once stated, however, that had he ever relented he would have insisted on Fred Astaire playing the lead.) Berlin was probably influenced by the filmed stories of his contemporaries, rarely too satisfying dramatically. What they did provide though, was the opportunity to present a string of marvellous standards, performed by top stars, orchestrated and played by top Hollywood musicians, and this was more than enough justification. The Gershwin biography, *Rhapsody in Blue,* introduced Robert Alda to film audiences as the composer, with Herbert Rudley as his brother and lyricist Ira Gershwin. It took the Gershwin story from his childhood to his death, from his first song hit "Swanee," recreated in the film by Al Jolson (q.v.) to his concert pieces and *Porgy and Bess. Night and Day* was the Cole Porter story, with Cary Grant the actor personally chosen by Porter for the lead. Porter's wife also personally asked for Warner contract star Alexis Smith to be her film counterpart.

Jerome Kern, just before he died, had assisted M-G-M in assigning songs to the many stars featured in *Till the Clouds Roll By.* Robert Walker played Kern in a film that, except for the Minnelli sequences, was sometimes dull to watch but was always gorgeous to listen to. As well as presenting first-class performances of many Kern standards, including a fifteen-minute condensation of *Show Boat* which opened the film, the background score made beautiful use of Kern's music, including the polka from

35

his rarely-heard "Mark Twain Suite." *Words and Music,* the story of Richard Rodgers (Tom Drake) and Lorenz Hart (Mickey Rooney), was dramatically disastrous, the script completely failing to come to terms with the enigmatic character of the temperamental Hart, but the songs and a series of lavish production numbers provided moments of much pleasure.

Lesser-known composers sometimes fared better for overall film success. *Three Little Words,* with Fred Astaire as Bert Kalmar and Red Skelton as Harry Ruby (qq.v.) was lively and amusing, besides having the decided advantage of dancers in leading roles—Vera-Ellen (q.v.) was the heroine. *I'll See You in My Dreams* was the only screen biography with a lyricist (Gus Kahn, q.v.) as its sole hero, and was one of Hollywood's best—well-paced, funny and touching in turn and with a fine period atmosphere. Danny Thomas (q.v.) played Kahn, with Frank Lovejoy as his chief composer Walter Donaldson (q.v.). Doris Day (q.v.) was Kahn's wife Grace, who composed the music for his first hit, "I Wish I Had a Girl." It was made in black-and-white, a rarity for its time (1951) and a possible factor in its comparatively modest box-office performance.

The majority of composer biographies take a hit song as their title, as did *The Best Things in Life Are Free.* Gordon Macrae, Ernest Borgnine and Dan Dailey played the team of DeSylva, Brown and Henderson (qq.v.) respectively in a film combining a witty script, lively direction, good Twenties atmosphere and well-staged numbers. "Yankee Doodle Boy" George M. Cohan, who combined the talents of composer, lyricist, playwright and performer, was given an outstanding tribute in *Yankee Doodle Dandy.* (See also "Entertainers' Biographies.") Two

of Cohan's hit songs, "Little Nellie Kelly" and "Give My Regards to Broadway" lent their names to Hollywood musicals. Jimmy Walker, who in 1925 became Mayor of New York City, had been an occasional lyricist and in 1905 wrote his major success, "Will You Love Me in December as You Do in May?" to the music of Ernest R. Ball. The royalties from the song put Walker through law school. His story was told in *Beau James* with Bob Hope (q.v.). Ball, whose sentimental successes also included "Mother Machree" and "Let the Rest of the World Go By," was played by Dick Haymes (q.v.) in *Irish Eyes Are Smiling.*

Chauncey Olcott was an Irish balladeer and composer, a former blackface minstrel, who was particularly associated with the songs of Ernest R. Ball but wrote many himself, the biggest hit lending its title to Warner's biography *My Wild Irish Rose,* starring Dennis Morgan (q.v.) as the tenor-songwriter. Other composers whose lives and songs were the subject of movie musicals are Joe Howard, who wrote his first big hit "Hello My Baby" in 1900, played by Mark Stevens in *I Wonder Who's Kissing Her Now;* Fred Fisher, composer of "Chicago," "Come Josephine in My Flying Machine" and "Peg O' My Heart," portrayed by S. Z. Sakall in *Oh You Beautiful Doll* (Fisher's daughter Doris, also a composer, wrote "Put the Blame on Mame" for Rita Hayworth, q.v.); John Philip Sousa, best known composer of martial music, played by Clifton Webb in *Stars and Stripes Forever/Marching Along;* Sigmund Romberg (q.v.), played by Jose Ferrer in *Deep in My Heart;* and Negro "father of the Blues" W. C. Handy, played by Nat "King" Cole in a film titled after his 1914 standard *St. Louis Blues* (58); and country music composer Hank Williams, played by George

Hamilton in *Your Cheating Heart*. Hollywood has not always been strictly fair in presenting some composers on screen, bolstering the one or two hit tunes written by the film's subject with new songs by studio composers. Paul Dresser, played by Victor Mature in *My Gal Sal*, wrote "On the Banks of the Wabash" and the title tune, both given production numbers, but apart from these, a brief prologue medley and a chorus of "Liza Jane" from Mature, the rest of the film's numbers were new songs attributed in the film to Dresser. *The Star Maker*, Hollywood's tribute to Gus Edwards, also had a primarily new score. Bing Crosby (q.v.) played Edwards, who wrote "By the Light of the Silvery Moon," "School Days" and "Strolling through the Park One Day" but was perhaps better known as a vaudevillian who produced a string of shows with talented youngsters, his discoveries including Ray Bolger, Eddie Buzzell, Eddie Cantor, Ann Dvorak, George Jessell, Mervyn LeRoy and Eleanor Powell (qq.v.). Crosby played another pioneering composer, Daniel Decatur Emmett, one of the creators of the American minstrel show, in *Dixie*. The classic number that gave the film its title was written quickly by Emmett on a rainy Sunday in 1859 when asked for a "walk-around" closing song for the following night's minstrel show. Though uninfluenced by the war (Emmett was actually a Northerner) "Dixie" soon became the rallying song of the South. Besides being a far from accurate biography, Crosby's film used many new songs in its score. *The Great Victor Herbert* used that composer's melodies for its score but, despite its title, was hardly about Herbert at all (he was played by Walter Connolly) but used his songs as a peg for the love story of two singers.

Hollywood's rare ventures into classical biography have met with mixed success. They also share a fondness for the use of "Song" in their titles. *A Song to Remember* is the most notorious, with Cornel Wilde coughing blood on the piano keys as Frederick Chopin, and Merle Oberon wearing trousers as George Sand. *Song of Scheherazade* had French actor Jean-Pierre Aumont as Russian composer Rimsky-Korsakoff, new lyrics by Jack Brooks for some of the melodies, and was accepted by some people as a comedy. *Song of My Heart* was a solemn, low-budget account of Tchaikovsky's life, with Frank Sundstrom as the composer, and *Song of Love* told the equally depressing story of Robert Schumann's fight against failure and illness. Paul Henreid played Schumann, with Katharine Hepburn as Clara Wieck, his pianist wife, Robert Walker as Johannes Brahms, who falls in love with Clara, and Henry Daniell as Franz Liszt, who recognised Schumann's talent. Liszt's own story was told in *Song without End*, and star Dirk Bogarde summed up some of the problems of classical biography when he said of George Cukor (q.v.), who took over direction of the film mid-way, "The first thing he did was go through the script and cut out all the lines like 'Hi Ya, Mendelssohn.'" Wagner, another Liszt championed, played by Lyndon Brook in the Liszt biography, was portrayed by Alan Badel in *Magic Fire*, like *Song without End* European-made. These films benefited from their locations, and the latest composer biography, the mammoth production of *Tchaikovsky*, was primarily filmed in the composer's own country Russia, making use of the Bolshoi Ballet and starring Innokenti Smoktunovsky in the title role. A smaller-scale version of the same composer's life, Ken Russell's *The Music*

*Lovers*, featured American Richard Chamberlain as Tchaikovsky.

**83 CONNOLLY, BOBBY** (1890–    ). Choreographer, former stage director (inc. *Ziegfeld Follies*) who directed several musical shorts as well as staging dances for features.

Films: *Moonlight and Pretzels, Take a Chance, Sweet Adeline, Sweet Music, Go into Your Dance, Broadway Hostess, Stars over Broadway* (co.), *Colleen, The Singing Kid, Cain and Mabel, Sons O'Guns* (also wrote story), *Ready Willing and Able, The King and the Chorus Girl, Swing Your Lady, Honolulu* (co.), *At the Circus, The Wizard of Oz, Broadway Melody of 1940, Two Girls on Broadway* (co.).

**84 CONRAD, CON** (1891–1938) RN: Conrad K. Dober. Composer of first film song to win an Oscar, "The Continental," was successful Broadway composer when William Fox brought him to Hollywood in 1929 to write for talkies.

Films: *Fox Movietone Follies, The Cockeyed World, Broadway* (29), *Happy Days, Fox Movietone Follies of 1930, Let's Go Places, Palmy Days, Wine Women and Song, The Gift of Gab, I Like It That Way, The Gay Divorcee, Here's To Romance, Reckless, King Solomon of Broadway, The Story of Vernon and Irene Castle* ("Only When You're In My Arms").

**85 CONRIED, HANS** (1917–    ). Tall comic actor who created the memorable Doctor Terwilliker in *The Five Thousand Fingers of Dr. T*.

Other films: *Bitter Sweet, Crazy House, His Butler's Sister, My Friend Irma* (cs), *Nancy Goes to Rio, The Barkleys of Broadway, Summer Stock/If You Feel like Singing, Texas Carnival, Rich Young*

*and Pretty, Affairs of Dobie Gillis, Peter Pan* (voice of Captain Hook and Mr. Darling), *You're Never Too Young* (cs), *The Birds and the Bees* (cs), *The Big Beat, Juke Box Rhythm*.

**86 COSLOW, SAM** (1905–    ). Lyricist, occasional producer, given Paramount contract 1929.

Films: Lyrics: *Why Bring That Up?, Dance of Life, Fast Company, Honey* (inc. "Sing You Sinners"), *College Humour, College Coach* (inc. "Just One More Chance"), *Too Much Harmony, From Hell to Heaven* (ds), *The Way to Love, Hello Everybody, Murder at the Vanities, You Belong to Me* (ds), *Belle of the Nineties* (inc. "My Old Flame"), *Many Happy Returns, Goin' to Town, Coronado, Klondike Annie* ("My Medicine Man"), *Poppy* (title song only), *Rhythm on the Range* ("Mr. Paganini," music also), *Every Day's a Holiday, Mountain Music* (music also), *Hideaway Girl, One Hundred Men and a Girl* ("It's Raining Sunbeams"), *This Way Please, The Champagne Waltz, Thrill of a Lifetime, Turn Off the Moon, Love on Toast, You and Me* (ds), *Dreaming Out Loud* (also co-prod.); *Song of the South* (title tune), *Carnegie Hall; His Kind of Woman* (ds). Prod. *Out of This World, Copacabana* (also music and lyrics).

**87 COY, JOHNNY** (c. 1924–    ). Skilful tap dancer who had brief career in youthful brash roles. Canadian-born, dancing in Broadway show with Mary Martin (q.v.) when signed by Paramount.

Films: *Bring on the Girls* (début), *That's the Spirit, On Stage Everybody, Duffy's Tavern, Earl Carroll Sketch Book/Hats Off to Rhythm, Ladies' Man* (47); *Top Banana*.

**88 CRAIN, JEANNE** (1925–    ). Charming ingenué of Forties who starred in several musicals, though her voice was dubbed. Tested by Orson Welles for *The Magnificent Ambersons* (non-musical) while still at school, she lost the part but started modelling. Made a trainee at Fox, her first major role in *Home in Indiana* (later re-made as musical *April Love*) made her a star.

Films: *The Gang's All Here/The Girls He Left Behind* (bit), *State Fair* (45), *Centennial Summer, Margie, You Were Meant for Me, Cheaper By the Dozen* (cs), *I'll Get By* (guest), *Belles on Their Toes* (cs), *Gentlemen Marry Brunettes, The Second Greatest Sex* (as a Western-style Lysistrata), *The Joker Is Wild* (ds).

## 89 CRAWFORD, JOAN (1904– ).
RN: Billie Cassin (also known as Lucille LeSueur). Best known as one of the screen's great female emoters, but also a fine dancer. Started in silents in 1925, became noted for wild Charleston and

*Joan Crawford dances with director-choreographer Charles Walters in TORCH SONG*

Black Bottom. Remained star for over forty years.

Films: *Hollywood Revue* (performed first tap dance ever *heard* on screen, sang "Gotta Feeling for You" and part of group who introduced "Singing in the Rain"), *Untamed* (ds), *Montana Moon* (ws), *Dance Fools Dance, Dancing Lady* (danced with Astaire), *Sadie McKee, Ice Follies of 1939, Hollywood Canteen* (as herself), *Humoresque* (ds), *It's a Great Feeling* (guest), *Torch Song*.

## 90 CROSBY, BING (1901– ). RN:
Harry Lillis Crosby. Best-known crooner of all time, who in the Thirties set a new style in popular song delivery and was an acknowledged influence on such singers as Perry Como and Frank Sinatra (qq.v.). Took name Bing from comic-strip he read as child, later nick-named "The Groaner." Started as drummer-vocalist with college band, formed double act with member of group Al Rinker whose sister, singer Mildred Bailey, got them started in New York. Signed by Paul Whiteman, who added singer Harry Barris to form trio known as "Rhythm Boys." As such, appeared with Whiteman in *King of Jazz*. Going solo, made several Sennett shorts. Hit radio show, with theme song "When the Blue of the Night," led to Paramount contract. Relaxed style, likeable personality, casual way with a comedy line and smooth, unmistakable voice made him top box-office star for over twenty years. Has also sold more records than any other singer.

Films: *King of Jazz, Check and Double Check, Reaching for the Moon, The Big Broadcast* (first film in which he received billing, intro. "Please"), *College Humour* (intro. "Down the Old Ox Road"), *Too Much Harmony, Going Hollywood* (intro. "Temptation"), *We're Not Dressing* (intro. "Love Thy Neighbour," "She

Reminds Me of You"), *She Loves Me Not* (intro. "Love in Bloom"), *Here Is My Heart* (intro. "June in January," "Love Is Just around the Corner"), *Mississippi* (intro. "Easy to Remember"), *Two for Tonight, Big Broadcast of 1936* (intro. "I Wished on the Moon"), *Anything Goes* (36, intro. "Sailor Beware"), *Rhythm on the Range* (intro. "I'm an Old Cowhand"), *Pennies from Heaven* (intro. "One Two Button My Shoe," "Pennies from Heaven"), *Waikiki Wedding* (intro. "Blue Hawaii") and "Sweet Leilani," the latter a song Crosby had heard in Hawaii and interpolated into the film—it went on to win that year's Oscar), *Double or Nothing* (intro. "It's the Natural Thing to Do," "The Moon Got in My Eyes"), *Doctor Rhythm, Sing You Sinners* (intro. "A Pocketful of Dreams," "Small Fry"), *Paris Honeymoon, East Side of Heaven* (intro. "Sing a Song of Moonbeams"), *The Star Maker* (intro. "An Apple for the Teacher"), *Road to Singapore* (40, intro. "Too Romantic"), *If I Had My Way* (intro. "The Pessimistic Character with the Crab-apple Face," "April Played the Fiddle" and revived 1913 title song), *Rhythm on the River* (intro. "Only Forever"), *Road to Zanzibar, Birth of the Blues* (intro. "The Waiter, the Porter and the Upstairs Maid" with Mary Martin, q.v., and Jack Teagarden), *Holiday Inn* (intro. "Be Careful It's My Heart" and his biggest record hit "White Christmas"), *Road to Morocco* (intro. "Moonlight Becomes You"), *Star Spangled Rhythm, Dixie* (as minstrel man-composer Dan Emmett, intro. "Sunday Monday and Always"), *Going My Way* (intro. "Swinging on a Star" and revived the 1913 "Too-ra-loo-ra-loo-ral"), *Here Come the Waves* (intro. "Accentuate the Positive" with Sonny Tufts, "Let's Take the Long Way Home" and sang "That Old Black Magic," introduced by Johnny Johnston, q.v., in *Star Spangled Rhythm*), *Out of This World* (voice only), *Duffy's Tavern* (reprised "Swinging on a Star"), *The Bells of St. Mary's* (intro. "Aren't You Glad You're You?"), *Road to Utopia, Blue Skies* (intro. "You Keep Coming Back like a Song"), *Welcome Stranger* (intro. "Country Style"),

*Bing Crosby with Shirley Ross in WAIKIKI WEDDING*

*Variety Girl, Road to Rio* (intro. "But Beautiful," "You Don't Have to Know the Language"), *The Emperor Waltz, A Connecticut Yankee in King Arthur's Court* (intro. "Once and for Always," "If You Stub Your Toe on the Moon"), *Top O' The Morning, Ichabod and Mr. Toad* (voice only), *Riding High* (50, intro. "Sunshine Cake"), *Mr. Music* (intro. "Accidents Will Happen," "High on the List"), *Here Comes the Groom* (intro. "In the Cool Cool Cool of the Evening" with Jane Wyman, q.v.), *Just for You* (intro. "Zing a Little Zong" with Wyman), *Road to Bali, Little Boy Lost* (ds), *White Christmas* (intro. "Counting My Blessings," "Snow"), *The Country Girl* (ds, intro. "The Search Is Through"), *Anything Goes* (56), *High Society* (intro. "I Love You Samantha," "True Love" with Grace Kelly, "Now You Has Jazz" with Louis Armstrong, q.v.), *Man on Fire* (ds, only singing was

behind credit titles), *Say One for Me, Let's Make Love* (guest), *High Time* (intro. "The Second Time Around"), *Pepe* (guest), *Road to Hong Kong, Robin and the Seven Hoods* (intro. "Mr. Booze"). Two compilation films, *Road to Hollywood* (46) and *Down Memory Lane* (49) include early Crosby shorts.

**91 CROSLAND, ALAN** (1894–1936). Director who started in 1914 and made the first screen musical, *The Jazz Singer*. Had earlier directed first film with synchronised music, *Don Juan*. His musicals lack imaginative flair, being mainly vehicles for Broadway stars of the time.

Films: *The Jazz Singer* (27), *On with the Show, Big Boy, Song of the Flame, Viennese Nights, Children of Dreams, King Solomon of Broadway*.

**92 CUKOR, GEORGE** (1899–    ). Director of great taste and style, famous for his handling of actresses (Garbo, Crawford, Hepburn, Holliday). Was Broadway producer before becoming dialogue director in Hollywood. Chosen to bring *My Fair Lady* to screen, but his best musical remains Garland's *A Star Is Born*.

Films: *One Hour with You* (co-dir. with Lubitsch, q.v.), *Dinner at Eight* (cs), *Zaza* (cs), *Two-Faced Woman* (cs), *Adam's Rib* (cs), *It Should Happen to You* (cs), *A Star Is Born, Les Girls, Let's Make Love, Song without End* (finished by Cukor after death of Charles Vidor, q.v.), *My Fair Lady*.

**93 CUMMINGS, IRVING** (1888– 1959). Director who started as film actor 1909. Wrote, dir., prod. and acted in

41

series of two-reelers, and dir. last twenty-six episodes of *Diamonds from the Sky*, longest serial ever made. Most notable musicals were Technicolored successes with Betty Grable (q.v.), including *Down Argentine Way*, the film which established her as Fox's musical queen.

Films: *Romance of the Underworld* (ds), *Cameo Kirby* (ds), *On the Level* (ds), *I Believed in You* (ds), *Curly Top, Poor Little Rich Girl, Merry-go-round of 1938, Walter Wanger's Vogues of 1938, Hollywood Cavalcade, Just around the Corner, Little Miss Broadway* (38), *Everything Happens at Night, Down Argentine Way, Lillian Russell, Louisiana Purchase, That Night in Rio, My Gal Sal, Springtime in the Rockies, Sweet Rosie O'Grady, The Dolly Sisters, Double Dynamite/It's Only Money* (cs).

**94 CUMMINGS, JACK** (1900–    ). Producer associated in the Forties with M-G-M's second-league musicals, but graduated to major stars and budgets in Fifties. Office boy, script boy, asst. dir., prod. of shorts before given features.

Films: *Born to Dance, Broadway Melody of 1938, Listen Darling, Honolulu, Broadway Melody* (40), *Two Girls on Broadway, Go West, Ship Ahoy, I Dood It/By Hook or by Crook, Broadway Rhythm, Bathing Beauty, Easy to Wed, Fiesta* (47), *It Happened in Brooklyn, Neptune's Daughter, Two Weeks with Love, Three Little Words, Texas Carnival, Excuse My Dust, Sombrero, Lovely to Look At, Kiss Me Kate, Give a Girl a Break, Seven Brides for Seven Brothers, Interrupted Melody*.

**95 CURTIZ, MICHAEL** (1888–1962). RN: Mihaly Kertesz. Director, a superb professional and one of the great names of Hollywood, under contract to Warners for nearly thirty years. As well as some

splendid musicals, his work includes the best of all *genres (Charge of the Light Brigade, Robin Hood, Elizabeth and Essex, Casablanca, Mildred Pierce)*. Born in Hungary, turned from acting to directing for Ufa in Berlin, and brought to Hollywood by Warners.

Films: *Mammy, Bright Lights* (31), *Yankee Doodle Dandy, This Is the Army, Janie* (cs), *Night and Day, Romance on the High Seas/It's Magic* (also prod.), *My Dream Is Yours* (also prod., re-make *Twenty Million Sweethearts*), *Young Man with a Horn/Young Man of Music, I'll See You in My Dreams, The Jazz Singer* (52), *White Christmas, We're No Angels* (cs), *The Vagabond King* (56), *The Best Things in Life Are Free, The Helen Morgan Story/ Both Ends of the Candle, King Creole*.

**96 DAILEY, DAN** (1915–    ). Tall dancer and leading man popularly teamed with Betty Grable (q.v.) in a series of back-stage musicals. Vaudeville and musical comedy background, spotted by M-G-M talent scout, but became star at Fox after war service.

Films: *Hullabaloo, Ziegfeld Girl, Lady Be Good, Panama Hattie, Moon over Her Shoulder* (cs), *Give Out Sisters, Mother Wore Tights, When My Baby Smiles at Me, You Were Meant for Me, Give My Regards to Broadway, A Ticket to Tomahawk* (cs), *I'll Get By* (guest), *My Blue Heaven, Call Me Mister, Meet Me at the Fair, The Girl Next Door, You're My Everything* (cs), *There's No Business like Show Business, It's Always Fair Weather, Meet Me in Las Vegas/Viva Las Vegas, The Best Things in Life Are Free* (as composer Ray Henderson, q.v.), *Pepe*.

**97 DALE, GROVER** (1936–    ). RN: Grover Robert Aitken. Broadway chorus boy and juvenile lead *(Sail Away)*, who played prominent dancing roles in musicals of Sixties.

Films: *The Unsinkable Molly Brown, Les Demoiselles de Rochefort/Young Girls of Rochefort* (French), *Half a Sixpence.*

**98 DALE, VIRGINIA** (c. 1919–    ). Dancer best remembered as Fred Astaire's (q.v.) partner in *Holiday Inn.*

Other films: *Start Cheering, Buck Benny Rides Again, The Quarterback, Love Thy Neighbour, Las Vegas Nights, Dancing on a Dime, Kiss the Boys Goodbye.*

**99 DALEY, CASS** (1915–    ). RN: Catherine Dailey. Gawky, buck-toothed comedienne whose madcap numbers were a staple of Paramount musicals in the Forties.

Films: *The Fleet's In, Crazy House, Star Spangled Rhythm, Riding High/ Melody Inn, Duffy's Tavern, Out of This World, Ladies' Man* (47), *Variety Girl; Here Comes the Groom, Red Garters; Norwood.*

**100 D'AMBOISE, JACQUES** (1934–    ). RN: Jacques Ahearn. Dancer and choreographer, *premier danseur* of the New York City Ballet, who has made telling dance contributions to the film musical.

Films: *Seven Brides for Seven Brothers* (as Ephraim), *Oklahoma, Carousel* (as the Ring-master), *The Best Things in Life Are Free.*

**101 DAMONE, VIC** (1925–    ). RN: Vito Farinola. Italian-American singer, a fine interpreter of popular music who played leading roles at M-G-M. Has recently taken dramatic parts.

Films: *Rich Young and Pretty* (début), *The Strip, Hit the Deck, Athena, Deep in My Heart, Meet Me in Las Vegas/Viva Las Vegas* (guest), *Kismet* (55); *Spree.*

**102 DANDRIDGE, DOROTHY** (1923–1965). Negro dancer turned band vocalist and night club singer who scored major screen success as Carmen Jones, also played Gershwin's (q.v.) Bess. Other film parts routine.

Films: *A Day at the Races* (as child), *Sun Valley Serenade, Atlantic City; Remains to Be Seen* (cs), *Bright Road* (ds), *Carmen Jones, Porgy and Bess.* In last two musicals, singing voice was dubbed.

**103 DANIELS, BEBE** (1901–    ). RN: Phyllis Daniels. Texas-born singer and leading lady on stage since childhood, Harold Lloyd's co-star when thirteen. After film musicals of Thirties scored equal success in British radio and vaudeville.

Films: *Rio Rita* (29), *Dixiana, Love Comes Along, Reaching for the Moon* (ds), *Forty-Second Street* (intro. "You're Getting To Be a Habit with Me"), *Cocktail Hour* (ds), *Music Is Magic.*

**104 DANIELS, WILLIAM** (1895–1970). Veteran photographer in Hollywood from 1917, worked on von Stroheim's *Foolish Wives* and *Greed.* Signed by M-G-M in 1924, remained there many years.

Films: *Broadway to Hollywood, Dinner*

*at Eight* (ds), *Naughty Marietta, Rose Marie* (36), *Broadway Melody of 1938; For Me and My Gal; For the Love of Mary; The Glenn Miller Story, The Girl Rush* (55), *The Benny Goodman Story, Can Can, A Hole in the Head* (cs), *Come September* (cs), *How the West Was Won* (ws, co.), *Billy Rose's Jumbo, Robin and the Seven Hoods, Valley of the Dolls* (ds).

**105 DARBY, KEN** (1909– ) RN: Kenneth Lorin. Vocal arranger and supervisor, occasional composer, who in early Thirties was part of vocal quartet and later formed large choral group, the Ken Darby Singers. Arranged for Bing Crosby (q.v.) in Thirties, devised the voices of the Munchkins in *The Wizard of Oz,* later worked at Fox as arranger and vocal coach.

As singer with The King's Men Quartet: *Sweetie, We're Not Dressing, Thanks a Million, Alexander's Ragtime Band, Girl of the Golden West, Ice Follies of 1939, Honolulu, Broadway Serenade, New Moon, Bitter Sweet, Pinnochio, Dumbo, Bambi.* As vocal arranger: *The Wizard of Oz, Higher and Higher, Step Lively, Make Mine Music* (also comp.), *Song of the South, Fun and Fancy Free, So Dear To My Heart, The Beautiful Blonde from Bashful Bend, Oh You Beautiful Doll, Dancing in the Dark, My Blue Heaven, A Ticket to Tomahawk* (cs), *Meet Me after the Show, Tonight We Sing, With a Song in My Heart, Call Me Madam, River of No Return* (also comp.), *There's No Business like Show Business, Carousel, The King and I, Bus Stop* (ds, also comp.), *Love Me Tender* (also comp.), *South Pacific, Hound Dog Man* (also comp.), *Porgy and Bess, Flower Drum Song, State Fair* (62), *How the West Was Won* (ws, also comp.), *Camelot, Finian's Rainbow.* As composer: *Rancho Notorious* (ws).

**106 DARE, DANNY** (1905– ). Choreographer-producer, former stage actor in Twenties who became dance director and producer. Worked in Hollywood from 1935, notably at Paramount in early Forties. Now works in TV, night clubs.

Films: Ch. *Three Cheers for Love, Fifty-second Street, Start Cheering, Holiday Inn, Star Spangled Rhythm, Bring On the Girls, Incendiary Blonde, Duffy's Tavern* (also ass. prod.). Prod., ch. *Road to Utopia, My Favourite Brunette* (cs), *Variety Girl, Road to Rio, Isn't It Romantic?*

**107 DARIN, BOBBY** (1936– ). RN: Robert Walden Cassotto. Pop singer and composer with brash style featured in several musicals, but made stronger impressions in his straight roles.

Films: *Come September* (cs, also comp.), *Pepe, State Fair* (61). Comp. *The Lively Set.*

**108 DAVIES, MARION** (1897–1961). RN: Marion Douras. One of the silent stars who was as great a success in talkies, an appealing heroine of M-G-M musicals of Thirties. Left convent school to dance in stage production of *Chu Chin Chow* before screen *début* in 1918.

Films: *Hollywood Revue, Marianne* (also prod.), *Blondie of the Follies* (also prod.), *Going Hollywood, Peg O' My Heart, Operator 13, Cain and Mabel, Hearts Divided, Ever Since Eve.*

**109 DAVIS, JOAN** (1908–1961). RN: Madonna Josephine Davis. One of Hollywood's few truly funny lady comics, who could handle slapstick, wisecracks and song numbers with equal aplomb. Stage *début* when three, at six toured as "The Toy Comedienne." Sennett short *Way Up Thar* started film career. In Fifties had hit TV show "I Married Joan."

Films: *Roman Scandals, Life Begins in College, Love and Hisses, Sing and Be Happy, Thin Ice/Lovely To Look At, Hold That Co-Ed, On the Avenue, Wake Up and Live, You Can't Have Everything, Just around the Corner, Josette, My Lucky Star, Sally Irene and Mary, Tail Spin, Sun Valley Serenade, Two Latins from Manhattan, Hold That Ghost, Yokel Boy, Sweetheart of the Fleet, Around the World, He's My Guy, Time Out for Romance, Manhattan Heartbeat, Beautiful but Broke, Kansas City Kitty, Show Business, George White's Scandals of 1945, If You Knew Susie, Make Mine Laughs, The Travelling Saleswoman.*

**110 DAVIS, SAMMY, jr.** (1925–    ). Negro entertainer whose film performances have generally been less dynamic than his stage ones. Professional *début* at two in family vaudeville act.

Films: *Meet Me in Las Vegas/Viva Las Vegas, Ocean's 11* (ds), *Pepe, Porgy and Bess, Robin and the Seven Hoods, A Man Called Adam* (ds), *Salt and Pepper* (cs), *Sweet Charity, One More Time* (cs).

**111 DAY, DENNIS** (1917–    ). RN: Eugene Denis McNulty. Irish-American tenor with a wide grin and gauche acting style. *Début* on Jack Benny radio show.

Films: *Buck Benny Rides Again, Sleepy Lagoon, The Powers Girl, Music in Manhattan, Melody Time* (voice only), *Make Mine Laughs, I'll Get By, Golden Girl, The Girl Next Door.*

**112 DAY, DORIS** (1924-    ). RN: Doris Kappelhoff. Blonde, freckled singer with cheerful personality, a star since first film 1948. Was child tap-dancer till car accident, when she took up singing. While band vocalist with Les Brown made hit record "Sentimental

*"It's Magic" : Doris Day in her first film ROMANCE ON THE HIGH SEAS/IT'S MAGIC*

Journey." When Michael Curtiz (q.v.) was unable to borrow Ava Gardner (q.v.) from M-G-M for *Romance on the High Seas* he took a chance with Doris, who was an overnight success with press and public. After series of lively musicals she shrewdly evolved straight comedy image in mid-Fifties. Own TV series 1969.

Films: *Romance on the High Seas/It's Magic* (début), *My Dream Is Yours, It's a Great Feeling, Young Man with a Horn/Young Man of Music, Tea for Two* (first of several teamings with Gordon Macrae, q.v.), *West Point Story/Fine and Dandy, Lullaby of Broadway, On Moonlight Bay, Starlift, I'll See You in My Dreams, April in Paris, By the Light of the Silvery Moon, Calamity Jane* (intro. "Secret Love"), *Lucky Me, Young at Heart, Love Me Or Leave Me* (as torch singer Ruth Etting), *The Man Who Knew Too Much* (ds, intro. "Que Sera, Sera"), *The Pajama*

Game, *It Happened to Jane* (cs), *Please Don't Eat the Daisies* (cs), *Lover Come Back* (cs), *Billy Rose's Jumbo, Do Not Disturb* (cs).

**113 DE HAVEN, GLORIA** (1925– ). Pert actress-singer, a charming ingenué who never quite attained star status. A child actress (in Chaplin's *Modern Times*) she later became vocalist with Bob Crosby and Jan Savitt bands. Signed by M-G-M 1940.

Films: *Best Foot Forward, Broadway Rhythm, Thousands Cheer, Two Girls and a Sailor, Step Lively, Summer Holiday, Yes Sir That's My Baby, Three Little Words* (guest role as her own mother, a musical comedy star), *Summer Stock/If You Feel like Singing, I'll Get By, Two*

*Gloria De Haven (left) with June Allyson and a young Stanley Donen in BEST FOOT FORWARD*

Tickets to Broadway, Down among the Sheltering Palms, So This Is Paris, The Girl Rush (55).

**114 DEL RIO, DOLORES** (1905– ). RN: Lolita Dolores Asunsolo de Martinez. Exotic Mexican actress and dancer, a silent star whose greatest talkie successes were made in her native Mexico.

Films: *Flying Down to Rio, Wonder Bar, In Caliente, I Live for Love, International Settlement* (ds); *Flaming Star* (ws). Also popularised song "Ramona," which she sang at personal appearances with her silent film of same name.

**115 DEL RUTH, ROY** (1895–1961). Prolific director who injected vitality and charm into many of his musicals. Former journalist, became writer for Sennett 1915, started directing 1917 with Ben Turpin films.

Films: *The Desert Song* (29), *Gold Diggers of Broadway* (29), *Hold Everything, Life of the Party* (30), *Blonde Crazy, Blessed Event* (cs), *Kid Millions, Broadway Melody of 1936, Folies Bergere, Thanks a Million, Born to Dance, Broadway Melody of 1938, On the Avenue, Happy Landing, My Lucky Star, The Star Maker, Tail Spin, The Chocolate Soldier, Maisie Gets Her Man* (cs), *DuBarry Was a Lady, Broadway Rhythm, It Happened on Fifth Avenue* (cs), *Always Leave Them Laughing* (cs), *West Point Story/Fine and Dandy, On Moonlight Bay, Starlift, About Face, Stop You're Killing Me* (cs), *Three Sailors and a Girl.*

**116 DEPAUL, GENE** (1919– ). Composer who with lyricist Don Raye wrote many scores at Universal. Major film success *Seven Brides for Seven Brothers* with Johnny Mercer (q.v.) as lyricist.

Films with Don Raye: *Hellzapoppin'* (inc. "Watch the Birdie"), *In the Navy, Keep 'Em Flying* (inc. "You Don't Know What Love Is"), *Moonlight in Hawaii, San Antonio Rose, Almost Married, Behind the Eight Ball, Private Buckaroo, Ride 'Em Cowboy* (inc. "I'll Remember April"), *Pardon My Sarong, Who Done It?* (inc. "He's My Guy"), *What's Cooking?, When Johnny Comes Marching Home, Follow the Band, Hi' Ya Chum, Hi Buddy, I Dood It/By Hook or By Crook* ("Star Eyes"), *Larceny with Music, What's Buzzin' Cousin?, Broadway Rhythm* (also voc. arr.), *Hi Good Lookin', Lost in a Harem, Night Club Girl, The Reckless Age, The Singing Sheriff, Song of the Sarong, A Date with Judy, A Song Is Born, Ichabod and Mr. Toad, Alice in Wonderland* (51, "Twas Brillig"). With Johnny Mercer: *Seven Brides for Seven Brothers*, (inc. "Bless Yore Beautiful Hide," "Lonesome Polecat," "Goin' Courtin'," "Spring Spring Spring"), *Li'l Abner*.

**117 DESYLVA, BUDDY** (1896–1950). RN: George Gard. Producer and songwriter. Was ukelele player and ballad singer till Al Jolson (q.v.) used one of his songs. Teamed with Ray Henderson and Lew Brown (qq.v.) to form one of most successful song-writing partnerships ever till they split in 1930, DeSylva staying in Hollywood as producer and writer. Prod. five Shirley Temple (q.v.) films, later production head at Paramount.

Films as lyricist: *The Singing Fool, Say It with Songs, Sunny Side Up, Follow the Leader, Good News* (30 and 47), *Follow Through, Just Imagine, Take a Chance, The Best Things in Life Are Free* (biography). Prod: *The Little Colonel, The Littlest Rebel, Captain January, Poor Little Rich Girl, Stowaway, You're a Sweetheart, Birth of the Blues, Aloma of the South Seas* (ds), *Lady in the Dark, The Stork Club*.

**118 DEUTSCH, ADOLPH** (1897– ). London-born conductor, occasional composer, for both musicals and dramas. MD for shows of Berlin, Gershwin and Rodgers and Hart (qq.v.) on Broadway prior to Hollywood.

Films as orchestrator: *Fools for Scandal; Take Me Out to the Ball Game/Everybody's Cheering, Annie Get Your Gun, Pagan Love Song, Show Boat* (51), *Belle of New York, Million Dollar Mermaid/The One-Piece Bathing Suit, The Band Wagon, Torch Song* (ds), *Seven Brides for Seven Brothers, Deep in My Heart, Interrupted Melody, Oklahoma* (mus. adapt. only), *Funny Face, Les Girls, Some Like It Hot* (cs, 59). Comp. *Lili* ("Hi-Lili, Hi-Lo" w. Bronislau Kaper).

**119 DIETRICH, MARLENE** (1901– ). RN: Maria Magdalene Dietrich. German-born singer-actress, legendary for her ageless glamour and her seductive way with a song. None of her films true musicals, but she has sung memorably in many of them.

Films: *The Blue Angel* (German, intro. "Falling in Love Again," "I'm Naughty Little Lola"), *Morocco, Blonde Venus, Song of Songs* (intro. "Johnny"), *The Devil Is a Woman, Desire, Destry Rides Again* (intro. "See What the Boys in the Backroom Will Have"), *Seven Sinners, The Flame of New Orleans, Manpower, The Lady Is Willing, Follow The Boys* (44), *Kismet* (44), *Golden Earrings, A Foreign Affair, Stage Fright* (intro. "The Laziest Gal in Town"), *Rancho Notorious, Witness for the Prosecution*.

**120 DIETZ, HOWARD** (1896– ). Lyricist who worked mainly with Arthur Schwartz (q.v.). As advertising executive he thought up "Leo the Lion" trademark and slogan "Ars gratia artis" for Samuel Goldwyn (q.v.) who made him head of publicity at M-G-M.

Films: *Battle of Paris, Hollywood Party, The Girl from Missouri, Under Your Spell, Three Daring Daughters/The Birds and the Bees* ("The Dickey-Bird Song"), *Dancing in the Dark* (this used songs from the Broadway revue *The Band Wagon*), *The Band Wagon, Torch Song* ("Two-Faced Woman").

**121  DOLAN, ROBERT EMMETT** (1908–    ). One of Paramount's chief arrangers and background music composers for many years, later producer. Broadway conductor from 1928 (inc. *Good News, Louisiana Purchase*), films from 1941.

Films as MD: *Birth of the Blues, Louisiana Purchase, Holiday Inn, Star Spangled Rhythm, Happy Go Lucky* (43), *Dixie, Let's Face It, Going My Way, Lady in the Dark, Here Come the Waves, Incendiary Blonde, Duffy's Tavern, Bring On the Girls, The Bells of St. Mary's, The Stork Club, Blue Skies, Cross My Heart.* Prod: *White Christmas, The Girl Rush* (55), *Anything Goes* (56).

**122  DONALDSON, WALTER** (1893–1947). Composer of Al Jolson's (q.v.) "Mammy" and Eddie Cantor's (q.v.) "Yes Sir That's My Baby." Had first hit in 1915 and had written many standards by time he went to Hollywood in 1929.

Films: *Glorifying the American Girl, Hot for Paris, Cameo Kirby, Kid Millions, Million Dollar Ransom, Operator 13, Hollywood Party, The Girl from Missouri, Here Comes the Band, The Great Ziegfeld* (inc. "You Never Looked So Beautiful"), *That's Right You're Wrong, Broadway Serenade, Two Girls on Broadway,* *Panama Hattie* ("At the Savoy"), *Give Out Sisters, Beautiful but Broke, Follow the Boys* (44), *It's a Pleasure.* Songs also featured prominently in Gus Kahn's (q.v.) biography *I'll See You in My Dreams.*

**123  DONEN, STANLEY** (1924–    ). Director and choreographer who once specialised in musicals. Learned dancing as child (after seeing *Flying Down to Rio*). New York *début* 1940 as chorus boy in *Pal Joey* starring Gene Kelly (q.v.). In chorus of *Best Foot Forward* and assistant ch. to Kelly. One of several members of that show's creative team signed by M-G-M to work on film version. When Kelly went to Columbia to make *Cover Girl* he asked for Donen as assistant. Stayed at studio to work on B musicals, returned to M-G-M to work with Kelly on choreography for *Anchors Aweigh.* Four years as dance director, 1949 co-ch. and dir. one sequence *Take Me Out to the Ball Game*, after which producer Arthur Freed (q.v.) asked him to co-dir. *On the Town* with Kelly. First solo dir. *Royal Wedding* (50). After *Damn Yankees* (59), abandoned musicals for romantic comedies/thrillers.

Films: Co-ch. *Best Foot Forward* (also only film appearance, as chorus boy), *Cover Girl.* Ch. *Hey Rookie, Jam Session, Kansas City Kitty.* Co-ch. *Anchors Aweigh.* Ch. *Holiday in Mexico, No Leave No Love.* Co-ch. *Living in a Big Way* (also dir. one sequence). Ch. *This Time for Keeps, Killer McCoy* (ds), *Big City, A Date with Judy, The Kissing Bandit.* Co-ch. *Take Me Out to the Ball Game/Everybody's Cheering* (also dir. one sequence). Co-dir. *On the Town* (also co-ch.). Dir. *Royal Wedding/Wedding Bells.* Co-dir. *Singin' in the Rain* (also co-ch.). Dir. *Give a Girl a Break* (also co-ch.), *Seven Brides for Seven Brothers,*

*Deep in My Heart* (made prior to *Brides* but released after). Co-dir. *It's Always Fair Weather* (also co-ch.). Dir. *Funny Face* (and staged songs). Co-dir and co-prod. *The Pajama Game, Damn Yankees/ What Lola Wants.*

**124 DONOHUE, JACK** (1912–    ). RN: John Francis Donohue. Irish-American dancer, choreographer and director who was bank clerk and iron worker before becoming chorus boy in *Ziegfeld Follies* 1928. Staged dances for several Broadway shows before joining Fox 1934, later Paramount, M-G-M, Warners.

Films: Ch. *George `White's Scandals* (34), *Music in the Air, Lottery Lover, Under Pressure, The Little Colonel, Under the Pampas Moon, Curly Top, Music Is Magic, The Littlest Rebel, Thanks a Million, Captain January ; Louisiana Purchase, You're in the Army Now, The Fleet's In, The Powers Girl, Girl Crazy* (43, co.), *Best Foot Forward* (co.), *Bathing Beauty, Anchors Aweigh* (co.), *Easy to Wed, It Happened in Brooklyn, On an Island with You, The Duchess of Idaho, Calamity Jane, Top Banana.* Dir., ch. *Lucky Me, Babes in Toyland* (61).

**125 DOUGLAS, GORDON** (c. 1910–    ). Director, former comedy writer and actor with Hal Roach, dir. "Our Gang" comedies. Not particularly at ease with the musical.

Films: *Road Show* (co-dir.), *The Girl Rush* (44), *If You Knew Susie, She's Back on Broadway, So This Is Love/The Grace Moore Story, Young at Heart, Sincerely Yours, Follow That Dream, Robin and the Seven Hoods.*

**126 DOWNS, JOHNNY** (1913–    ). Dancer-actor. Member of "Our Gang" series, then went into vaudeville prior to B musicals.

Films: *Babes in Toyland* (34), *Hold That Girl, Coronado, Pigskin Parade, The First Baby, Thrill of a Lifetime, Turn off the Moon, Swing Sister Swing, Hawaiian Nights, Laugh It Off, I Can't Give You Anything but Love Baby, Sing Dance and Plenty Hot/Melody Girl, Melody and Moonlight, All-American Co-Ed, Moonlight in Hawaii, Sing Another Chorus, Red Head, Behind the Eight Ball, Campus Rhythm, Harvest Melody, They Shall Have Faith, Trocadero, Twilight on the Prairie, Rhapsody in Blue, The Kid from Brooklyn, Cruising Down the River.*

**127 DRAKE, DONA** (1920–    ). RN: Rita Novello. (Once known as Rita Rio.) Bouncy little Mexican performer, former band singer, who provided lively support in Paramount musicals.

Films: *Louisiana Purchase, Aloma of the South Seas* (ds), *Star Spangled Rhythm, Road to Morocco, Let's Face It, Salute for Three, Hot Rhythm.*

**128 DREIFUSS, ARTHUR** (1908–    ). German-born director of second-features aimed mainly at juvenile market. Child prodigy as conductor, pianist, later choreographer and Broadway producer.

Films: *The Sultan's Daughter, Sarong Girl* (both these were vehicles for burlesque star Ann Corio), *Campus Rhythm, Melody Parade, Nearly Eighteen, Ever since Venus, Eadie Was a Lady, Junior Prom, Freddie Steps Out, Gay Senorita, High School Hero, Betty Co-Ed, Vacation Days, Little Miss Broadway* (47), *Sweet Genevieve, Two Blondes and a Redhead, Glamour Girl, Mary Lou, I Surrender Dear, An Old Fashioned Girl, Manhattan Angel, There's a Girl in My Heart* (also prod.), *Juke Box Rhythm.*

**129 DUBIN, AL** (1891–1945). Swiss-born lyricist, former singing waiter, who teamed with Harry Warren (q.v.) to write scores for most Warner musicals of Thirties.

Films: *Gold Diggers of Broadway* (29, inc. "Tip-toe Through the Tulips"), *Sally, Dancing Sweeties, She Couldn't Say No, Oh Sailor Behave, Hold Everything, Top Speed, Big Boy, Blessed Event* (cs), *The Crooner, Roman Scandals* (inc. "Keep Young and Beautiful"), *Gold Diggers of 1933* (inc. "My Forgotten Man"), *Footlight Parade* (inc. "Shanghai Lil"), *Forty-Second Street* (inc. "Shuffle Off to Buffalo," "You're Getting To Be a Habit with Me"), *Moulin Rouge, Twenty Million Sweethearts, Dames* (inc. "I Only Have Eyes for You"), *Wonder Bar, Go Into Your Dance, Gold Diggers of 1935* (35 Oscar "Lullaby of Broadway"), *In Caliente, Broadway Gondolier* (inc. "Lulu's Back in Town"), *Shipmates Forever, Stars over Broadway, Colleen, Sons O'Guns, Sing Me a Love Song, Hearts Divided, Cain and Mabel, Gold Diggers of 1937* (inc. "With Plenty of Money and You"), *San Quentin* (ds), *Mr Dodd Takes the Air* (inc. "Remember Me?"), *The Singing Marine, Melody for Two, Gold Diggers in Paris, Stage Door Canteen.*

**130 DUKE, VERNON** (1903–1969). RN: Vladimir Dukelsky. Russian-born composer of both popular and classical music (the latter under his original name). More prolific in theatre than cinema.

Films: *Goldwyn Follies* (completed score after death of George Gershwin, q.v.); *Cabin in the Sky; April in Paris, She's Working Her Way through College.*

**131 DUNN, JAMES** (1905–1967). Actor, song-and-dance man who started as extra. Career declined after Thirties, but returned to win Oscar for *A Tree Grows in Brooklyn* (non-musical).

Films: *Bad Girl, Dance Team, Jimmy and Sallie, Take a Chance, Sailor's Luck, Stand Up and Cheer, Baby Take a Bow* (took its title from number he and Shirley Temple, q.v., performed in previous film), *Bright Eyes, Change of Heart, Have a Heart, Hold That Girl, Three Hundred and Sixty-Five Nights in Hollywood, George White's Scandals of 1935, Living on Love* (cs), *Walking Down Broadway; Killer McCoy* (ds).

**132 DUNNE, IRENE** (1904–    ). Actress-singer who created dignified ladylike image which she could sometimes drop for good comic effect. Soprano voice first heard in touring versions of musicals. Seen by Ziegfeld and given role in touring *Show Boat* which brought offers from Hollywood.

Films: *Stingaree* (ws), *Sweet Adeline, Roberta, Show Boat* (36), *The Awful Truth* (cs), *High Wide and Handsome*

*Irene Dunne with Allan Jones in SHOW BOAT*

(intro. "The Folks Who Live on the Hill"), *Joy of Living, Love Affair* (ds), *A Guy Named Joe* (ds), *Never a Dull Moment* (50, cs).

**133 DURANTE, JAMES "SCHNOZZLE"** (1893–    ). Individual comedian famous for his strut, his gravel voice and the size of his "proboscis." From music halls and night clubs to Broadway and Hollywood, became one of America's great entertainers. In films from 1929.

*"Schnozzle" Durante with Margaret O'Brien*

Films: *Roadhouse Nights* (début), *Sally Irene and Mary, Cuban Love Song, Blondie of the Follies, The Phantom President, Broadway to Hollywood, Meet the Baron* (cs), *George White's Scandals* (34), *Hollywood Party, Palooka, Strictly Dynamite, Student Tour, Little Miss Broadway* (38), *Start Cheering, Melody Ranch; Two Girls and a Sailor, Music for Millions, Ziegfeld Follies* (sketch cut from release print), *Two Sisters from Boston, It Happened in Brooklyn, This Time for Keeps, On an Island with You, The Great Rupert, The Milkman* (cs); *Beau James* (cs), *Billy Rose's Jumbo.*

**134 DURBIN, DEANNA** (1921–    ). RN: Edna Mae Durbin. Soprano who as a 'teenager became one of screen's biggest

attractions with her happy musicals in which she managed to sort out all the adults' problems while warbling popular arias and light music (e.g. "Ave Maria," "Last Rose of Summer"). Tested by M-G-M at the same time as Judy Garland (q.v.) she was snapped up by Joe Pasternak (q.v.) for Universal and her films are said to have saved that studio from bankruptcy. Adult miscasting as night club singer in *Christmas Holiday* marked start of decline in material and popularity. Retired 1948.

Films: *Every Sunday* (short), *Three Smart Girls, One Hundred Men and a Girl, Mad about Music, Three Smart Girls Grow Up, That Certain Age* (intro. "My Own"), *First Love, It's a Date, Spring Parade, Nice Girl?* (intro. "Beneath the Lights of Home"), *It Started with Eve, Hers to Hold* (intro. "Say a Prayer for the Boys over There"), *The Amazing Mrs. Holliday, His Butler's Sister, Christmas*

*Holiday* (ds, intro. "Spring Will Be a Little Late This Year"), *Can't Help Singing, Lady on a Train* (ds), *Because of Him, I'll Be Yours, Something in the Wind, Up in Central Park, For the Love of Mary.*

**135 DVORAK, ANN** (1912– ). RN: Ann McKim. Actress, singer and dancer whose musical talents were used only rarely by Hollywood. After first film, M-G-M retained her as dancing instructor, giving her small parts. Success in *Scarface* (non-musical) brought stardom, often as chorus girl or night club singer.

Films: *Hollywood Revue* (début), *Lord Byron of Broadway/What Price Melody?, The Crooner, Bright Lights* (35), *Folies Bergère, Thanks a Million, Manhattan Merry-go-round/Manhattan Music-Box; Masquerade in Mexico* (cs), *Abilene Town* (ws), *The Bachelor's Daughters* (cs).

**136 DWAN, ALLAN** (1885– ). Canadian-born director, active since silents, who adapted himself equally to Fairbanks swashbucklers, Stanwyck Westerns and Shirley Temple (q.v.) musicals.

Films: *The Song and Dance Man, Heidi, Rebecca of Sunnybrook Farm, Josette, The Three Musketeers, Young People, Rise and Shine, Here We Go Again* (also prod.), *Around the World* (also prod.), *Calendar Girl* (also assoc. prod.), *Northwest Outpost/End of the Rainbow, The Wild Blue Yonder/Thunder across the Pacific* (ds), *I Dream of Jeanie* (biog. of composer Stephen Foster), *Montana Belle* (ws), *Sweethearts on Parade.*

**137 EBSEN, BUDDY** (c. 1906– ). RN: Christian Rudolf Ebsen. Dancer and comedian, former soda jerk who became Broadway chorus boy (*Whoopee*), formed dancing team with sister Vilma. Film success mid-Thirties, later TV success

as head Beverly Hillbilly.

Films: *Broadway Melody of 1936, Born to Dance, Banjo on My Knee* (ws), *Captain January* (danced "At the Codfish Ball" with Shirley Temple q.v.), *Broadway Melody of 1938, Girl of the Golden West, My Lucky Star, They Met in Argentina, Sing Your Worries Away; Red Garters; Breakfast at Tiffany's* (cs), *The One and Only Genuine Original Family Band.*

**138 EDDY, NELSON** (1901–1967). Tenor who with Jeanette MacDonald (q.v.) formed the screen's most successful operetta team. Graduated from boy soprano to Gilbert & Sullivan, then opera. Metropolitan *début* 1924, signed by M-G-M 1933 after concert success. An uneasy actor whose first roles were inauspicious until *Naughty Marietta* started the now legendary partnership. Still singing (in night clubs) at time of death.

Films: *Dancing Lady* (début), *Broadway to Hollywood, Student Tour, Naughty Marietta, Rose Marie* (36), *Maytime, Rosalie, Girl of the Golden West, Sweethearts, Let Freedom Ring, Balalaika, New Moon* (40), *Bitter Sweet, The Chocolate Soldier, I Married an Angel* (last and least successful of teamings with MacDonald), *Phantom of the Opera* (ds), *Knickerbocker Holiday* (also wrote some lyrics), *Make Mine Music* (all voices for "Jonah and the Whale" sequence), *Northwest Outpost/End of the Rainbow.*

**139 EDENS, ROGER** (1905–1970). Musical supervisor, arranger, composer, lyricist and producer long associated with M-G-M and with Judy Garland (q.v.) for whom he wrote special material and selected properties. Started as pianist, accompanying ballroom dancers Tony and Renee DeMarco, played in pit for *Girl Crazy* starring Ethel Merman (q.v.) for whom he later wrote vocal arrangements and special material. Went to Hollywood 1933 to write special material for Merman's films *Kid Millions* and *We're Not Dressing,* joined M-G-M as musical supervisor—taking scripts and deciding where music should be inserted and in what form, also doing some arrangements, mainly for singers. Became associate to Arthur Freed (q.v.) 1940, produced first film 1954. In following filmography MS = music supervision.

Special material: *Kid Millions, We're Not Dressing.* MS: *Reckless, Broadway Melody of 1936, The Great Ziegfeld, San Francisco* (ds), *Born to Dance, A Day at the Races, Rosalie.* MS, comp. *Broadway Melody of 1938* ("Dear Mr. Gable," originally written for Garland to sing at a studio birthday party for Clark Gable). MS: *Everybody Sing, Listen Darling.* MS, comp. *Love Finds Andy Hardy* (cs, "In-Between"). MS: *Ice Follies of 1939.* Arr. and comp. vocal interpolations: *The Wizard of Oz.* Mus. adapt. and comp. interpolations: *Babes in Arms.* MS: *Honolulu, Society Lawyer* (ds), *Broadway Melody* (40). Arr., comp. interpolations: *Andy Hardy Meets Debutante.* MS, comp. *Strike Up the Band* ("Nobody's Got Me" also, music only, "Our Love Affair"), *Go West, Little Nelly Kelly* (inc. "It's a Great Day for the Irish," "A Pretty Girl Milking Her Cow"), *Two Girls on Broadway, Ziegfeld Girl* (inc. "Minnie from Trinidad"), *Lady Be Good, Babes on Broadway* (inc. "Hoe Down," music only), *Panama Hattie* ("Good Neighbours"), *Maisie Gets Her Man* (cs). MS: *For Me and My Gal, Cabin in the Sky.* MS, comp. *Presenting Lily Mars, DuBarry Was a Lady.* MS: *Girl Crazy* (43). Voc. arr., comp. *Thousands Cheer.* MS, assoc. prod. *Meet Me in St. Louis, Yolanda and the Thief, The Harvey Girls.* MS, comp. *Ziegfeld Follies* ("Bring on the Beautiful Girls," "Madam Cremation [A Great Lady Meets the Press]" music only). Voc. arr. *Till The Clouds Roll By.* Assoc. prod., comp. *Good News* ("The French Lesson," music only). Assoc. prod., mus. adapt. *The Pirate, Easter Parade, Words and Music.* Ass. prod., comp. *Take Me Out to the Ball Game/Everybody's Cheering* (inc. "It's Fate Baby, It's Fate," "Strictly USA," "Yes Indeedy" music only). Ass. prod. *The Barkleys of Broadway.* Ass. prod., comp. *On the Town* (inc. "Main Street," "Prehistoric Man," "On the Town" music only). MS (co.), ass. prod. *Annie Get Your Gun.* Staged "Happy Harvest" number: *Summer Stock/If You Feel like Singing.* Ass. prod., comp. *Pagan Love Song.* Ass. prod. *Royal Wedding/Wedding Bells, Show Boat* (51), *An American in Paris.* Ass. prod., comp. *Belle of New York* ("Let a Little Love Come In"), *Singin' in the Rain* ("Moses," music only). Assoc. prod. *The Band Wagon.* Prod. *Deep in My Heart.* Voc. arr. comp. *A Star Is Born* ("Born in a Trunk," music only). Prod. comp. *Funny Face* (inc. "Bonjour Paris," "On How to Be Lovely," "Think Pink" music only). Ass. prod. *The Unsinkable Molly Brown, The Sound of Music, Hello Dolly!*

**140 EDWARDS, BLAKE** (1922–     ). An excellent director of glossy escapist fare ideally suited to musicals, though has made few since becoming "name" director. Started as radio writer and actor. Engaged as actor by Richard Quine (q.v.) who then asked him to be writer on his pictures.

Films: wrote: *Sound Off, Rainbow Round My Shoulder, Cruisin' down the River, All Ashore* (also acted), *My Sister Eileen.* Dir: *Bring Your Smile Along* (also

53

sc.), *He Laughed Last* (also sc.), *High Time, Breakfast at Tiffany's* .(cs), *The Great Race* (cs), *Darling Lili*.

**141 EDWARDS, CLIFF** (1895–    ). Comedian known as "Ukelele Ike" who made a hit with "Singing in the Rain" in his first film and had long career of supporting roles in musicals and Westerns.

Films: *Hollywood Revue, So This Is College, The Prodigal* (ds), *Marianne, Way Out West* (ws), *Dance Fools Dance, Stepping Out, Shipmates, Good News* (30), *Montana Moon, Lord Byron of Broadway/What Price Melody?, Take a Chance, Those Three French Girls, George White's Scandals* (34), *George White's Scandals of 1935, Girl of the Golden West ; Pinocchio* (voice of Jiminy Cricket), *Salute for Three, Fun and Fancy Free* (voice).

**142 ENRIGHT, RAY** (1896–1965). Director of many and varied, but mainly routine, films. Started as editor and Sennett gagman, became dir. with Rin-Tin-Tin film in 1927.

Films: *Dancing Sweeties, Golden Dawn, Song of the West, Dames, Twenty Million Sweethearts, We're in the Money, Sing Me a Love Song, Ready Willing and Able, The Singing Marine, Going Places, Gold Diggers in Paris, Swing Your Lady, Hard to Get, Naughty but Nice, On Your Toes*.

**143 ENTERTAINERS' BIOGRA-PHIES.** Many of America's great headliners of vaudeville, revue and musical comedy have had their stories told on the screen, but it is fitting that one of the most successful Hollywood biographies and one of the biggest commercial successes of all time should have been the story of the man who starred in the first talkie, Al Jolson (q.v.). *The Jolson Story* also repaid Hollywood's debt to Jolson, for it revived

his career, which was in the doldrums, and made a new generation, who had grown up in the war years and barely knew his name, aware of the Jolson magic. Though Larry Parks (q.v.) played Al, it was Jolson's voice singing the songs, and for one number, "Swanee," it is Jolson himself, in blackface, who is seen in the film. It also prompted that rarity for biographical films, a sequel, *Jolson Sings Again* which carried the story up to the making of the first film and showed Parks (as Jolson) being introduced to Parks (as Parks)!

Actually, Jolson's own first film, *The Jazz Singer,* had been said to be loosely autobiographical, but the first Hollywood musical to be completely biographical was M-G-M's 1936 *The Great Ziegfeld,* a mammoth three-hour production originally road-shown complete with interval. William Powell played the great impresario with Luise Rainer as Anna Held, the French-born beauty who became a Broadway star in the first show Ziegfeld produced (1896) and married him a year later. Myrna Loy played Billie Burke, Ziegfeld's second wife, one of Broadway's biggest stars of the Twenties and later a character actress (notably as the Good Fairy in *The Wizard of Oz*). The Castles, famous dancing team of the early part of the century, were the first performers to have a Hollywood musical based entirely on their lives, with *The Story of Vernon and Irene Castle.* Fred Astaire and Ginger Rogers (qq.v.) played the pair who introduced the Tango and Fox-trot to America, and the film's fidelity to the facts made it the only Astaire–Rogers movie to have a tragic ending. The same year, 1939, saw a thinly-disguised but far from factual account of Fanny Brice's (q.v.) career in *Rose of Washington Square,* starring Alice Faye (q.v.) who the following year played the beautiful Broadway star of the 1890s *Lillian Russell*. George M. Cohan, patriotic composer, entertainer and playwright, who had himself starred in a Hollywood musical *The Phantom President* in 1932, was immortalised by James Cagney (q.v.) in *Yankee Doodle Dandy* (42), which besides being a superbly made film also captured the patriotic fervour being felt by the American public in the early years of the Second World War. In 1944 Ann Sheridan (q.v.) played the great vaudeville performer Nora Bayes in *Shine On Harvest Moon,* titled after the song Bayes wrote with her husband Jack Norworth and which she introduced in *Ziegfeld Follies of 1908.* Norworth, whose other lyrics include the baseball anthem "Take Me Out to the Ball Game," was played by Dennis Morgan (q.v.).

Two 1945 biographies were among the biggest successes of their respective stars. *Incendiary Blonde,* starring Betty Hutton (q.v.) as famed night club owner Texas Guinan, re-created the world of prohibition, racketeers and bootleg liquor, while *The Dolly Sisters* went back to the early part of the century for the *Follies* stars who were as notorious for their glamorous off-stage exploits as their singing and dancing. Betty Grable (q.v.) played the tempestuous Jenny Dolly, and June Haver (q.v.) was Rosie. Betty Hutton went back to silent screen days in 1947 playing Pearl White, heroine of cliff-hanging serials, in *The Perils of Pauline,* distinguished by its excellent Frank Loesser (q.v.) score. 1949 saw Hollywood's tribute to Broadway star of the Twenties Marilyn Miller (q.v.) in *Look for the Silver Lining* starring June Haver. *The Great Caruso* (51) inevitably offended purists who remembered the Italian tenor, but with Mario Lanza (q.v.) as the legendary Enrico and a first-class production it was a tremendous success. In 1952 Betty Hutton played a star of the past for the third time, giving a surprisingly subdued performance as Blossom Seeley, vaudeville star, in *Somebody Loves Me,* which besides the title tune revived the 1924 hit "Jealous." Blossom's husband was Benny Fields, a debonair top-hat-and-tails singer known as "Your Minstrel Man," who starred in two movies *Big Broadcast of 1936* and *The Minstrel Man.* He was played in Hutton's movie by Ralph Meeker. The hit biographical film of 1952 though, was *With a Song in My Heart,* with Susan Hayward (q.v.) as singer Jane Froman, whose courageous fight against injuries received in a wartime aircrash gave a dramatic background to the score of standards revived in the film and sung by Froman herself.

Eva Tanguay was a vaudeville star who in 1905 made famous, and was made famous by, the song, "I Don't Care." In 1953 Mitzi Gaynor (q.v.) starred in *The I Don't Care Girl,* which proved shallow as biography but had some fine production numbers. In the same year David Wayne (q.v.) played impresario Sol Hurok in *Tonight We Sing,* a peg on which to hang a series of extracts from opera and ballet. *So This Is Love/The Grace Moore Story* failed to get much drama or excitement from the life of Grace Moore (q.v.), played by Kathryn Grayson (q.v.), and *The Eddie Cantor Story,* another 1953 film, failed to do for Cantor what had earlier been done for Jolson, though Cantor's own voice was heard on the soundtrack going through his old hits. Keefe Braselle was the miscast leading man. In the mid-Fifties, when it seemed the biographical formula was becoming tired, a new element of realism was injected with a frank treatment of problems with booze, gangsters and corruption. First of these "warts-and-all" movies was *Love Me or Leave Me* in which Doris Day (q.v.), in her first film away from her home studio Warners, played a far from glamourised Ruth Etting. Etting had been a night club singer who became a star in the 1927 *Ziegfeld Follies,* introduced "Love Me or Leave Me" in Broadway's *Whoopee* (28) and "Ten Cents a Dance" in *Simple Simon* (30). She acted in films *Roman Scandals* and *Gift of Gab* as well as several shorts including the 1931 *Broadway's Like That* in which an unknown Humphrey Bogart made a walk-on. *Love Me or Leave Me* was particularly outspoken regarding her rise to fame and her relationship with her gangster-protector, played by James Cagney (q.v.). It was followed by *I'll Cry Tomorrow* (57) with Susan Hayward as Lillian Roth (qq.v.) facing problems with alcohol, and *The Helen Morgan Story/Both Ends of the Candle* (57) with Ann Blyth as Helen Morgan (qq.v.) and Gogi Grant providing some superb singing on the soundtrack. Besides their new realism, these three films had in common their high standard as musical dramas. *The Joker Is Wild* (57) with Frank Sinatra (q.v.) as comedian-singer Joe E. Lewis, was patchy as drama, but gave Sinatra the chance to sing a brace of standards in the early part of the film, as well as the Oscar-winning "All the Way."

With the decline in musical production by Hollywood, biographies seemed to have disappeared and it took the Broadway theatre to bring them back. In 1963 Mervyn LeRoy (q.v.) produced and directed a faithful transcription of *Gypsy,* the brilliant stage hit about the early life of Gypsy Rose Lee (q.v.). Natalie Wood (q.v.) played the famous stripper, but the story was really about her ambitious mother, given a fiercely intense, energetic

and effective portrayal by Rosalind Russell (q.v.). The emergence of two major musical stars during the Sixties, Julie Andrews and Barbra Streisand (qq.v.) was responsible for the revival of the biographical musical at the end of the decade. Andrews played the British stage and screen star Gertrude Lawrence in the shakily-scripted *Star!*, later re-titled *Those Were the Happy Times,* in which Daniel Massey made a strong impression as the young Noël Coward. From Broadway came Barbra Streisand's *Funny Girl,* the Fanny Brice story again told with more fidelity (the stage version had been produced by Brice's nephew) and reviving for its climax the soulful "My Man," a French song introduced by Brice in the 1921 *Ziegfeld Follies.*

**144  EPHRON, HENRY** (1912–      ) and **PHOEBE** (1914–      ). Husband-and-wife writing team, mainly of light comedy and musicals. Henry also producer. Was stage manager when he met Phoebe, a writer and secretary to theatrical agent.

Films: co-sc. *Look for the Silver Lining, On the Riviera, Belles on Their Toes* (cs), *There's No Business like Show Business, Daddy Long Legs, Carousel.* Henry dir. *Sing Boy Sing,* prod. *Carousel, The Best Things in Life Are Free* (Phoebe co-sc. with William Bowers).

**EVANS, RAY.** See **LIVINGSTON, JAY.**

**145  FAIN, SAMMY** (1902–      ). Composer, former pianist and radio entertainer. First song 1925.

Films: *Romance of the Underworld, It's a Great Life, Dangerous Nan McGrew, Follow the Leader, Young Man of Manhattan, The Big Pond* (inc. "You Brought a New Kind of Love to Me"), *The Crooner, Footlight Parade* (inc. "By a

Waterfall"), *College Coach, Moonlight and Pretzels, Dames, Strictly Dynamite, Fashion Follies of 1934, Harold Teen, Happiness Ahead, Sweet Music, Goin' to Town, New Faces of 1937, Tarnished Angel* (cs), *Swing Fever, Meet the People, Two Girls and a Sailor, Maisie Goes to Reno/You Can't Do That to Me* (cs), *Lost in a Harem* (cs), *I'll Be Seeing You* (non-musical, title song), *Thrill of a Romance, George White's Scandals of 1945, Anchors Aweigh* ("The Worry Song"), *Weekend at the Waldorf* (ds), *Two Sisters from Boston, No Leave No Love, The Un-finished Dance, This Time for Keeps, Three Daring Daughters/The Birds and the Bees, The Milkman* (cs), *Call Me Mister, Alice in Wonderland, Peter Pan, The Jazz Singer* (53), *Calamity Jane* (inc. 53 Oscar "Secret Love"), *Three Sailors and a Girl, Lucky Me, Young at Heart, Ain't Mis-behavin', Love Is a Many-Splendoured Thing* (non-musical, 55 Oscar title tune), *April Love, Marjorie Morningstar* (ds), *Made in Paris* (cs), *Myra Breckinridge* (cs).

**146 FALKENBURG, JINX** (1919– ). RN: Eugenia Falkenburg. Spanish-born swimming and tennis champion turned model and cover girl, featured in Columbia musicals and comedies in Forties. Later a popular TV personality.

Films: *Song of the Buckaroo, Two Latins from Manhattan, Sing for Your Supper, Laugh Your Blues Away, Sweet-heart of the Fleet, She Has What It Takes, Lucky Legs, Cover Girl* (as herself), *Tahiti Nights, Meet Me on Broadway, The Gay Senorita.*

**147 FAPP, DANIEL.** Photographer not particularly noted for musicals, but 1961 Oscar-winner for colour work on *West Side Story.*

Films: *Glamour Boy/Hearts in Spring-time, Golden Earrings* (ds); *Knock on Wood* (cs), *Living It Up, The Five Pennies, West Side Story, The Unsinkable Molly Brown, Fun in Acapulco, The Pleasure Seekers* (cs), *I'll Take Sweden* (cs).

**148 FARRELL, CHARLES** (1901– ). Romantic lead who graduated from crowd work to star teaming with Janet Gaynor (q.v.) 1927. Success in both silents and talkies.

Films: *Sunny Side Up, Happy Days, High Society Blues, Delicious, Girl without a Room, Change of Heart, Just around the Corner, Tail Spin.*

**149 FAYE, ALICE** (1912– ). RN: Alice Leppert. Fox's big musical star of the late Thirties, whose mellow contralto was one of the finest crooning voices to be heard in movies. Started as blonde Harlow-type till studio polished and refined her personality. Went straight from school into chorus line. In Broadway chorus of *George White's Scandals of 1931* when spotted by Rudy Vallee (q.v.) and given job singing with his orchestra. Vallee persuaded Fox to use her in film of *Scandals* and when star Lillian Harvey (q.v.) walked out she was given lead. Work led to contract. Performed intricate tap routine with Shirley Temple and Jack Haley (qq.v.) in *Poor Little Rich Girl* but danced less and sang more as films increased in stature. Teamed with Betty Grable (q.v.), who was to replace her as musical star at studio, in *Tin Pan Alley.* After marriage to Phil Harris (q.v.), birth of daughters and mis-casting in *Fallen Angel* (non-musical), retired from films but for brief come-back in *State Fair* re-make. Occasionally guests on TV.

Films: *George White's Scandals* (34, début), *Now I'll Tell* (ds), *She Learned*

*Alice Faye with Jack Oakie (left) and John Payne in* THE GREAT AMERICAN BROADCAST

*about Sailors, Three-hundred and Sixty-five Nights in Hollywood, George White's Scandals of 1935, Every Night at Eight, Music Is Magic, King of Burlesque* (intro. "I'm Shooting High"), *Poor Little Rich Girl, Sing Baby Sing* (intro. "You Turned the Tables on Me"), *Stowaway* (intro. "Goodnight My Love"), *On the Avenue* (intro. "This Year's Kisses"), *Wake Up and Live* (intro. "There's a Lull in My Life"), *You Can't Have Everything, You're a Sweetheart, Sally Irene and Mary, In Old Chicago* (ds, a role originally intended for Jean Harlow), *Alexander's Ragtime Band* (intro. "Now It Can Be Told"), *Tail Spin* (ds), *Rose of Washington Square* (as thinly disguised Fanny Brice q.v.), *Hollywood Cavalcade, Barricade* (ds), *Little Old New York* (ds), *Tin Pan Alley* (intro. "You Say the Sweetest Things"), *That Night in Rio, The Great American Broadcast* (intro. "Where You Are," "I Take to You"), *Weekend in Havana, Hello Frisco Hello* (intro. "You'll Never Know"), *The Gang's All Here/The Girls He Left Behind* (intro. "No Love No Nothing"), *Four Jills in a Jeep* (as herself); *State Fair* (62).

**150  FELIX, SEYMOUR** (1892–1961). Choreographer and director in movies from 1929. Vaudeville dancer at fifteen, later Broadway dance director (inc. *Whoopee, Hit the Deck*).

Films as dir: *Stepping Sisters*. Ch. *Sunny Side Up, Hollywood Party* (co.), *The Great Ziegfeld* (36 Oscar for gigantic "A Pretty Girl Is like a Melody" sequence), *Alexander's Ragtime Band, Rose of Washington Square, Tin Pan Alley, After the Thin Man* (cs), *Yankee Doodle Dandy* (w. Leroy Prinz q.v.), *Let's Face It, Cover Girl* (w. Donen q.v., Kelly q.v.), *Greenwich Village, Three Little Girls in Blue, Golden Girl, The I Don't Care Girl, Down among the Sheltering Palms.*

**151  FIELDS, DOROTHY** (1905–   ). Lyricist, daughter of a comedian and sister of librettist Herbert Fields, with whom she collaborated on musical comedies and screenplays. Wrote poetry at college, persuaded by Jimmy McHugh (q.v.) to write lyrics for his music.

Films: *Love in the Rough, Dance Fools Dance, Cuban Love Song, Flying High, Dancing Lady, Meet the Baron* (cs),

*Dinner at Eight* (ds, inc. "Don't Blame Me"), *Have a Heart, Every Night at Eight* (inc. "I'm in the Mood for Love," "I Feel a Song Coming On"), *Nitwits, Hooray for Love, I Dream Too Much, Roberta* ("Lovely to Look At"), *In Person, The Smartest Girl in Town, The King Steps Out, Swing Time* (inc. 36 Oscar "The Way You Look Tonight," also "A Fine Romance," "Never Gonna Dance," "Bojangles of Harlem"), *Living on Love* (cs), *When You're in Love, The Joy of Living* (inc. "You Couldn't Be Cuter"), *One Night in the Tropics* (inc. "Remind Me"); *Up in Central Park, Excuse My Dust, Mr. Imperium/You Belong to My Heart, Texas Carnival, The Farmer Takes a Wife; Sweet Charity* (inc. "My Personal Property").

**152 FINE, SYLVIA.** Composer and lyricist, wife of Danny Kaye (q.v.) for whom she has written many speciality numbers.

Films: *Up in Arms* ("The Lobby Song"), *Wonder Man* ("Bali Boogie"), *The Kid from Brooklyn* ("Pavlova"), *The Secret Life of Walter Mitty* (inc. "Anatole of Paris"), *The Inspector General* (inc. "Happy Times"), *On the Riviera* (inc. "Popo the Puppet," "Rhythm of a New Romance"), *Knock on Wood, The Court Jester, On the Double.*

**153 FINKLEHOFFE, FRED F.** (1911– ). Writer-producer, former law student.

Films: St., co-sc. *Strike Up the Band, Babes on Broadway.* Co-sc. *For Me and My Gal.* Sc. *Girl Crazy* (43). Co-sc. *Best Foot Forward, Meet Me in St. Louis.* Sc. *Words and Music;* St., sc., prod. *At War with the Army* (cs), *The Stooge* (cs).

**154 FITZGERALD, ELLA** (1918– ). Negro jazz singer, a fine interpreter of popular songs who started

singing 1935 with Chick Webb's band. Occasional film appearances.

Films: *Ride 'Em Cowboy, Pete Kelly's Blues, St. Louis Blues* (58), *Let No Man Write My Epitaph* (ds).

**155 FLOREY, ROBERT** (1900– ). French-born director who made two-reel comedies in Hollywood, went back to Europe to make features, returned to Hollywood with offer of better films but generally kept in second-feature bracket. TV in Fifties.

Films: *The Cocoanuts* (co-dir.), *Battle of Paris, Ship Café, Going Highbrow, Preview Murder Mystery* (ds), *Mountain Music, This Way Please, The Desert Song* (44).

**156 FOLSEY, GEORGE J.** (c. 1900– ). Veteran cameraman, as proficient with colour (notably at M-G-M in Forties) as he had been with black-and-white.

Films: *The Cocoanuts* (cs), *Applause, The Smiling Lieutenant, Going Hollywood, Operator 13, Reckless, The Great Ziegfeld, Thousands Cheer, A Guy Named Joe* (ds), *Meet Me in St. Louis, The Harvey Girls, Ziegfeld Follies* (co.), *Till the Clouds Roll By* (co.), *Take Me Out to the Ball Game/Everybody's Cheering, Mr Imperium/You Belong to My Heart, Lovely to Look At, Million Dollar Mermaid/The One-Piece Bathing Suit, Seven Brides for Seven Brothers.*

**157 FORREST, SALLY** (1928– ). RN: Katherine Scully Feeney. Dancer in M-G-M chorus who shortly after becoming a leading player switched to dramatic roles.

Films: *Till the Clouds Roll By, Are You With It?, The Pirate, Take Me Out to the Ball Game/Everybody's Cheering, The Strip, Excuse My Dust.*

59

**158 FOSSE, BOB** (1927– ). Dancer and choreographer, now a director of stage and film musicals. Started dancing when thirteen, had brief career at M-G-M before turning to Broadway. His choreography for *How to Succeed in Business without Really Trying* was restaged for screen version by Dale Moreda.

Films as actor: *The Affairs of Dobie Gillis, Kiss Me Kate, Give a Girl a Break, My Sister Eileen, Damn Yankees/What Lola Wants.* Ch. *My Sister Eileen, The Pajama Game, Damn Yankees/What Lola Wants.* Dir. and Ch. *Sweet Charity.*

**159 FOSTER, SUSANNA** (1924– ). RN: Suzan Larsen. Soprano who starred in two good horror-musicals *The Phantom of the Opera* (w. Claude Rains) and *The Climax* (w. Boris Karloff). Her last two films were mediocre and followed by retirement.

Films: *The Great Victor Herbert* (début), *Glamour Boy/Hearts in Springtime, There's Magic in Music, Top Man, Phantom of the Opera* (ds), *Follow the Boys* (44), *This Is the Life* (44), *The Climax* (ds), *Bowery to Broadway, Frisco Sal, That Night with You.*

**160 FOY, EDDIE jnr.** (c. 1908– ). Comedian, son of famous vaudevillian, raised in theatre.

Films: *Broadway through a Keyhole, Turn off the Moon; Scatterbrain, Yankee Doodle Dandy* (as his own father), *Yokel Boy, Joan of Ozarks, Moonlight Masquerade, And the Angels Sing; Honeychile, The Farmer Takes a Wife, Lucky Me, The Pajama Game, Bells Are Ringing.*

**161 FRANCIS, CONNIE** (1938– ). RN: Concetta Franconero. Italian-American singer whose disc success in early Sixties led to attempt by M-G-M to make her a musical film star.

Films: *Where the Boys Are* (début), *Follow the Boys* (63), *Looking for Love, When the Boys Meet the Girls.* Sang on soundtrack of *Rock Rock Rock.*

**162 FRAZEE, JANE** (1918– ). RN: Mary Jane Frahse. Spirited popular singer and an attractive leading lady of "B" musicals of Forties. Night clubs and radio before films.

Films: *Melody and Moonlight, Angels with Broken Wings, Buck Privates/Rookies, Hellzapoppin, San Antonio Rose, Moonlight in Hawaii, Sing Another Chorus, Don't Get Personal, What's Cooking?, Almost Married, Get Hep to Love/She's My Lovely, Moonlight in Havana, When Johnny Comes Marching Home, Moonlight Masquerade, Hi Ya Chum, Rhythm of the Islands, Beautiful but Broke, Cowboy Canteen, Rosie the Riveter, Kansas City Kitty, Swing in the Saddle/Swing and Sway, She's a Sweetheart, Ten Cents a Dance/Dancing Ladies, Swingin' on a Rainbow, A Guy Could Change, Calendar Girl, Gay Ranchero, Under California Stars, Grand Canyon Trail, Rhythm Inn.*

**163 FREED, ARTHUR** (1894– ). RN: Arthur Grossman. Outstanding producer of Hollywood musicals, responsible for the tremendous repertory company of talent at M-G-M throughout the Forties. As a song-writer, wrote lyrics for first M-G-M musical *Broadway Melody.* Was associate producer of *The Wizard of Oz* and for first solo production bought stage musical *Babes in Arms* as a vehicle for Judy Garland and Mickey Rooney (qq.v.). Showed such a sure touch in selection of properties and creative talent that Louis B. Mayer allowed him to make such daring (for their time) projects as *Cabin in the Sky, Yolanda and the Thief* and *The Pirate* (all

*Arthur Freed (left) with Jules Styne*

directed by Minnelli, q.v., one of Freed's "discoveries"). Also responsible for greatest movie successes of Garland, Gene Kelly, Cyd Charisse, and Fred Astaire (qq.v.) in second phase of his career. Started own career as song plugger till Minnie Marx hired him as part of Marx Brothers act in vaudeville. Wrote special material for night club revues, had first hit 1923 with lyrics of "I Cried for You." Was directing plays at Hollywood theatre when hired by Irving Thalberg to work at M-G-M.

Films as lyricist: *Broadway Melody, Marianne, Hollywood Revue* (inc. "Singin' in the Rain"), *Untamed* (ds), *The Pagan* (ds), *Those Three French Girls, Lord Byron of Broadway/What Price Melody?, Montana Moon* (ws), *Blondie of the Follies, The Barbarian* (ds), *Peg O' My Heart, Going Hollywood* (inc. "Temptation"), *Stage Mother* (ds), *Sadie McKee* (ds), *Hollywood Party, Student Tour, Broadway Melody of 1936* (inc. "You Are My Lucky Star"), *A Night at the Opera, San Francisco* (ds, "Would You?"), *After the Thin Man* (cs), *Broadway Melody of 1938* (inc. "Broadway Rhythm"), *Thoroughbreds Don't Cry, Babes in Arms* ("Good Morning"), *Two Girls on Broadway, Strike Up the Band* ("Our Love Affair"), *Lady Be Good, Ziegfeld Follies* ("This Heart of Mine"), *Singin' in the Rain* (this film utilised many of Freed's past hits). Ass. prod. *The Wizard of Oz*. Prod. *Babes in Arms, Strike Up the Band, Little Nelly Kelly, Lady Be Good, Babes on Broadway, Panama Hattie, For Me and My Gal, Cabin in the Sky, DuBarry Was a Lady, Best Foot Forward, Girl Crazy* (43), *Meet Me in St. Louis* (also sang "You and I" as voice of Leon Ames), *Yolanda and the Thief, The Harvey Girls, Ziegfeld Follies, Till the Clouds Roll By, Good News* (47), *Summer Holiday, The Pirate, Easter Parade, Words and Music, Take Me Out to the Ball Game/Everybody's Cheering, The Barkleys of Broadway, On the Town, Annie Get Your Gun, Pagan Love Song, Royal Wedding/Wedding Bells, Show Boat* (51), *An American in Paris, Belle of New York, Singin' in the Rain, The Band Wagon, Brigadoon, It's Always Fair Weather, Kismet* (55), *Invitation to the Dance, Silk Stockings, Gigi, Bells Are Ringing, The Subterraneans* (ds).

**164 FREED, RALPH.** Lyricist in Hollywood from mid-Thirties.

Films: *Careless Lady, College Holiday, Hideaway Girl, Double or Nothing, Swing High Swing Low, Cocoanut Grove, She Married a Cop, It's a Date, Babes on Broadway* (inc. "How About You?"), *DuBarry Was a Lady, Swing Fever, Meet the People, Seven Sweethearts, Two Girls and a Sailor* (inc. "Young Man with a Horn"), *Maisie Goes to Reno/You Can't Do That to Me* (cs), *Lost in a Harem* (cs), *Thrill of a Romance, Anchors Aweigh* ("The Worry Song"), *Yolanda and the Thief* (inc. "Coffee Time"), *Ziegfeld Follies* ("Bring on the Beautiful Girls"),

61

*Two Sisters from Boston, No Leave No Love, This Time for Keeps, My Dream Is Yours.*

**165 FREELAND, THORNTON** (1898–    ). Director, former juvenile actor in travelling company. Joined Vitagraph at sixteen, learned all aspects of film-making. Frequently dir. in Britain.

Films: *Whoopee, Be Yourself, Flying down to Rio, George White's Scandals* (34), *Too Many Blondes.*

**166 FRIML, RUDOLF** (1879–    ). Operetta composer, born in Prague, studied under Dvorak. U.S. *début* as pianist 1906, first stage success *The Firefly* 1912. As well as composing for Hollywood (inc. dramatic scores) supervised filming of his stage musicals in Thirties.

Films: *The Vagabond King* (30 and 55), *Rose Marie* (36, 54), *The Firefly* (inc. "The Donkey Serenade"), *Music for Madame, Northwest Outpost/End of the Rainbow.*

*Ava Gardner in SHOW BOAT*

**167 FUNICELLO, ANNETTE** (1942–    ). Disney juvenile discovery who became 'teenage lead of pop musicals.

Films: *Babes in Toyland* (61), *Beach Party, Muscle Beach Party, Bikini Beach, Beach Blanket Bingo, How to Stuff a Wild Bikini/How to Fill a Wild Bikini, Pajama Party.*

**168 GARDNER, AVA** (1922–    ). One of Hollywood's most beautiful actresses who created a memorable Julie in the 1951 *Show Boat.* A farmer's daughter, her photograph got her a screen test at M-G-M and series of bit roles from 1942.

Films: *DuBarry Was a Lady, Swing Fever, Two Girls and a Sailor, Maisie Goes to Reno/You Can't Do That to Me* (cs), *Music for Millions; One Touch of Venus; Show Boat* (51), *The Band Wagon* (guest).

**169 GARLAND, JUDY** (1922–1969). RN: Frances Gumm. The quintessential musical star—actress, comedienne, dancer and above all, singer. Stage *début* when three as part of sister act in vaudeville. M-G-M 1935, the only star in history of studio to be given contract without a screen test. Hit singing "Dear Mr. Gable (You Made Me Love You)" in *Broadway Melody of 1938.* Role of Dorothy in *The Wizard of Oz* and popular teamings with Mickey Rooney (q.v.) revealed comedy flair and touching dramatic ability in addition to vibrant and distinctive voice. Under Vincente Minnelli (q.v.) in *Meet Me in St. Louis* displayed qualities of depth and charm that placed her among greats of Hollywood, while *The Pirate* revealed supreme comic ability. Film triumphs in Forties were mingled with personal and professional problems that climaxed with breakdown during abortive filming of *Annie Get Your Gun* (50). Two years

*Judy Garland with (above) Margaret O'Brien in MEET ME IN ST. LOUIS ("Under the Bamboo Tree"), and (right) in A STAR IS BORN ("The Man That Got Away")*

later staged comeback on stages of London Palladium and New York Palace, but despite triumphs of *A Star Is Born* (54), appearance at Carnegie Hall (61) and a faithful and ever-adulatory legion of followers, was never able to regain box-office cinema following among mass public. Took straight dramatic role in *Judgment at Nuremberg* (this and *The Clock* 45, were her only completely non-musical roles). Final film 1963, after which concentrated on concert and cabaret appearances. Own TV series 1963.

Films: *Every Sunday* (short), *Pigskin Parade, Broadway Melody of 1938, Thoroughbreds Don't Cry, Everybody Sing, Listen Darling, Love Finds Andy Hardy* (intro. "In-Between"), *The Wizard of Oz* (intro. "Over the Rainbow"), *Babes in Arms* (intro. "Good Morning"), *Andy Hardy Meets Debutante* (cs), *Strike Up the Band* (intro. "Our Love Affair"), *Little Nelly Kelly* (intro. "It's a Great

Day for the Irish," also played first adult role in early sequences of film in which she had dual role), *Ziegfeld Girl* (intro. "Minnie from Trinidad"), *Life Begins for Andy Hardy* (cs), *Babes on Broadway* (intro. "How about You?"), *We Must Have Music* (a short describing work of studio's music department and using a Garland number cut from *Ziegfeld Girl*), *For Me and My Gal, Presenting Lily Mars* (included a memorable duetting of 1910 oldie "Every Little Movement" with Connie Gilchrist), *Girl Crazy, Thousands Cheer, Meet Me in St. Louis* (intro. "The Trolley Song," "The Boy Next Door," "Have Yourself a Merry Little Christmas"), *The Harvey Girls* (intro. "On the Atchison, Topeka and the Santa Fe"), *Ziegfeld Follies* (a speciality number parodying film star interviews and the roles played by Greer Garson), *Till the Clouds Roll By* (as Marilyn Miller q.v.), *The Pirate* (intro. "Love of My Life,"

"Mack the Black," "You Can Do No Wrong," "Be a Clown"), *Easter Parade* (intro. "Better Luck Next Time," "A Couple of Swells"), *Words and Music, In the Good Old Summertime, Summer Stock/ If You Feel like Singing* (intro. "Happy Harvest"); *A Star Is Born* (intro. "The Man That Got Away," "Gotta Have Me Go with You," "Born in a Trunk"); *Pepe* (voice only), *Gay Purr-ee* (voice only), *A Child Is Waiting* (ds), *I Could Go On Singing* (in G.B.).

**170 GARRETT, BETTY** (1919–     ). Comedienne who chased Frank Sinatra (q.v.) with wry good humour in two

*"There's Nothing Like Love" : Betty Garrett (left) with Janet Leigh in MY SISTER EILEEN*

*"If I had a Talking Picture of You" : Janet Gaynor with Charles Farrell in SUNNY SIDE UP*

M-G-M musicals. Won theatre scholarship in teens, danced with Martha Graham, acted with Mercury Theatre then Broadway hit with *Call Me Mister* (46). Films followed. Now works in theatre with husband Larry Parks (q.v.).

Films: *Big City* (début), *Words and Music, Take Me Out to the Ball Game/ Everybody's Cheering* (intro. "It's Fate Baby, It's Fate"), *Neptune's Daughter, On the Town, My Sister Eileen*.

**171 GAXTON, WILLIAM** (1894–1963). Dapper leading man of musical comedies (*Anything Goes, Of Thee I Sing* etc.) who made a few films.

Films: *Fifty Million Frenchmen, Some-*

*thing to Shout About, Best Foot Forward, The Heat's On/Tropicana, Diamond Horseshoe.*

**172  GAYNOR, JANET** (1904–    ). RN: Laura Gainer. One of early sweethearts of screen. Started as extra 1924, became star with silent *Seventh Heaven* (its theme song "Diane" becoming associated with her).

Films: *Sunny Side Up* (intro. "If I Had a Talking Picture of You"), *Happy Days, High Society Blues, Delicious, Adorable, Carolina, Change of Heart; Bernadine.*

**173  GAYNOR, MITZI** (1930–    ). RN: Francesca Mitzi Marlene de Charney von Gerber. Vivacious dancer-actress who studied dancing as child and at fourteen was in production of *Roberta* and touring U.S.O. shows. Spotted by Fox scout in Los Angeles production of *The Great Waltz* and given contract. First starring role *Golden Girl* a success but career never really took fire. Played Nellie Forbush in *South Pacific,* has since scored big success in night clubs and TV.

Films: *My Blue Heaven* (début), *Golden Girl, Bloodhounds of Broadway, The I Don't Care Girl* (as Broadway star Eva Tanguay), *Down among the Sheltering Palms, There's No Business like Show Business, Anything Goes* (56), *The Birds and the Bees* (cs), *Les Girls, The Joker Is Wild* (ds), *South Pacific.*

**174  GERSHENSEN, JOSEPH** (1904–    ). Russian-born conductor, head of Universal's music department since 1941. Theatre conductor in Twenties, joined Universal 1933 as ass. prod. and musical director of shorts. (Early credits as Joseph G. Sanford.)

Films as MD: *Has Anybody Seen My Gal?, The Glenn Miller Story, So This Is Paris, The Benny Goodman Story, Summer Love, Never Steal Anything Small, Come September* (cs), *I'd Rather Be Rich* (cs).

**175  GERSHWIN, GEORGE** (1898–1937). Composer whose work embraced Broadway and Hollywood scores, symphonic and concert music and a folk-opera *(Porgy and Bess).* Studied piano and composition as child, heavily influenced by music of Berlin and Kern (qq.v.). First hit came when Al Jolson (q.v.) sang his "Swanee" on stage. One of America's half-dozen most renowned composers of popular music.

Films: *Song of the Flame, Delicious* (his first score written directly for screen), *Girl Crazy* (32 and 43), *Damsel in Distress* (inc. "A Foggy Day"), *Shall We Dance?* (inc. "They Can't Take That Away from Me," "Let's Call the Whole Thing off," "They All Laughed"), *Goldwyn Follies* (inc. "Love Walked In," "Our Love Is Here to Stay"), *Lady Be Good; Rhapsody in Blue* (biography), *The Shocking Miss Pilgrim* (score posthumously compiled from unpublished manuscripts); *The Barkleys of Broadway* (revived "They Can't Take That Away from Me"), *An American in Paris; Funny Face, Porgy and Bess; When the Boys Meet the Girls* (another version of *Girl Crazy), Kiss Me Stupid* (cs).

**176  GERSHWIN, IRA** (1896–    ). Lyricist, first to win a Pulitzer Prize (stage musical *Of Thee I Sing* 1932), who has collaborated with several top composers besides brother George (q.v.).

Films: *Delicious, Girl Crazy* (32 and 43), *Damsel in Distress* (inc. "Nice Work If You Can Get It"), *Shall We Dance?* (inc. "They Can't Take That Away from Me," "Let's Call the Whole Thing Off," "They All Laughed"), *Goldwyn Follies*

65

(inc. "Our Love Is Here to Stay"), *Lady Be Good, Lady in the Dark, Cover Girl* (inc. "Put Me to the Test," a lyric first written for *Damsel in Distress* and not used, also "Long Ago and Far Away," "A Sure Thing," "Who's Complaining?"), *Rhapsody in Blue* (biography of George in which Ira was played by Herbert Rudley), *The Shocking Miss Pilgrim* (inc. "Aren't You Kind of Glad We Did?," "Back Bay Polka"), *The Barkleys of Broadway* (inc. "Shoes with Wings On"), *An American in Paris, Give a Girl a Break* (inc. "Applause, Applause"), *A Star Is Born* (inc. "The Man That Got Away," "It's a New World," "Gotta Have Me Go with You"), *The Country Girl* (ds), *Funny Face, Porgy and Bess, When the Boys Meet the Girls* (re-make *Girl Crazy*), *Kiss Me Stupid* (cs).

**177 GHOSTING.** If *Singin' in the Rain* is accurate the practice of ghosting—mating an unseen person's voice to the lip movements of the performer on screen—has been going on since the movies learned to speak and some silent stars discovered their voices were unsuitable for sound reproduction. Musically, ghosting is particularly useful, and has probably gone on since numbers started to be pre-recorded, but these were the days when Hollywood was surrounded by glamour and mystery and if some top stars were ghosted the public rarely knew. It was not until the late Forties that "ghosts" themselves began receiving publicity, and a prime factor was the advent of the soundtrack recording as a lucrative sideline for the companies. Earlier, notable film vocalists such as Bing Crosby and Judy Garland (qq.v.) had re-recorded their film songs in record studios, but when M-G-M launched their record label, issuing albums of complete film scores, there was the problem of labelling and several non-singers had their secret revealed. Cyd Charisse and Vera-Ellen (qq.v.) were two notable examples of dancing stars who did not sing for themselves, and were also two fine reasons for justifying the practice, for with their glamour and dancing skills no-one really cared if they were ghosted. Earlier, it had been a fairly open secret that Rita Hayworth (q.v.) was unhappy singing. Her ghosts included NAN WYNN, MARTHA MEARS, ANITA ELLIS and JO ANN GREER, the last, a former vocalist with Les Brown's orchestra, being her most frequent screen voice. Martha Mears was also regular standby for Veronica Lake, singing her songs in *This Gun for Hire, Isn't It Romantic?* and *Star Spangled Rhythm*. She also sang for Lucille Ball (q.v.) in *DuBarry Was a Lady* and *The Big Street*. Anita Ellis, who had her own night club act, also did a lot of work behind the screen. She sang for Vera-Ellen in *Three Little Words* and *Belle of New York,* and for Jeanne Crain (q.v.) in *Gentlemen Marry Brunettes*. TRUDY STEVENS provided Vera-Ellen's singing voice in *White Christmas,* while CAROLE RICHARDS sang for Vera-Ellen in *Call Me Madam* and for Cyd Charisse in *Silk Stockings*. Charisse's other ghosts have included BETTY WILSON in *The Harvey Girls* and INDIA ADAMS in *The Band Wagon*. Miss Adams, a singer and actress in her own right (she understudied Ginger Rogers, q.v., in the London production of *Mame*) also sang for Joan Crawford (q.v.) in *Torch Song*.

EILEEN WILSON did one of the oddest ghosting jobs when she sang for Ava Gardner (q.v.) in *Show Boat*. Although Ava's voice was considered unsuitable for the two ballads she had in the film, she was allowed to sing them on the "soundtrack" album issued commercially. Eileen Wilson also sang for Gardner in *The Hucksters* and for Barbara Bel Geddes in *The Five Pennies*.

Early ghosts are VIRGINIA VERRILL, who used to sing for Eleanor Powell (q.v.), Jean Harlow and Myrna Loy in their M-G-M movies, and BUDDY CLARK, the popular crooner who sang for Jack Haley (q.v.) in *Wake Up and Live*. When Lynn Bari (q.v.) appeared in front of the Glenn Miller orchestra in *Sun Valley Serenade* and *Orchestra Wives* it was the voice of PAT FRIDAY on the soundtrack, while LOUANNE HOGAN sang the Oscar-winning "It Might As Well Be Spring" for Jeanne Crain in *State Fair* (45) and sang for the same actress in *Centennial Summer*. Susan Hayward's (q.v.) voice in her early hit *Smash-Up/Woman Destroyed* was PEGGY LACENTRA, while twenty years later when she took over the role of a musical comedy star in *Valley of the Dolls* her big number, originally written for Judy Garland (q.v.), was belted out by husky-voiced MARGARET WHITING, daughter of composer Richard Whiting (q.v.).

Male ghosts are more rare, but two notable instances are JIM BRYANT, who sang for Richard Beymer in *West Side Story*, and BILL LEE, who sang all those choruses of "Edelweiss" for Christopher Plummer in *The Sound of Music*. When *South Pacific* was filmed GEORGIO TOZZI sang for Rosanno Brazzi, but the oddest case of dubbing in this film involved the role of Bloody Mary. It was decided to use the original Broadway creator of the part, Juanita Hall, but since her voice was not what it once was her two numbers "Bali Ha'i" and "Happy Talk" were sung by the London creator of the same role,

MURIEL SMITH. Best-known ghost voice, though, is undoubtedly MARNI NIXON, who did a series of well-publicised ghosting jobs in large-budget musicals. She was the voice of Deborah Kerr in *The King and I*, Natalie Wood (q.v.) in *West Side Story* and Audrey Hepburn (q.v.) in *My Fair Lady*. Earlier she sang for Jeanne Crain in *Cheaper By the Dozen*. She also acted, and sang for herself, in *The Sound of Music*. But when it was suggested that dubbed actresses should not be eligible for acting awards (like Oscars) the secrecy veil was lowered once more. Record albums now list song titles as sung by the *characters* in the film, leaving the question of the singer open. And even Marni Nixon has not managed to overcome one hurdle that faces the movie ghost. There is a moment in *Singin' in the Rain* when the beautiful but dumb Lina Lamont screams in horror, "You mean it's going to say up there on the screen that I don't talk and sing for myself?" As yet, no soundtrack ghost has ever been given credit up there on the screen.

**178 GIBSON, VIRGINIA.** Dancer who provided pleasant support in Fifties musicals.

Films: *Tea for Two* (début), *Painting the Clouds with Sunshine*, *About Face*, *Starlift*, *She's Working Her Way through College*, *Stop You're Killing Me* (cs), *She's Back on Broadway*, *Athena*, *Seven Brides for Seven Brothers*.

**179 GILBERT, PAUL** (1924– ). RN: Paul MacMahon. Singer-comic, more active in night clubs than movies.

Films: *So This Is Paris*, *The Second Greatest Sex*, *You Can't Run Away from It*.

**180 GOLDWYN, SAM** (1882– ). RN: Samuel Goldfisch. Warsaw-born producer of highly polished entertainments. Formed production company with Jesse Lasky 1910, later formed Goldwyn Picture Corporation. Sold interest to Metro and became independent. Most of his musicals feature bevy of beauties known as "Goldwyn Girls." Brought Busby Berkeley (q.v.) to Hollywood, and specially helpful to film careers of Eddie Cantor (q.v.) and Danny Kaye (q.v.).

Films: *The Awakening* (silent, Goldwyn used Irving Berlin's q.v. "Marie" as theme song), *Whoopee, Palmy Days, The Kid from Spain, Roman Scandals, Kid Millions, Strike Me Pink, The Hurricane* (ds), *Goldwyn Follies, They Shall Have Music/Melody of Youth, Ball of Fire* (cs), *Up in Arms, The Princess and the Pirate* (cs), *Wonder Man, The Kid from Brooklyn, The Secret Life of Walter Mitty, A Song Is Born, Hans Christian Andersen, Guys and Dolls, Porgy and Bess.*

**181 GOODRICH, FRANCES** (c. 1896–    ) and **HACKETT, ALBERT** (1900–    ). Husband-and-wife writing team, both one-time actors who married in 1931 and moved to Hollywood. Best known for *Thin Man* series and play *The Diary of Anne Frank*, but have written many amusing comedy and musical scripts.

Films: co-sc. *Naughty Marietta, Rose Marie* (36), *After the Thin Man* (cs), *The Firefly, Society Lawyer; Lady in the Dark, Summer Holiday, The Pirate, Easter Parade* (also st.), *In the Good Old Summertime, Grounds for Marriage, Give a Girl a Break, Seven Brides for Seven Brothers, Gaby* (ds), *A Certain Smile* (ds).

**182 GOODWINS, LESLIE** (1899–    ). British-born director of second features. Started as director and writer of shorts.

Films: *Tarnished Angel* (ds), *The Girl from Mexico* (cs), *Let's Make Music, They Met in Argentina, Silver Skates, Gals Incorporated, The Singing Sheriff, Casanova in Burlesque, Murder in the Blue Room* (ds), *Hi Beautiful, I'll Tell the World, Radio Stars on Parade, An Angel Comes to Brooklyn, Riverboat Rhythm, Paris Follies of 1956.*

**183 GORDON, MACK** (    –1959). Lyricist who was vaudeville performer before teaming with Harry Revel (q.v.). One of Hollywood's most prolific and consistent lyricists.

Films: *Pointed Heels, Swing High, Broadway through a Keyhole, The Gay Divorcee* (inc. "Let's K-nock K-nees"), *We're Not Dressing* (inc. "She Reminds Me of You"), *She Loves Me Not, Shoot the Works, College Rhythm* (inc. "Stay as Sweet as You Are"), *Love in Bloom, Stolen Harmony, Paris in the Spring, Two for Tonight, Collegiate, Poor Little Rich Girl, Florida Special* (cs), *Stowaway* (inc. "Goodnight My Love"), *Head over Heels* (Brit.), *This Is My Affair* (ds), *Wake Up and Live* (inc. "There's a Lull in My Life"), *Danger Love at Work* (cs), *You Can't Have Everything, Ali Baba Goes to Town, Love and Hisses, Hold That Co-ed, Josette, My Lucky Star, Love Finds Andy Hardy* (cs), *Sally Irene and Mary, Thanks for Everything, Young People, Johnny Apollo* (also comp.), *Rose of Washington Square* ("I Never Knew Heaven Could Speak"), *Down Argentine Way, Star Dust, Tin Pan Alley, That Night in Rio* (inc. "I Yi Yi Yi Yi Yi"), *The Great American Broadcast, Weekend in Havana* (inc. "When I Love I Love"), *Sun Valley Serenade* (inc. "I Know Why," "Chatanooga Choo Choo"), *Springtime in the Rockies, Orchestra Wives* (inc. "I've Got a Gal in Kalamazoo"), *Song of the Islands* (inc. "Down on Ami-

Ami-Oni-Oni Isle''), *Iceland* (inc. "There Will Never Be Another You''), *Hello Frisco Hello* (44 Oscar "You'll Never Know''), *Sweet Rosie O'Grady* (inc. "My Heart Tells Me''), *Pin Up Girl* (inc. "The Story of the Very Merry Widow''), *Sweet and Low Down, Diamond Horseshoe* (inc. "The More I See You''), *The Dolly Sisters* (inc. "I Can't Begin to Tell You''), *Three Little Girls in Blue* (inc. "You Make Me Feel So Young''), *Mother Wore Tights, When My Baby Smiles at Me* (inc. "What Did I Do?''), *Beautiful Blonde from Bashful Bend* (cs), *Come to the Stable* (ds), *Wabash Avenue, Summer Stock/If You Feel like Singing* (inc. "Dig Dig Dig''), *I'll Get By, Call Me Mister, I Love Melvin* (inc. "Where Did You Learn to Dance?''), *The Girl Next Door, Young at Heart* ("You My Love''), *Bundle of Joy*. Prod. *Three Little Girls in Blue*.

**184 GOULD, DAVE** (1905–    ). Hungarian-born choreographer of early musicals. Active in theatre prior to Hollywood.

Films: *Melody Cruise, Flying Down to Rio, Hips Hips Hooray, The Gay Divorcee, Hollywood Party* (co.), *Folies Bergere, Broadway Melody of 1936, A Perfect Gentleman* (cs), *Born to Dance, A Day at the Races, Broadway Melody of 1938, Everything's on Ice, It All Came True* (ds), *The Boys from Syracuse, Rhythm Parade* (also co-dir.).

**185 GOULDING, EDMUND** (1891–1959). A thoughtful drama director whose musicals do not represent his best work. British-born, acted and wrote for theatre before films. Dir. first film 1925.

Films: sc. *Broadway Melody* (29). Dir. *Paramount on Parade* (excerpt), *Reaching for the Moon* (ds), *Blondie of the Follies;*

*Down among the Sheltering Palms, Mardi Gras.*

**186 GRABLE, BETTY** (1916–    ). Blonde pin-up-girl of the Forties, owner of the most famous legs in the world and in 1948 the highest salaried woman in the U.S.A. Though first to admit neither great singer nor dancer, possessed pleasantly melodic voice and an above-average hoofer when material demanded (e.g. Apache number in *Pin Up Girl*). Trained at Hollywood Professional School and

*Betty Grable in the aptly-titled PIN UP GIRL*

made film *début* as chorus girl when thirteen. After spell as Goldwyn Girl and many small roles gained attention in *The Gay Divorcee* singing and dancing with Edward Everett Horton. Signed by Fox prior to Broadway role in *Du Barry Was a Lady*, she replaced ailing Alice Faye (q.v.) as star of *Down Argentine Way* which established her image as queen of lavish, gaudy Technicolor extravaganzas. After *Mother Wore Tights*, her biggest hit, material declined. Studio refused to buy *Guys and Dolls* for her, and inadequate vehicles led to suspension and ultimate release from contract. Still active in theatres, night clubs.

Films: *Let's Go Places* (début), *Fox Movietone Follies, Happy Days, Whoopee, Palmy Days, The Kid from Spain, Child of Manhattan* (ds), *Sweetheart of Sigma Chi* (33), *Cavalcade* (ds), *Student Tour, The Gay Divorcee, Hips Hips Hooray, Nitwits* (cs), *Old Man Rhythm, Collegiate, Follow the Fleet, Pigskin Parade, This Way Please, Thrill of a Lifetime, College Swing/Swing Teacher Swing, Give Me a Sailor, Man about Town, Million Dollar Legs, Down Argentine Way, Tin Pan Alley, Moon over Miami, A Yank in the RAF* (ds), *I Wake Up Screaming/Hot Spot* (ds), *Footlight Serenade, Song of the Islands, Springtime in the Rockies* (intro. "Run Little Raindrop Run"), *Coney Island, Sweet Rosie O'Grady* (intro. "My Heart Tells Me"), *Four Jills in a Jeep* (as herself), *Pin Up Girl, Diamond Horseshoe* (intro. "Acapulco"), *The Dolly Sisters, Do You Love Me?* (brief guest appearance), *The Shocking Miss Pilgrim* (intro. "Changing My Tune"), *Mother Wore Tights* (intro. "Kokomo Indiana"), *That Lady in Ermine, When My Baby Smiles at Me* (intro. "By the Way"), *The Beautiful Blonde from Bashful Bend* (cs), *Wabash Avenue* (re-make of same star's *Coney Island*), *My Blue Heaven, Call Me*

70

*Above : Dolores Gray in* IT'S ALWAYS FAIR WEATHER. *Below : Kathryn Grayson in* TWO SISTERS FROM BOSTON

*Mister, Meet Me after the Show, The Farmer Take a Wife* (intro. "Today I Love Everybody"), *Three for the Show, How to Be Very Very Popular* (re-make *She Loves Me Not*).

**187 GRAY, DOLORES** (1924– ). Musical comedy star (notably in London production of *Annie Get Your Gun*) whose vibrant voice and buoyant sense of humour have been featured too rarely on screen.

Films: *It's Always Fair Weather, Kismet* (55), *The Opposite Sex, Designing Woman* (cs).

**188 GRAYSON, KATHRYN** (1922– ). RN: Zelma Hedrick. M-G-M's resident soprano of the Forties. Sang on Eddie Cantor's (q.v.) radio show before signed by M-G-M, who groomed her for two years before first film. Now in theatres and night clubs, frequently in double-act with Howard Keel (q.v.).

Films: *Andy Hardy's Private Secretary* (cs, début), *The Vanishing Virginian* (ds), *Seven Sweethearts, Rio Rita* (42), *Thousands Cheer, Anchors Aweigh, Ziegfeld Follies, Two Sisters from Boston, Till the Clouds Roll By, It Happened in Brooklyn, The Kissing Bandit* (intro. "Love Is Where You Find It"), *That Midnight Kiss, Grounds for Marriage, The Toast of New Orleans, Show Boat* (51), *Lovely to Look At, The Desert Song* (53), *So This Is Love/The Grace Moore Story, Kiss Me Kate, The Vagabond King* (56).

**GREEN, ADOLPH.** See **COMDEN, BETTY.**

**189 GREEN, ALFRED E.** (1889–1960). Director of mostly minor films. Started in silents 1912 and dir. George Arliss's first three Hollywood films. His best musical *The Jolson Story* had musical numbers directed by Joseph H. Lewis, an above-average B-picture director.

Films: *Road to Singapore* (31), *Sweet Music, Here's to Romance, Colleen, Mr. Dodd Takes the Air, Thoroughbreds Don't Cry, The Gracie Allen Murder Case* (cs), *Shooting High, Mayor of 44th Street, The Jolson Story, Tars and Spars, Copacabana, The Fabulous Dorseys, Two Gals and a Guy, The Eddie Cantor Story, Top Banana.*

**190 GREEN, JOHNNY** (1908– ). Conductor, arranger and composer, one-time General Music Director at M-G-M. Started as rehearsal pianist, formed own band in Thirties. Signed by M-G-M 1934, Universal 1947 briefly, then back to M-G-M for *Easter Parade,* for which he won first of several scoring Oscars. Now freelances in films, also active in concerts and TV.

Films: Comp. *The Sap from Syracuse, Dude Ranch* ("Out of Nowhere"), *Bachelor of Arts* ("Easy Come, Easy Go"), *Cockeyed Cavaliers, The First Baby; Bathing Beauty, Something in the Wind; Everything I Have Is Yours.* MD and music supervision: *Broadway Rhythm, Bathing Beauty, Easy to Wed, It Happened in Brooklyn, Fiesta* (47), *Easter Parade, Summer Stock/If You Feel like Singing, Royal Wedding/Wedding Bells, The Great Caruso, An American in Paris* (w. Saul Chaplin q.v.), *Because You're Mine, Brigadoon, Invitation to the Dance, I'll Cry Tomorrow* (ds); *West Side Story* (w. Chaplin), *Pepe, Bye Bye Birdie; Oliver* (in G.B.).

**191 GREEN, MITZI** (1920–1969). Child musical star, a mimic at six, given Paramount contract two years later. Starred in *Babes in Arms* on Broadway.

Films: *Honey, Paramount on Parade,*

*Love among the Millionaires, Dude Ranch, Girl Crazy* (32), *Transatlantic Merry-go-round; Lost in Alaska* (cs), *Bloodhounds of Broadway.*

## 192 GREENWOOD, CHARLOTTE

(1893–    ). Statuesque comedienne-dancer with an impressive high kick and engaging style. Started as eccentric acrobatic dancer, silent film *début* 1918. After success in theatre re-entered films 1928 starring in series of "Letty" comedies. In later musicals often the good-natured chaperone with a roving eye herself.

Films: *So Long Letty, She Couldn't Say No, Stepping Out, Flying High, Palmy Days, Happy Landing, Young People, Down Argentine Way, Star Dust, Tall Dark and Handsome, Moon over*

*"Ain't Nature Grand"*: Charlotte Greenwood in DANGEROUS WHEN WET

*Miami, Springtime in the Rockies, The Gang's All Here/The Girls He Left Behind, Wake Up and Dream* (46), *Oh You Beautiful Doll; Dangerous When Wet, Oklahoma, Glory* (cs), *The Opposite Sex.*

## 193 GUIZAR, TITO (c. 1910–    ).

RN: Frederick Guizar. Mexican singer-guitarist, former opera singer, who starred in Latin-flavoured musicals at Republic.

Films: *Under the Pampas Moon, The Big Broadcast of 1938, Tropic Holiday, St. Louis Blues* (39), *Blondie Goes Latin, Brazil, Mexicana, The Gay Ranchero.*

## HACKETT, ALBERT. See GOODRICH, FRANCES.

## 194 HAGEN, JEAN (c. 1925–    ).

RN: Jean Verhagen. Actress usually better than her material, but as dumb blonde Lina Lamont in *Singin' in the Rain* she had a superb role and played it to the hilt.

Films: *Adam's Rib* (cs), *Singin' in the Rain, Latin Lovers.*

## 195 HALEY, JACK (1902–    ).

Wide-eyed comedian-singer with vaudeville and musical comedy experience. In recent years has been active in affairs of American Guild of Variety Artists.

Films: *Follow Through, Sitting Pretty, Hold That Girl, Coronado, The Girl Friend, Red Heads on Parade, Pigskin Parade, Poor Little Rich Girl, Danger Love at Work, Pick a Star, Rebecca of Sunnybrook Farm, Alexander's Ragtime Band, Thanks for Everything, The Wizard of Oz* (as the Tin Man), *Moon over Miami, Navy Blues, Beyond the Blue Horizon* (ds), *Higher and Higher, Take It Big, George White's Scandals of 1945, Sing Your Way Home, People Are Funny, Make Mine Laughs; Norwood*

**196 HALL, ALEXANDER** (1895–). Comedy director who came to films from stage 1932.

Films: *The Torch Singer* (co.), *Little Miss Marker/Girl in Pawn, Goin' to Town, Give Us This Night; Down to Earth* (included three characters from same director's straight comedy *Here Comes Mr. Jordan*); *The Great Lover* (cs), *Because You're Mine, Let's Do It Again* (cs, re-make *The Awful Truth*), *Forever Darling* (cs).

**197 HAMMERSTEIN II, OSCAR** (1895–1960). Lyricist whose work was variable but at its best had a poetic lyricism that made him a worthy collaborator with Jerome Kern and Richard Rodgers (qq.v.).

Films: *The Desert Song* (29, 43 and 53), *Show Boat* (29, 36 and 51), *Golden Dawn, Song of the Flame, New Moon* (30 and 40), *Sunny* (30 and 41), *Song of the West, Three Sisters, Viennese Nights, Children of Dreams, Music in the Air, Reckless* (title song), *The Night Is Young, Rose Marie* (36 and 54), *Give Us This Night, Sweet Adeline, Roberta, High Wide and Handsome* (inc. "The Folks Who Live on the Hill"), *The Lady Objects, Lady Be Good* (41 Oscar "The Last Time I Saw Paris"), *State Fair* (45 and 62 inc. "That's For Me" and 45 Oscar-winner "It Might as Well Be Spring"), *Centennial Summer* (inc. "All through the Day"), *Oklahoma, Carousel, South Pacific, The King and I, Flower Drum Song, The Sound of Music*. Co-sc. *Swing High Swing Low*. Acted (as himself) in *Main Street to Broadway* (ds).

**198 HANEY, CAROL** (1928–1964). Dancer and choreographer with pixie-ish quality. Was chorus girl, joined Jack Cole (q.v.) troupe. Gene Kelly (q.v.) made her his dance assistant on *An*

*Carol Haney in KISS ME KATE*

*American in Paris, Singin' in the Rain, Brigadoon* and *Invitation to the Dance*. Danced in latter and in *Kiss Me Kate* ("From This Moment On" sequence) with Bob Fosse (q.v.) who remembered her when staging *The Pajama Game* on Broadway and recommended her for role of Gladys, which she repeated in film version.

**199 HARBURG, E. Y.** (1898–    ). Lyricist, former electrician, who started with lyrics for Earl Carroll and Ziegfeld shows and soon had contract with Paramount. A master of tricky internal rhymes, his most consistent collaborator has been Harold Arlen (q.v.).

Films: *Glorifying the American Girl* ("What Wouldn't I Do for That Man"), *Follow the Leader, The Sap from Syracuse, Roadhouse Nights, Moonlight and Pretzels, Take a Chance* ("It's only a

73

Paper Moon"), *The Singing Kid, Stage Struck, Gold Diggers of 1937, The Wizard of Oz* (inc. "If I Only Had a Brain," "Ding Dong the Witch Is Dead," and 39 Oscar winner "Over the Rainbow"), *At the Circus* (inc. "Lydia the Tattooed Lady"), *Babes in Arms* ("God's Country"), *Cairo, Ship Ahoy* (inc. "I'll Take Tallulah"), *Thousands Cheer, Cabin in the Sky* (inc. "Happiness Is a Thing Called Joe," "Life's Full O' Consequence"), *Kismet* (ds, 44), *Can't Help Singing* (inc. "Californ-i-ay"), *Meet the People* (also prod.), *California* (ds); *Gay Purr-ee, I Could Go On Singing, Finian's Rainbow.*

**200 HARRIS, PHIL** (1906–    ). Comedian and singer of patter songs, former bandleader. Married to Alice Faye (q.v.).

Films: *Melody Cruise* (début, with orchestra), *Turn Off the Moon, Man about Town, Buck Benny Rides Again, Dreaming Out Loud, Memory for Two, I Love a Bandleader, Wabash Avenue, Here Comes the Groom* (guest), *The Wild Blue Yonder/Thunder across the Pacific* (ds, intro. "The Thing"), *Starlift, Anything Goes* (56), *The Jungle Book* (voice only).

**201 HARRISON, REX** (1906–    ). RN: Reginald Carey. Debonair English actor on stage and screen since 1930. Worked with Korda, then had spell with Fox in Hollywood. Returned to films after tremendous stage success in *My Fair Lady,* won Oscar for repeating role on screen. Broke tradition by insisting his songs be recorded during actual photography.

Films: *Main Street to Broadway* (ds, cameo), *My Fair Lady, Doctor Dolittle.*

**202 HART, LORENZ** (1895–1943). Lyricist whose words are literate, witty,

sensitive, sharp and unmatched for consistent brilliance. Having excelled in literature and languages, started writing lyrics at college. Was translating German operettas into English when he met Richard Rodgers (q.v.) to form the most successful partnership in song-writing history, though it was five years before their first success. Conscious of his height (five feet), temperamental, disorganised and undisciplined, he was the epitome of the difficult genius. The team was less happy in Hollywood than on Broadway, probably because of the restrictions imposed by film *mores.* Even when their stage musicals were filmed, Hart's lyrics would often be bowdlerised by Hollywood censors. In *Babes in Arms* "The Lady Is a Tramp" was used simply as background music, while "I Wish I Were in Love Again" and "My Funny Valentine" were considered too sophisticated for inclusion. *On Your Toes* reduced all the songs merely to background music, while in *The Boys from Syracuse* one of the few retained songs "He and She" had its last line altered so that not only was the point of the lyric completely lost—the new line didn't even scan. For *I Married an Angel* Hart completely re-wrote one song to suit Nelson Eddy (q.v.), and even as late as 1960 the team's masterpiece *Pal Joey* had most of its score deleted for the screen, with safer standards substituted. Hart collaborated with Gus Kahn (q.v.) on new lyrics for M-G-M's 1934 *The Merry Widow.* For all his other films see RODGERS, RICHARD.

**203 HART, MOSS** (1904–1961). Writer, best known for his stage achievements as playwright and director.

Films: sc. *Frankie and Johnny* (35), *Broadway Melody of 1936.* St., sc. *Lady*

*in the Dark. Sc. Hans Christian Andersen,
A Star Is Born.*

**204  HARVEY, LILLIAN** (1907–    ).
British-born actress. In Germany when
war broke out, became dancer on German
stage. Made reputation in Ufa films,
*Congress Dances* having particular success in States, and made a few Hollywood
musicals.

Films: *My Lips Betray, My Weakness,
I Am Suzanne, Let's Live Tonight.*

**205  HAVER, JUNE** (1926–    ). RN:
June Stovenour. Blonde actress-singer
who had own radio show when eleven.
Sang with bands, made Universal shorts
before Fox contract. Left films to enter
convent, now married to Fred Mac
Murray (q.v.).

Films: *Sweet and Low Down, Irish
Eyes Are Smiling, Where Do We Go from
Here?, The Dolly Sisters, Three Little
Girls in Blue, Wake Up and Dream* (46),
*I Wonder Who's Kissing Her Now?, Look
for the Silver Lining* (as Marilyn Miller
q.v.), *Oh You Beautiful Doll, The Daugh-
ter of Rosie O'Grady, I'll Get By, The
Girl Next Door.*

**206  HAVOC, JUNE** (1916–    ). RN:
June Hovick. Former child vaudeville
performer (the Baby June of *Gypsy*) who
graduated via marathon dances to Broadway and Hollywood. A good all-round
performer with a neat line in wisecracks.

Films: *Four Jacks and a Jill, Sing Your
Worries Away, Hello Frisco Hello,
Casanova in Burlesque, When My Baby
Smiles at Me, Red Hot and Blue.*

**207  HAWKS, HOWARD** (1896–
   ). Director, former prop boy, story
editor.

Films: *Ball of Fire* (cs), *To Have and
Have Not* (ds); *A Song Is Born* (re-make

of *Ball of Fire* tailored for Danny Kaye
q.v.), *Gentlemen Prefer Blondes.*

**208  HAYMES, DICK** (1916–    ).
Argentine-born crooner with a rich baritone voice but dull acting style who
enjoyed period of popularity at Fox.

Films: *Irish Eyes Are Smiling* (début),
*Four Jills in a Jeep, Diamond Horseshoe*
(intro. "The More I See You"), *State
Fair, Do You Love Me?, Centennial
Summer, The Shocking Miss Pilgrim,
Carnival in Costa Rica, Up in Central
Park, One Touch of Venus, St. Benny the
Dip* (ds), *All Ashore, Cruisin' down the
River.*

**209  HAYTON, LENNIE.** Conductor-
arranger, one of M-G-M's chief music
directors in Forties. Arranged for Paul
Whiteman, led own large dance band in
New York during Thirties before migrat-
ing to Hollywood 1941. Married to Lena
Horne (q.v.).

Films as MD: *Born to Sing* (co.), *Best
Foot Forward, Meet the People, Yolanda
and the Thief, The Harvey Girls, Ziegfeld
Follies, Till the Clouds Roll By, Living in
a Big Way, Good News* (47), *Summer
Holiday, The Pirate, Words and Music,
The Barkleys of Broadway, On the Town,
Strictly Dishonourable, Singin' in the*

*Rain, Easy to Love* (co.); *Star!/Those Were the Happy Times, Hello Dolly!* (co.). Comp. *Maisie Gets Her Man* (cs, "Cookin' with Gas").

### 210 HAYWARD, SUSAN (1918–

). RN: Edythe Marrener. Dramatic actress, three of whose biggest successes have been portrayals of singers. Won first Oscar nomination as alcoholic vocalist in *Smash-Up* and further nominations for playing Jane Froman (dubbed) and Lillian Roth (q.v.) using her own voice. After poverty-stricken childhood became model. When George Cukor (q.v.) brought her picture to attention of David Selznick she went to Hollywood to test for Scarlett O'Hara and stayed.

Films: *One Thousand Dollars a Touch-down, Sis Hopkins* (sang duet with Bob Crosby), *Forest Rangers* (cs), *Star Spangled Rhythm, Hit Parade of 1943* (later re-edited and reissued as *Change of Heart*), *Canyon Passage* (ds), *Smash-Up/ A Woman Destroyed* (ds), *With a Song in*

*My Heart* (as Froman), *I'll Cry To-morrow* (as Roth); *Valley of the Dolls* (ds, replaced Judy Garland q.v. as fading Broadway star and was again dubbed).

### 211 HAYWORTH, RITA (1918–

). RN: Marguerite Cansino. Red-haired beauty, the "Love Goddess" of the Forties. Part of dancing act with Spanish father 1932 appearing in stage prologues to movies. Film *début* 1935 in *Dante's Inferno* (non-musical) for Fox but after year as Egyptian, Argentine, Irish and Russian dancers respectively, contract terminated. Many B-pictures as Mexican and Indian princesses followed. Had made thirty-two films when given lead in *You'll Never Get Rich* in which her dancing with Astaire (q.v.) won praise. Several big-budget musicals followed and throughout Forties she was Columbia's biggest asset. Singing voice always dubbed.

Films: *Under the Pampas Moon, Paddy O'Day, Who Killed Gail Preston?* (ds),

76

*Music in My Heart, You'll Never Get Rich, My Gal Sal, Tales of Manhattan* (ds), *You Were Never Lovelier, Cover Girl, Tonight and Every Night, Gilda* (ds), *Down to Earth, The Loves of Carmen* (ds); *Affair in Trinidad* (ds), *Salome* (performed dance of seven veils), *Miss Sadie Thompson* (ds); *Pal Joey*.

**212 HEALY, MARY** (c. 1917–     ). Singer-actress who was working as stenographer for Fox when given contract. Irving Berlin (q.v.) heard her sing and got her second-lead in *Second Fiddle* (début). Also *Star Dust, Zis Boom Bah, Strictly in the Groove, The Five Thousand Fingers of Dr. T.*

**213 HEINDORF, RAY** (c. 1910–     ). Conductor-arranger long associated with Warners. Head of their music department from mid-Forties.

Films: arr. *Sweet Music, Colleen, Stage Struck* (cs), *The Singing Kid, Gold Diggers of 1937, On Your Toes.* MD: *Hard to Get.* Co-MD: *Yankee Doodle Dandy, The Hard Way* (ds), *The Desert Song* (43), *This Is the Army, Hollywood Canteen, Up in Arms, Wonder Man, Rhapsody in Blue, Cinderella Jones, Night and Day, My Wild Irish Rose.* MD: *April Showers, Romance on the High Seas/It's Magic, My Dream Is Yours, Look for the Silver Lining, It's a Great Feeling, Always Leave Them Laughing, Tea for Two, West Point Story/Fine and Dandy, Lullaby of Broadway, On Moonlight Bay, Painting the Clouds with Sunshine, Starlift, I'll See You in My Dreams, About Face, She's Working Her Way through College, April in Paris, The Jazz Singer* (53, co.), *The Eddie Cantor Story, The Desert Song* (53), *She's Back on Broadway, By the Light of the Silvery Moon, Calamity Jane, Lucky Me, A Star Is Born, Pete Kelly's Blues, The Helen Morgan Story/Both*

*Ends of the Candle, The Pajama Game, Damn Yankees/What Lola Wants, The Music Man, Gypsy, Finian's Rainbow.*

**214 HENDERSON, RAY** (1896–     ). Composer who wrote many hits of Twenties and Thirties. Trained as serious musician, played piano with jazz groups, worked as song plugger till his melodies got him commission from impresario George White. "Bye Bye Blackbird" and "Alabamy Bound" among hits prior to teaming with lyricists Buddy

*Sonja Henie in THIN ICE/LOVELY TO LOOK AT*

DeSylva (q.v.) and Lew Brown (q.v.) to write for Broadway and Hollywood.

Films: with DeSylva and Brown: *The Singing Fool* (inc. "Sonny Boy," "There's a Rainbow Round My Shoulder"), *Say It with Songs, Sunny Side Up* (inc. "If I Had a Talking Picture of You," "I'm a Dreamer, Aren't We All?"), *Follow the Leader, Good News* (30 and 47), *Follow Through, Just Imagine; The Best Things in Life Are Free* (biography). With Jack Yellen and Irving Caesar: *George White's Scandals* (34). With Ted Koehler (q.v.) and Irving Caesar: *Curly Top* (inc. "Animal Crackers").

**215 HENIE, SONJA** (1913–1969). Norwegian ice skater, the screen's only major skating star. Won Norwegian championship at eleven, gained many world championships before signed by Fox, where she starred in series of sparkling entertainments.

Films: *One in a Million* (début), *Thin Ice/Lovely to Look At, Happy Landing, My Lucky Star, Second Fiddle, Everything Happens at Night, Sun Valley Serenade, Iceland, Wintertime, It's a Pleasure, Countess of Monte Cristo.*

**216 HEPBURN, AUDREY** (1929– ). RN: Edda Hepburn van Heemstra. Belgian-born actress who after small parts in England was chosen by William Wyler for *Roman Holiday* (non-musical). Early training as dancer and work in stage musicals served her brilliantly when starred with Astaire (q.v.) in *Funny Face.*

Films: *Funny Face, Breakfast at Tiffany's* (cs, intro. "Moon River"), *Paris When It Sizzles* (cs), *My Fair Lady.*

**217 HILLIARD, HARRIET** (1914– ). Wry musical comedy actress of late Thirties, former band singer, who later became popular radio and television star with husband Ozzie Nelson.

Films: *Follow the Fleet* (intro. "Get Thee Behind Me Satan"), *New Faces of 1937, Cocoanut Grove, Sweetheart of the Campus, Juke Box Jennie, Gals Incorporated, Honeymoon Lodge, Hi Good Lookin', Swingtime Johnny, Take It Big.*

**218 HOLLANDER, FREDERICK** (1892– ). RN: Friedrich Hollaender. London-born composer who studied music in Berlin and wrote score for *The Blue Angel,* his music catching the flavour of Germany in the Thirties. Hollywood 1934 to work at Paramount, often with Marlene Dietrich and Ernst Lubitsch (qq.v.).

Films: *The Blue Angel* (30, inc. "They Call Me Naughty Lola," "Falling in Love Again," the latter also used in 59 remake), *Song of Songs* (ds, inc. "Johnny"), *I Am Suzanne, Million Dollar Baby, Desire* (ds), *Anything Goes* (36 inc. "My Heart and I"), *Poppy* (title song only), *Rhythm on the Range, The Jungle Princess* (ds, "Moonlight and Shadows"), *The Champagne Waltz, This Way Please, Thrill of a Lifetime, One Hundred Men and a Girl* ("It's Raining Sunbeams"), *You and Me* (ds), *Cocoanut Grove* ("You Leave Me Breathless"), *Her Jungle Love* (ds), *Man about Town, Destry Rides Again* (ws, inc. "See What the Boys in the Backroom Will Have"), *Zaza* (ds), *The Farmer's Daughter* (cs), *Typhoon* (ds, "Palms of Paradise"), *A Night at Earl Carroll's, Moon over Burma* (cs), *Seven Sinners* (ds, inc. "I've Been in Love Before"), *Manpower* (ds), *Aloma of the South Seas* (ds), *Forest Rangers* (ds, "Tall Grows the Timber"); *A Foreign Affair* (cs), *We're No Angels* (cs).

**219 HOLLIDAY, JUDY** (1923–1965). RN: Judith Tuvim. Delightfully dizzy

blonde comedienne who started with group of night club performers in Thirties inc. Betty Comden and Adolph Green (q.v.) who were to write book and lyrics for her Broadway musical *Bells Are Ringing*, later filmed by M-G-M.

Films: *Something for the Boys* (début), *Adam's Rib* (cs, first sizeable film role), *It Should Happen to You* (cs), *Bells Are Ringing*.

**220 HOPE, BOB** (1903–    ). RN: Leslie Townes Hope. London-born wise-cracking comedian who also sings attractively. Hollywood's most successful comic, has starred steadily since 1938, after vaudeville and musical comedy (*Roberta*, *Ziegfeld Follies*). Made several two-reelers inc. *Paree Paree* (34) based on Cole Porter's (q.v.) *Fifty Million Frenchmen*. Most of his films have a song or two.

Films listed are those closest to musicals or particularly memorable for song content: *Big Broadcast of 1938* (feature début—intro. "Thanks for the Memory"), *College Swing/Swing Teacher Swing, Give Me a Sailor, Thanks for the Memory* (intro. "Two Sleepy People"), *Never Say Die, Some Like It Hot* (39, intro. "The Lady's in Love with You"), *Road to Singapore* (40), *Road to Zanzibar, Louisiana Purchase, Road to Morocco, Star Spangled Rhythm* (as himself), *They Got Me Covered* (cs), *Let's Face It, The Princess and the Pirate, Road to Utopia, My Favourite Brunette, Variety Girl* (as himself), *Road to Rio, The Paleface* (intro. "Buttons and Bows"), *Sorrowful Jones, The Great Lover, Fancy Pants* (intro. "Home Cookin'"), *The Lemon Drop Kid* (intro. "Silver Bells"), *My Favourite Spy* (51), *The Greatest Show on Earth* (fleeting unbilled appearance), *Son of Paleface* (intro. "Am I in Love?"), *Road to Bali, Off Limits/Military Policeman, Here Come the Girls, The Seven Little Foys* (as vaudeville star Eddie Foy), *That Certain Feeling, Beau James* (as New York's song-writing Mayor Jimmy

*Bob Hope with Shirley Ross in SOME LIKE IT HOT*

Walker), *Paris Holiday*, *The Five Pennies* (as himself), *Alias Jesse James* (intro. "Ain't A-Hankerin'"), *Road to Hong Kong*, *I'll Take Sweden*.

**221  HORNE, LENA** (1917–    ). Negro singer with smouldering style that had her once labelled "the tigress." After band and night club work M-G-M signed her on recommendation of Roger Edens (q.v.) but rarely gave her more than speciality spots that could be edited out in Southern states.

Films: *Panama Hattie* (début), *Cabin in the Sky* (best film role), *I Dood It*/*By Hook or By Crook*, *Stormy Weather*, *Broadway Rhythm*, *Thousands Cheer*, *Swing Fever*, *Two Girls and a Sailor*, *Ziegfeld Follies* (intro. "Love"), *Till the Clouds Roll By*, *Words and Music*; *Meet Me in Las Vegas*/*Viva Las Vegas*.

**222  HOVICK, LOUISE** (also known as **GYPSY ROSE LEE**) (1914–1970). RN: Rose Louise Hovick. Best-known stripper in show business who also had limited film career and some success as writer. Child act in vaudeville with sister June Havoc (q.v.). Small parts in Fox musicals preceded writing of book "G-

String Murders" filmed as *Lady of Burlesque* (and banned by National Legion of Decency). *Doll Face* was based on one of her plays, and her autobiography became hit Broadway musical and film *Gypsy*.

Films, as Louise Hovick: *Ali Baba Goes to Town*, *You Can't Have Everything*, *Sally Irene and Mary*, *Battle of Broadway*, *My Lucky Star*. As Gypsy Rose Lee: *Stage Door Canteen* (sketch satirising striptease), *Belle of the Yukon*.

**223  HUMBERSTONE,    BRUCE** (1903–    ). Skilled director of fast-moving musicals and thrillers, former script clerk, juvenile lead.

Films: *Charlie Chan at the Opera* (ds), *Rascals*, *Pack Up Your Troubles*, *The Quarterback* (cs), *Sun Valley Serenade*, *Tall Dark and Handsome*, *I Wake Up Screaming*/*Hot Spot* (ds), *Iceland*, *Hello Frisco Hello*, *Pin Up Girl*, *Wonder Man*, *Three Little Girls in Blue*, *South Sea Sinner*/*East of Java* (ds), *Happy Go Lovely* (Brit.), *She's Working Her Way through College*, *The Desert Song* (53).

**224  HUNTER, ROSS** (1921–    ). RN: Martin Fuss. Producer of glossy escapist movies. From school teaching became actor 1944.

Films as actor: *She's a Sweetheart*, *Louisiana Hayride*, *Ever since Venus*, *Sweetheart of Sigma Chi* (46). As prod: *Take Me to Town* (cs), *Flower Drum Song*, *I'd Rather Be Rich* (cs, re-make *It Started with Eve*), *Thoroughly Modern Millie*.

**225  HUTTON, BETTY** (1921–    ). RN: Betty Jane Thorburg. Madcap singer and comedienne known as Blonde Bombshell and top star at Paramount in late Forties. Sang on street corners as child to help support family and deve-

*"The Tunnel of Love" : Betty Hutton
with Fred Astaire in LET'S DANCE*

loped frantic style—tumbles, cartwheels and yells—to draw attention from prettier sister Marion (q.v.). Sang with band at thirteen, signed by Vincent Lopez who adapted his band's style to suit hers. Buddy DeSylva (q.v.) chose her for his Broadway production *Panama Hattie,* and later as executive at Paramount he signed her for *The Fleet's In.* Her rendition of "Arthur Murray Taught Me Dancing in a Hurry" had immediate impact. Straight comedy role in *The Miracle of Morgan's Creek* a success, and later roles often mixed drama with music. Energy and material both seemed to be weakening when chosen to replace Judy Garland (q.v.) in *Annie Get Your Gun,* but despite this her career continued to falter.

Films: *The Fleet's In* (début), *Star Spangled Rhythm, Happy Go Lucky* (intro. "Murder He Says"), *Let's Face It, And the Angels Sing* (intro. "His Rocking Horse Ran Away"), *Here Come the Waves* (intro. "There's a Fellow Waiting in Poughkeepsie"), *Incendiary Blonde* (as night club queen Texas Guinan), *Duffy's Tavern* (intro. "Doin' It the Hard Way"), *The Stork Club* (intro. "Doctor, Lawyer, Indian Chief"), *Cross My Heart, The Perils of Pauline* (47, as silent serial star Pearl White, intro. "The Sewing Machine," "I Wish I Didn't Love You So"), *Variety Girl, Dream Girl* (cs), *Red Hot and Blue* (intro. "Hamlet"), *Annie Get Your Gun, Let's Dance* ("my first chance to dance like a lady"), *Sailor Beware* (cs, guest), *Somebody Loves Me* (as vaudeville star Blossom Seeley), *The Greatest Show on Earth* (ds), *Spring Reunion* (ds).

**226 HUTTON, MARION** (1919– ). RN: Marion Thorburg. Sister of Betty (q.v.), best known as band vocalist of Forties (notably with Glenn Miller) but made a few films. More subdued, conventional than her sister.

Films: *Orchestra Wives, Crazy House* (w. Glenn Miller Singers), *In Society* (intro. "My Dreams Are Getting Better"), *Babes on Swing Street, Love Happy.*

**227 ITURBI, JOSE** (1895– ). Spanish-born concert pianist, conductor of Rochester Symphony Orchestra in US 1936. Made a hit playing boogie along with classics in first film, and later played romantic lead opposite Jeanette MacDonald (q.v.).

Films: *Thousands Cheer* (début), *Two Girls and a Sailor, Music for Millions, A Song to Remember* (sound track only), *Anchors Aweigh, Holiday in Mexico,*

*Three Daring Daughters/The Birds and the Bees, That Midnight Kiss.*

**228 JEAN, GLORIA** (1928– ). RN: Gloria Jean Schoonover. Sweet young singer discovered by Joe Pasternak (q.v.) when only eleven and signed by Universal, playing ingenué lead in many B musicals.

Films: *The Underpup* (début), *If I Had My Way, A Little Bit of Heaven, Pardon My Rhythm, Never Give a Sucker an Even Break* (cs), *What's Cooking?, It Comes Up Love, When Johnny Comes Marching Home, Get Hep to Love/She's My Lovely, Moonlight in Vermont, Mr. Big, Ghost Catchers, The Reckless Age, Follow the Boys* (44), *Easy to Look At, I'll Remember April, An Old Fashioned Girl, Copacabana, I Surrender Dear, Manhattan Angel, There's a Girl in My Heart; Ladies' Man* (61).

**229 JERGENS, ADELE** (1922– ). Tall blonde, former New York model, who became the epitome of that musical staple, the worldly-wise, wise-cracking showgirl.

Films: *Tonight and Every Night, When a Girl's Beautiful, Down to Earth, Ladies of the Chorus, Slightly French, The Travelling Saleswoman, Show Boat* (51), *Aaron Slick from Pumkin Crick/Marshmallow Moon, Somebody Loves Me.*

**230 JESSEL, GEORGE** (1898– ). Actor, producer, singer and raconteur. In vaudeville from childhood, made two-reeler 1911 and starred in one of first talkies, but greatest movie success came as producer of Fox musicals, generally with show business setting.

Films as actor: *Lucky Boy* (intro. "My Mother's Eyes"), *Love Live and Laugh* (ds), *Happy Days; Stage Door Canteen, Four Jills in a Jeep; Juke Box Rhythm, Can Heironymous Merkin ever Forget Mercy Humppe and Find True Happiness?* As prod: *The Dolly Sisters, Do You Love Me?, I Wonder Who's Kissing Her Now, When My Baby Smiles at Me, Oh You Beautiful Doll, Dancing in the Dark, Meet Me after the Show, Golden Girl, Wait Till the Sun Shines Nellie* (ds), *Bloodhounds of Broadway, The I Don't Care Girl, Tonight We Sing.*

**231 JOHNSON, VAN** (1916– ). Freckle-faced actor who graduated from vaudeville and Broadway choruses to M-G-M where he became a top musical and romantic lead of Forties.

Films: *Too Many Girls, A Guy Named*

*"I Won't Dance": Van Johnson with Lucille Bremer in* TILL THE CLOUDS ROLL BY

*Al Jolson with Ruby Keeler in GO INTO YOUR DANCE/CASINO DE PARIS*

*Joe* (ds), *Two Girls and a Sailor, Thrill of a Romance, Weekend at the Waldorf* (ds), *Easy to Wed, No Leave No Love, Till the Clouds Roll By, In the Good Old Summertime, Grounds for Marriage, The Duchess of Idaho, Remains to Be Seen* (cs), *Easy to Love, Brigadoon, Kelly and Me* (cs).

**232 JOHNSTON, ARTHUR** (1898– ). Composer who was once chief arranger for Irving Berlin (q.v.). Went to Hollywood with Berlin and orchestrated scores of *Putting on the Ritz, Mammy* and *Reaching for the Moon.* When Berlin returned to Broadway, Johnston stayed in Hollywood to compose, and first song "Just One More Chance" (*College Coach*) was a hit.

Films: *College Coach, College Humour, Too Much Harmony* (inc. "Black Moon-

light"), *From Hell to Heaven* (ds), *The Way to Love* (title tune), *Hello Everybody* (inc. "Moon Song"), *Murder at the Vanities* (inc. "Cocktails for Two"), *Belle of the Nineties* (inc. "My Old Flame"), *Many Happy Returns* (inc. "Fare Thee Well"), *Thanks a Million* (inc. "Sitting High on a Hilltop"), *The Girl Friend, Go West Young Man, Pennies from Heaven, Double or Nothing* (inc. "It's the Natural Thing to Do"); *Song of the South* (title song).

**233 JOHNSTON, JOHNNY** (c. 1920– ). Personable leading man and singer, former radio singer and guitarist. More active in theatre and night clubs than films.

Films: *Sweater Girl* (début), *Star Spangled Rhythm, Priorities on Parade,*

*You Can't Ration Love, Till the Clouds Roll By, This Time for Keeps; Rock around the Clock.*

**234 JOLSON, AL** (c. 1882–1950). RN: Asa Yoelson. The man who started it all, star of the first talkie *The Jazz Singer* and several others, though his screen career never equalled his tremendous successes in vaudeville and musical comedy. Son of a cantor, made stage *début* when thirteen, toured with minstrel shows and circus troupes before Broadway. Became one of immortals of show business, epitomising larger-than-life entertainment with his broad gestures and blatantly emotional songs. His uniquely rich voice reached a new generation when he dubbed the soundtrack of *The Jolson Story*, one of the biggest film successes of all time. Married for a while to Ruby Keeler (q.v.). Died after returning from entertaining troops in Korea.

Films: *The Jazz Singer, The Singing Fool* (intro. "Sonny Boy"), *Say It with Songs, Mammy* (intro. "Let Me Sing and I'm Happy"), *Big Boy, Show Girl in Hollywood* (guest), *Hallelujah I'm a Bum, Wonder Bar, Go into Your Dance* (intro. "About a Quarter to Nine"), *The Singing Kid; Rose of Washington Square, Swanee River; Rhapsody in Blue* (as himself), *The Jolson Story* (voice only but for "Swanee" in which he appears in longshot), *Jolson Sings Again* (voice only, except for scene where he is introduced to Larry Parks q.v.).

**235 JONES, ALLAN** (1908–    ). Tenor who acted in several stage operettas before becoming leading man on screen.

Films: *Reckless* (début), *A Night at the Opera, Rose Marie* (36), *Show Boat* (36), *A Day at the Races, The Firefly* (intro. "The Donkey Serenade"), *Everybody Sing, The Great Victor Herbert, The Boys from Syracuse, One Night in the Tropics, There's Magic in Music, Moonlight in Havana, True to the Army, When Johnny Comes Marching Home, Crazy House* (guest), *Larceny with Music, Rhythm of the Islands, You're a Lucky Fellow Mr. Smith, Sing a Jingle/Lucky Days, Honeymoon Ahead, Senorita from the West.*

**236 JONES, SHIRLEY** (1934–    ). Actress-singer, acting in touring version of a Rodgers and Hammerstein musical when chosen for film lead in *Oklahoma.*

When musical roles became less effective, switched to straight drama (*Elmer Gantry*) and won Oscar.

Films: *Oklahoma* (début), *Carousel, April Love, Never Steal Anything Small, Pepe.*

**237 JUNE, RAY** (c. 1908–    ). Photographer active in Hollywood since start of talkies.

Films: *Lottery Bride, Puttin' On the Ritz, Reaching for the Moon, Horse Feathers, Roman Scandals, The Girl from Missouri, The Great Ziegfeld, Born to Dance, Honolulu, Babes in Arms, Strike Up the Band, Little Nelly Kelly, Ziegfeld*

*Girl, I Married an Angel, I Dood It/By Hook or By Crook, Three Daring Daughters/The Birds and the Bees, Nancy Goes to Rio, Strictly Dishonourable, Sombrero, Easy to Love, The Court Jester, Funny Face.*

**238 KAHN, GUS.** German-born lyricist whose words are simple, direct and effective. Chief collaborator in Twenties was Walter Donaldson (q.v.). Later resident at M-G-M where one of main chores was to provide new lyrics for established operettas.

Films: *Flying down to Rio, Cockeyed Cavaliers, Bottoms Up, Kid Millions, Stingaree* (ds), *The Merry Widow* (34, w. Lorenz Hart q.v.), *Operator 13, Hollywood Party* (inc. "I've Had My Moments"), *Reckless, Love Me Forever, Thanks a Million* (inc. "He Calls Me Sugar Plum"), *The Girl Friend, Let's Sing Again, Music for Madam, Maytime, Girl of the Golden West, Everybody Sing, Let Freedom Ring, Balalaika, Honolulu, Broadway Serenade, Bitter Sweet, Go West, Two Girls on Broadway, The Chocolate Soldier, Ziegfeld Girl* ("You Stepped Out of a Dream"); *I'll See You in My Dreams* (biography).

**239 KALMAR, BERT** (1884–1947). Lyricist and writer, former dancing comic till a knee injury led to his teaming with Harry Ruby (q.v.) to produce hit songs. For films see RUBY, HARRY.

**240 KANE, HELEN** (1904–1966). The "Boop-a-doop" girl of the Thirties. Stage *début* in Marx Brothers revue. Intro. "I Wanna Be Loved By You" 1928 in Broadway's *Good Boy*. Paramount contract 1929.

Films: *Sweetie* (intro. "He's So Unusual"), *Nothing but the Truth* (cs), *Pointed Heels, Dangerous Nan McGrew,* *Paramount on Parade, Heads Up.* Sang "I Wanna Be Loved By You" on soundtrack of *Three Little Words* (portrayed by Debbie Reynolds q.v.).

**241 KATZMAN, SAM** (1901–    ). Producer of quickly-made low-budget pictures whose musicals are usually aimed at 'teenage market, often built around current dance or music craze. Started as prop boy at Fox when thirteen, worked up to production manager. Prod. from 1931.

Films: *Freddie Steps Out, High School Hero, Betty Co-Ed, Sweet Genevieve, Two Blondes and a Redhead, Glamour Girl; Rock around the Clock, Don't Knock the Rock, Calypso Heat Wave, Going Steady, Juke Box Rhythm, Twist around the Clock, Don't Knock the Twist, Two Tickets to Paris, Hootenanny Hoot, Kissin' Cousins, Your Cheating Heart, Harum Scarum/Harem Holiday, When the Boys Meet the Girls* (re-make *Girl Crazy*), *Hold On.*

**242 KAYE, DANNY** (1913–    ). RN: David Daniel Kaminsky. Tall comedian who worked his way through vaudeville and summer shows to night clubs and Broadway revue. Signed by Moss Hart (q.v.) for *Lady in the Dark,* he stopped show with tongue-twisting "Tchaikowsky" number. Starred in *Let's Face It,* given contract by Sam Goldwyn (q.v.) who starred him in first feature. Had made two-reelers in Thirties.

Films: *Up in Arms* (feature *début*), *Wonder Man, The Kid from Brooklyn, The Secret Life of Walter Mitty, A Song Is Born, The Inspector General, On the Riviera, Hans Christian Andersen, Knock on Wood* (cs), *White Christmas, The Court Jester* (cs), *Merry Andrew, The Five Pennies* (as jazzman Red Nichols), *On the Double* (cs).

**243 KEEL, HOWARD** (1919–    ). RN: Harold Keel. Powerful singer, leading man at M-G-M through Fifties. Starred in London production *Oklahoma*, film *début* in British thriller then chosen for lead in film of *Annie Get Your Gun*. Less wooden than than many such singers, he tempered stoic roles with humour.

Films: *Annie Get Your Gun, Pagan Love Song, Show Boat* (51), *Texas Carnival, Callaway Went Thataway/The Star Said No* (cs), *Lovely to Look At, I Love Melvin* (guest), *Calamity Jane, Kiss Me Kate, Rose Marie* (54), *Seven Brides for Seven Brothers* (intro. "Bless Yore Beautiful Hide"), *Deep in My Heart, Jupiter's Darling, Kismet* (55).

**244 KEELER, RUBY** (1909–    ). RN: Ethel Keeler. Screen's first star hoofer, who started dancing as child and made stage *début* when thirteen. Did speciality at Texas Guinan's night club, signed by Ziegfeld as tap dancer in *Whoopee*, followed by star roles. Went to Hollywood with Al Jolson (q.v.) and offered role in *Forty-Second Street*. Often teamed with Dick Powell (q.v.) and specialised in ingenuous chorines who became a star on opening night.

Films: *Show Girl in Hollywood* (guest), *Forty-Second Street, Footlight Parade, Gold Diggers of 1933, Dames, Flirtation Walk, Go into Your Dance* (teamed with Jolson), *Shipmates Forever, Colleen, Ready Willing and Able; Sweetheart of the Campus*.

**245 KELLY, GENE** (1912–    ). RN: Eugene Joseph Kelly. Dancer, choreographer and director who revitalised dance musical in early Forties by injecting new form of joyous spontaneity and freshness to what was becoming a tired formula. Learned dancing as child, 1938 became Broadway chorus boy. Staged numbers for Billy Rose's Diamond Horseshoe night club, won star part in *Pal Joey* on Broadway. Staged dances for Broadway's *Best Foot Forward*, signed by David Selznick for Hollywood but contract bought by M-G-M on advice of Arthur Freed (q.v.). First major opportunity on loan to Columbia for *Cover Girl* with its two memorable routines: the dance trio through the streets to song "Make Way for Tomorrow" and Kelly's celebrated "Alter Ego" dance duet with himself. Former routine, with simple but unrestrained feeling of sheer *joie de vivre*, was forerunner of many similar sequences in years to come. Further breakthroughs followed: the extended "Nina" routine and balletic dream sequence in *The Pirate*, the "Slaughter on Tenth Avenue" ballet in *Words and Music* (again first of several such numbers) and tradition-shattering *On the Town* with its full-scale location shooting, fine ensemble playing and wholehearted communication through song and dance. Co-directed this, along with *Singin' in the Rain*. With decline in audience interest in musicals turned to direction of straight comedies, but returned to song and dance directing *Hello Dolly!*

Films as actor: *For Me and My Gal* (début), *DuBarry Was a Lady, Thousands Cheer, Cover Girl, Christmas Holiday* (ds), *Anchors Aweigh, Ziegfeld Follies* (his only screen teaming with Astaire q.v.), *Living in a Big Way, The Pirate, Words and Music, Take Me Out to the Ball Game/Everybody's Cheering, On the Town* (co-dir.), *Summer Stock/If You Feel like Singing, An American in Paris, Singin' in the Rain* (co-dir.), *Brigadoon, It's Always Fair Weather* (co-dir.), *Invitation to the Dance* (dir.), *Deep in My Heart* (guest), *Les Girls, Marjorie Morningstar* (ds),

*Let's Make Love* (guest), *What a Way to Go* (cs), *Les Demoiselles de Rochefort/Young Girls of Rochefort* (French). Worked on choreography of all Hollywood films from *Cover Girl* on. Dir. *Hello Dolly!*

**246 KELLY, PATSY** (1910–    ). Genial comedienne who was dancing teacher before Broadway stage and Hal Roach comedies. Reliable laugh-getter in Thirties musicals.

Films: *Going Hollywood, Every Night at Eight, Go into Your Dance, Thanks a Million, Pigskin Parade, Sing Baby Sing, Wake Up and Live, Nobody's Baby, Ever Since Eve, Pick a Star, Hit Parade of 1941, Playmates, Road Show, Sing Your Worries Away; Please Don't Eat the Daisies* (cs).

**247 KERN, JEROME** (1885–1945). Composer of exceptional tenderness, a master of compressed emotion and writer of some of America's most beautiful melodies. Left father's furniture business to work in publishing firm, composed songs for interpolation into European scores on Broadway. First hit "How'd You Like to Spoon with Me?" (1905) was re-created by Angela Lansbury (q.v.) in his film biography. Name established nine years later with "They Didn't Believe Me." Many stage scores preceded classic *Show Boat* (27), filmed three times.

Films: *Sally, Show Boat* (29, 36 and 51), *Sunny* (30 and 41), *Three Sisters* (inc. "Hand in Hand"), *The Cat and the Fiddle, Music in the Air, Reckless* (title tune), *I Dream Too Much, Sweet Adeline, Roberta* ("I Won't Dance" composed for Astaire and Rogers), *Swing Time* (36 Oscar "The Way You Look Tonight," also "A Fine Romance," "Bojangles of Harlem," "Pick Yourself Up," "Never Gonna Dance" and "Waltz in Swing Time"), *When You're in Love, High Wide and Handsome* (inc. "Can I Forget You?," "The Folks Who Live on the Hill"), *Joy of Living* (inc. "You Couldn't Be Cuter"), *One Night in the Tropics* (inc. "Remind Me"), *Lady Be Good* ("The Last Time I Saw Paris"), *You Were Never Lovelier* (inc. "I'm Old Fashioned," "Dearly Beloved"), *Cover Girl* (inc. "Long Ago and Far Away," "Sure Thing," "Make Way for Tomorrow"), *Can't Help Singing* (inc. "More and More"), *Centennial Summer* (last complete score inc. "In Love in Vain," "Up with the Lark" and "All through the Day"), *Till the Clouds Roll By* (biography). Songs also featured prominently in biographies of Marilyn Miller, q.v.

*Michael Kidd (left) with Sylvia Fine and Danny Kaye on the set of KNOCK ON WOOD*

(*Look for the Silver Lining*) and Helen Morgan, q.v. (*The Helen Morgan Story/Both Ends of the Candle*).

**248 KEYES, EVELYN** (1919–    ). Actress-dancer, former night club performer, signed to contract by Cecil B. DeMille without screen test.

Films: *Sing You Sinners, The Jolson Story* (as thinly disguised Ruby Keeler, q.v.), *Thrill of Brazil*.

**249 KIDD, MICHAEL** (1919–    ). Choreographer of energetic and humorous dance numbers. Started as ballet dancer 1937, ch. own original ballet "On Stage" 1945, Broadway musical *Finian's Rainbow* 1947.

Films as actor: *It's Always Fair Weather*. Ch. *Where's Charley?, The Band Wagon, Knock on Wood, Seven Brides for Seven Brothers, Guys and Dolls, Merry Andrew* (also dir.), *Li'l Abner* (his Broadway choreography re-staged by Dee Dee Wood), *Star!/Those Were the Happy Times, Hello Dolly!*

**250 KING, CHARLES** (1894–1944). Remembered for singing "You Were Meant for Me" to Bessie Love (q.v.) in *Broadway Melody,* he actually made more Westerns than musicals. At fifteen regarded child genius as singer, toured vaudeville, acted in Ziegfeld Follies and made 420 film shorts in ten years.

Films: *Broadway Melody, Hollywood Revue, Chasing Rainbows, Oh Sailor Behave.*

**251 KING, HENRY** (1892–    ). Veteran director who started in silents and has made every type of movie. Spent most of his career with Fox.

Films: *Carolina, Marie Galante* (ds), *Ramona, In Old Chicago* (ds), *Alexander's Ragtime Band, Little Old New York* (ds), *A Yank in the RAF* (ds), *Margie, Wait Till the Sun Shines Nellie* (ds); *Carousel.*

**252 KINGSLEY, DOROTHY** (c. 1908–    ). Writer long affiliated with M-G-M. Former radio writer for Bob Hope (q.v.).

Films: sc. *Broadway Rhythm* (co.), *Bathing Beauty* (co.), *Easy to Wed, A Date with Judy* (co.), *On an Island with You* (co.), *Neptune's Daughter, Two Weeks with Love* (co.), *Texas Carnival, Small Town Girl* (co.), *Dangerous when Wet, Kiss Me Kate, Seven Brides for Seven Brothers, Jupiter's Darling, Pal Joey, Can Can, Pepe, Half a Sixpence, Valley of the Dolls* (ds, co.).

**253 KOEHLER, TED** (1894–    ). Lyricist, former photo-engraver and song plugger.

Films: *Manhattan Parade, Let's Fall in Love, Curly Top, King of Burlesque* (inc. "I'm Shooting High"), *Dimples, The First Baby, Happy Go Lucky* (36), *Artists and Models* (37), *The King and the Chorus Girl* (cs), *Rainbow Island, Hollywood Canteen, Up in Arms* (inc. "Tess's Torch Song"), *Pillow to Post* (cs), *Week-end at the Waldorf* (ds), *Cheyenne* (ws), *Summer Stock/If You Feel like Singing* (revived "Get Happy," his 1930 hit with Harold Arlen, q.v.).

**254 KOSTAL, IRWIN** (c. 1915–    ). Arranger who scored Broadway musicals, now works on big-budget film scores.

Films: *West Side Story, Mary Poppins, The Sound of Music, Half a Sixpence.*

**255 KOSTER, HENRY** (1905–    ). RN: Herman Kosterlitz. German director, former cartoonist, who worked with Joe Pasternak (q.v.) in Europe, joined him at Universal to make Deanna Durbin (q.v.) musicals.

Films: *Three Smart Girls, One Hundred Men and a Girl, Three Smart Girls Grow Up, First Love, Spring Parade, It Started with Eve, Music for Millions, Two Sisters from Boston, The Unfinished Dance* (re-make of French ballet film *La Mort du Cygne*), *Come to the Stable* (ds), *The Inspector General, Wabash Avenue* (re-make *Coney Island*), *My Blue Heaven, Stars and Stripes Forever/Marching Along, Flower Drum Song, The Singing Nun*.

**256  LAHR, BERT** (1895–1967). RN: Irving Lahrheim. Ex-burlesque comedian, star of Broadway revue and musical comedy whose best film role was Cowardly Lion in *The Wizard of Oz*.

Films: *Flying High, Love and Hisses, Merry-go-round of 1938, Josette, Just around the Corner, The Wizard of Oz, Ship Ahoy, Sing Your Worries Away, Meet the People, Always Leave Them Laughing* (cs), *Rose Marie* (54), *The Second Greatest Sex, The Night They Raided Minsky's* (cs).

**257  LAINE, FRANKIE** (1913–    ). RN: Frank Paul Lo Vecchio. Husky pop singer who reached peak of popularity in early Fifties and starred in several minor musicals.

Films: *Make Believe Ballroom, When You're Smiling, The Sunny Side of the Street, Rainbow Round My Shoulder, Bring Your Smile Along, He Laughed Last, Meet Me in Las Vegas/Viva Las Vegas* (guest).

**258  LAMAS, FERNANDO** (1917–    ). Argentine-born romantic lead who had made many films in Buenos Aires from 1940 prior to Hollywood.

Films: *Rich Young and Pretty* (U.S. début, intro. "We Never Talk Much" w. Danielle Darrieux), *The Merry Widow* (52), *Dangerous When Wet* (intro. "Ain't

Nature Grand?"), *Rose Marie* (54), *The Girl Rush* (54). Married to Esther Williams (q.v.).

**259  LAMONT, CHARLES** (1898–    ). Veteran director who started with silents. Long at Universal where he specialised in Abbott and Costello comedies, the Ma and Pa Kettle series and zippy low-budget musicals.

Films: *Oh Johnny How You Can Love, Melody Lane, Moonlight in Hawaii, San Antonio Rose, Sing Another Chorus, Almost Married, Don't Get Personal, Hi Neighbour, Get Hep to Love/She's My Lovely, It Comes Up Love, When Johnny Comes Marching Home, Hit the Ice, Mr. Big, Top Man, Chip Off the Old Block, The Merry Monahans, Bowery to Broadway, That's the Spirit, Frontier Gal* (ws), *Curtain Call at Cactus Creek/Take the Stage, Comin' Round the Mountain, Untamed Heiress, Ricochet Romance*.

**260  LAMOUR, DOROTHY** (1914–    ). RN: Dorothy Kaumeyer. Paramount's glamour girl of Second World War, remembered as sarong girl of the movies and for "Road" films. Also a good singer and adept comedienne. Former Miss New Orleans beauty queen and radio singer.

Films: *Footlight Parade* (bit), *The Jungle Princess* (first major role, intro. "Moonlight and Shadows"), *College Holiday, High Wide and Handsome, Swing High Swing Low, Thrill of a Lifetime, The Hurricane* (ds, intro. "Moon of Manakoora"), *Big Broadcast of 1938, Her Jungle Love* (ds), *Spawn of the North* (ds), *Tropic Holiday, Man about Town, St. Louis Blues* (39), *Typhoon* (ds), *Johnny Apollo* (ds, intro. "Dancing for Nickels and Dimes"), *Road to Singapore* (40, intro. "The Moon and the Willow Tree"), *Moon over Burma* (cs), *Aloma of *the South Seas* (ds), *Road to Zanzibar, The Fleet's In* (intro. "I Remember You"), *Star Spangled Rhythm* (sang "A Sweater, a Sarong and a Peek-a-boo Bang" with Paulette Goddard and Veronica Lake), *Road to Morocco, Beyond the Blue Horizon* (ds), *Dixie, They Got Me Covered* (cs), *Riding High/Melody Inn* (43), *Rainbow Island, And the Angels Sing* (intro. "It Should Happen to You"), *Duffy's Tavern, Road to Utopia* (intro. "Personality"), *Masquerade in Mexico* (cs), *My Favourite Brunette* (cs), *Variety Girl, Road to Rio, Lulu Belle, Slightly French, Here Comes the Groom* (guest), *Road to Bali, The Greatest Show on Earth* (ds), *Road to Hong Kong, Pajama Party.*

*Dorothy Lamour with Bing Crosby in ROAD TO SINGAPORE*

**261  LANDIS, CAROLE** (1919–1948). RN: Frances Ridste. Former model and band singer who started playing bit roles in Hollywood 1937, eventually became second-league player at Fox. Despite consistent good work, was given only B pictures or second-leads in major ones. Personal and professional problems led to suicide.

Films: *A Day at the Races, Varsity Show, Hollywood Hotel, Gold Diggers in Paris, Road Show, Dance Hall, Moon over Miami, I Wake Up Screaming/Hot Spot* (ds), *Cadet Girl, My Gal Sal, Orchestra Wives, The Powers Girl, Wintertime, Four Jills in a Jeep.*

**262  LANE, BURTON** (1912–    ). Composer of Broadway and Hollywood scores inc. *Finian's Rainbow.* Wrote songs as child, worked as pianist for publisher and encouraged by Gershwin (q.v.). First show 1930, Hollywood from 1933.

Films: *Dancing Lady* (inc. "Everything I Have Is Yours"), *Bottoms Up, Strictly Dynamite, Palooka, Kid Millions, Folies Bergere, Reckless, A Perfect Gentleman, Here Comes the Band, College Holiday, Hideaway Girl, Double or Nothing, Artists and Models* (37), *Swing High Swing Low* (title tune), *Love on Toast, Spawn of the North* (ds), *College Swing/Swing Teacher Swing, Cocoanut Grove, St. Louis Blues* (39), *Some Like It Hot* (39, "The Lady's in Love with You"), *Cafe Society, She Married a Cop, Las Vegas Nights, Dancing on a Dime* (inc. "I Hear Music"), *Babes on Broadway* (inc. "How about You?"), *Ship Ahoy, Seven Sweethearts, DuBarry Was a Lady, Thousands Cheer* ("I Dug a Ditch in Wichita"), *Meet the People, Rainbow Island, Hollywood Canteen, Pillow to Post* (cs), *Feudin' Fussin' and a-Fightin'* (title tune), *Royal Wedding/Wedding Bells* (inc. "Every Night at Seven," "Too Late Now," "I Left My

Hat in Haiti," "The Liar Song"),
*Finian's Rainbow, On a Clear Day You
Can See Forever.*

**263 LANFIELD, SIDNEY** (1900–
). Comedy and musical director, in
films since 1930, particularly associated
with Bob Hope (q.v.) comedies. Former
jazz musician.

Films: *Cheer Up and Smile, Dance
Team, Hat Check Girl, Broadway Bad,
Moulin Rouge, King of Burlesque, One in
a Million, Sing Baby Sing, Love and
Hisses, Thin Ice/Lovely to Look At, Wake
Up and Live, Second Fiddle, Swanee
River, You'll Never Get Rich, Let's Face
It, Bring on the Girls;* Sorrowful Jones
(cs), *The Lemon Drop Kid* (cs), *Skirts
Ahoy.*

**264 LANG, WALTER** (1896–    ).
Veteran director, former stage actor, in
films since silent days. Long associated
with Fox musicals.

Films: *Hell Bound* (ds), *Meet the Baron*
(cs), *Hooray for Love, The Little Princess*
(ds), *The Blue Bird, Star Dust, Tin Pan
Alley, Moon over Miami, Weekend in
Havana, Song of the Islands, Coney
Island, Greenwich Village, State Fair*
(45), *Mother Wore Tights, When My
Baby Smiles at Me, You're My Every-
thing* (cs), *Cheaper by the Dozen* (cs), *On
the Riviera* (re-make *That Night in Rio*),
*With a Song in My Heart, Call Me
Madam, There's No Business like Show
Business, The King and I, Can Can.*

**265 LANGFORD, FRANCIS** (1913–
). Popular vocalist of war years, who
came to films via vaudeville, night clubs
and radio. Starred in many B pictures
and a frequent guest star in others.

Films: *Every Night at Eight* (début),
*Broadway Melody of 1936, Collegiate,
Palm Springs, Born to Dance, Hit Parade*

"*Hey Babe*" : *Frances Langford with
Buddy Ebsen in* BORN TO DANCE

(37), *Hollywood Hotel, Dreaming Out
Loud, Too Many Girls, Hit Parade of
1941, All American Co-Ed, Swing It
Soldier, Mississippi Gambler* (42), *Yankee
Doodle Dandy, Cowboy in Manhattan,
Follow the Band, This Is the Army, Never
a Dull Moment* (43), *Career Girl, Dixie
Jamboree, The Girl Rush* (44), *Radio Stars
on Parade, People Are Funny, Bamboo
Blonde, Beat the Band, Melody Time*
(voice only), *Make Mine Laughs, Deputy
Marshall* (ws), *Purple Heart Diary/No
Time for Tears; The Glenn Miller Story*
(as herself).

**266 LANSBURY, ANGELA** (1925–
). London born actress evacuated to
U.S.A. during Blitz. Impersonated
Beatrice Lillie in night club act, signed
by M-G-M who wanted British girl to
play Sibyl Vane in *The Picture of Dorian
Gray.* Consistently outstanding charac-
ter work for twenty years preceded
Broadway musical stardom as *Mame.*

Films: *The Picture of Dorian Gray* (ds,
sang "Little Yellow Bird"), *Till the
Clouds Roll By* (sang "How'd You Like
to Spoon with Me?"), *The Harvey Girls;
Remains to Be Seen* (cs), *The Court Jester*
(cs); *Blue Hawaii; Bedknob and Broomstick.*

*Angela Lansbury in TILL THE CLOUDS ROLL BY*

**267 LANZA, MARIO** (1921–1959). RN: Alfred Cocozza. Tenor signed by M-G-M after concert and opera experience. Tremendous popular success as Caruso, but career hampered by constant weight problems.

Films: *That Midnight Kiss* (début), *The Toast of New Orleans* (intro. "Be My

Love"), *The Great Caruso*, *Because You're Mine*, *The Student Prince* (voice only, role played by Edmund Purdom), *Serenade*, *The Seven Hills of Rome*, *For the First Time*.

**268 LAWFORD, PETER** (1923–    ). London-born actor, popular leading man in the Forties. Child actor in Europe, was on holiday in U.S.A. when war broke out, signed by M-G-M. Broke soft-spoken polite Englishman image with rendition of "Whose Baby Are You?" in *It Happened in Brooklyn* with such success that several musical roles followed.

Films: *The Picture of Dorian Gray* (ds), *Two Sisters from Boston*, *It Happened in Brooklyn*, *Good News* (47), *On an Island with You*, *Easter Parade* (intro. "A Fella with an Umbrella"), *Royal Wedding/Wedding Bells*; *It Should Happen to You* (cs); *Pepe* (guest), *Ocean's 11* (ds), *Salt and Pepper* (cs), *One More Time* (cs).

**269 LEAVITT, SAM.** Photographer active in Hollywood since 1952 and noted for his imaginative use of CinemaScope (*A Star Is Born*) when process was in early stages. Films: *A Star Is Born*, *Carmen Jones*, *The Right Approach*.

**LEE, GYPSY ROSE.** See **HOVICK, LOUISE.**

92

**270 LEE, PEGGY** (1920–    ). RN: Norma Dolores Egstrom. Singer and lyricist. Started with minor radio and club spots until chosen by Benny Goodman as vocalist with his orchestra. Later top recording star and acknowledged expert at popular song delivery.

Films: *Stage Door Canteen* (début, singing her hit with Goodman "Why

Don't You Do Right?"); *Mr. Music* (guest), *The Jazz Singer* (first leading role), *Pete Kelly's Blues*. Lyrics: *The Lady and the Tramp* (also sang on soundtrack), *tom thumb*.

**271 LEHMAN, ERNEST** (c. 1915–    ). Writer, producer, former short story writer whose magazine work brought him to attention of Hollywood.

Films: first script *Executive Suite* (non-musical) 1954. First prod. *Who's Afraid of Virginia Woolf?* (non-musical) 1966. Sc. *The King and I, West Side Story, The Sound of Music*. Sc. and prod. *Hello Dolly!*

**272 LEIGH, JANET** (1927–    ). RN: Jeanette Morrison. Blonde actress who became competent singer-dancer. No previous experience when spotted by actress Norma Shearer and brought to attention of M-G-M. Film *début* 1947.

Films: *Words and Music, Strictly*

*Dishonorable, Two Tickets to Broadway, Walking My Baby Back Home, Living It Up, My Sister Eileen, Pete Kelly's Blues, Pepe, Bye Bye Birdie.*

**273 LEISEN, MITCHELL** (1898–    ). Director of excellent sophisticated comedies (*Easy Living, Midnight*) and glossy melodramas (*Kitty, Frenchman's Creek*) who was less happy with musical fare. So disliked Kurt Weill's (q.v.) music for *Lady in the Dark* that he played down its most beautiful song, "My Ship." Former architect student, he became art director and assistant to DeMille, directed first film 1932. Frequently designed own films.

Films: *Murder at the Vanities, Big Broadcast of 1937, Swing High Swing Low, Artists and Models Abroad, Big Broadcast of 1938, The Lady Is Willing* (cs), *Lady in the Dark* (also sc.), *Masquerade in Mexico* (re-make of *Midnight*), *Golden Earrings* (ds), *Dream Girl* (cs), *Captain Carey USA/After Midnight* (ds), *Tonight We Sing ; The Girl Most Likely ; Spree* (co.). Acted in *Variety Girl*, and seen briefly as orchestra conductor in *Murder at the Vanities.*

**274 LEMMON, JACK** (1925–    ). Comedy actor on stage as child, later radio actor. Occasional singing roles.

Films: *It Should Happen to You* (cs, début), *Three for the Show, My Sister Eileen, You Can't Run Away from It, Some Like It Hot* (59, cs), *It Happened to Jane* (cs), *The Great Race* (cs).

**275 LENNART, ISOBEL.** Writer who specialises in musicals, and in dramas with strong female appeal. Many years with M-G-M.

Films: sc. *Anchors Aweigh, Holiday in Mexico, It Happened in Brooklyn, The Kissing Bandit* (co.), *Skirts Ahoy, The Girl Next Door, Latin Lovers, Love Me or*

*Alan Jay Lerner with Andre Previn at work on the new songs for PAINT YOUR WAGON*

*Leave Me* (co.), *Meet Me in Las Vegas/ Viva Las Vegas* (also story), *This Could Be the Night, Merry Andrew* (co.); *Please Don't Eat the Daisies* (cs); *Funny Girl.*

**276 LEONARD, ROBERT Z.** (1889–1968). Director, former stage actor and singer who entered films as actor 1910. Dir. many of Mae Murray's silent successes, spent most of career at M-G-M.

Films: *Marianne, In Gay Madrid, Dancing Lady, Peg O' My Heart, The Great Ziegfeld, The Firefly, Maytime, Girl of the Golden West, Broadway Serenade, New Moon* (40), *Ziegfeld Girl; Weekend at the Waldorf* (ds); *In the Good Old Summertime, Grounds for Marriage, Nancy Goes to Rio, The Duchess of Idaho, Everything I Have Is Yours; Kelly and Me* (cs). Acted in *In Hollywood.*

**277 LERNER, ALAN JAY** (1918– ). Lyricist and writer, former radio scriptwriter who teamed with Frederick Loewe (q.v.) to write scores for Broadway hits including *My Fair Lady.* Has also teamed notably with Burton Lane (q.v.).

Films: sc., lyrics *Royal Wedding/ Wedding Bells* (inc. "Too Late Now," "I Left My Hat in Haiti," "The Liar Song"). St., sc. *An American in Paris.*

Sc., lyrics *Brigadoon, Gigi* (inc. "I'm Glad I'm Not Young Any More," "I Remember It Well"), *My Fair Lady, Camelot, Paint Your Wagon* (inc. "The Ballad of No-Name City"), *On a Clear Day You Can See Forever.*

**278 LE ROY, MERVYN** (1900– ). Director, ex-vaudeville performer, who spent most of his career at Warners directing gangster films, dramas and comedies with equal professionalism.

Films: *Broadway Babies, Little Johnny Jones, Show Girl in Hollywood, Top Speed, Big City Blues, Gold Diggers of 1933, Happiness Ahead, Sweet Adeline, The King and the Chorus Girl* (also prod.), *Fools for Scandal; Lovely to Look At* (re-make *Roberta*), *Million Dollar Mermaid/The One-Piece Bathing Suit, Latin Lovers, Rose Marie* (54); *Gypsy* (also prod.). Prod. *A Day at the Circus, The Wizard of Oz.*

**279 LESLIE, JOAN** (1925– ). RN: Joan Brodell. Ex-childhood vaudeville performer who became Warner ingenué in Forties, usually playing the hero's faithful sweetheart. Best role as Astaire's (q.v.) partner in *The Sky's the Limit.* Retired.

Films: *Yankee Doodle Dandy, The Hard Way* (ds), *Thank Your Lucky Stars, This Is the Army, The Sky's the Limit, Hollywood Canteen, Where Do We Go from Here?, Rhapsody in Blue, Cinderella Jones, Janie Gets Married* (cs), *Two Guys from Milwaukee/Royal Flush* (cs); *The Toughest Man in Arizona* (ws), *Jubilee Trail* (ws), *The Revolt of Mamie Stover* (ds).

**280  LEVANT, OSCAR** (1906–    ). Accomplished pianist and occasional composer, also comic actor with cynical approach.

Films: as actor: *Dance of Life* (début); *Rhythm on the River, Kiss the Boys Goodbye, Rhapsody in Blue* (he was a good friend of Gershwin, q.v., and is noted interpreter of his music), *Humoresque* (ds), *You Were Meant for Me, Romance on the High Seas/It's Magic, The Barkleys of Broadway, An American in Paris* (again performing Gershwin's music), *The I Don't Care Girl, The Band Wagon.* Comp. *Tanned Legs, The Street Girl, Love Comes Along, In Person, Music Is Magic, Charlie Chan at the Opera, The Smartest Girl in Town, Living on Love.*

**281  LEVIEN, SONYA** (1886–1960). RN: Sonya Levien Hovey. Russian-born writer and story editor, former lawyer. Films: co-sc. *Cavalcade* (ds), *In Old Chicago* (ds), *Rebecca of Sunnybrook Farm, First Love* (also st.), *Ziegfeld Girl; Rhapsody in Blue, Three Daring Daughters/The Birds and the Bees, The Great Caruso, The Merry Widow* (52), *The Student Prince, Hit the Deck* (55), *Interrupted Melody* (also st.), *Oklahoma.* St. *The Amazing Mrs. Holliday.*

**282  LEVIN, HENRY** (1909–    ). Workmanlike director whose musicals are mainly routine. Entered films from theatre 1943 as dialogue director.

Films: *Jolson Sings Again, The Petty Girl/Girl of the Year, Belles on Their Toes* (cs), *The Farmer Takes a Wife, Let's Be Happy* (Brit.), *Bernardine, April Love, Where the Boys Are, The Wonderful World of the Brothers Grimm, Honeymoon Hotel* (cs).

**283  LEWIS, MONICA** (c. 1925–    ). Top radio, recording and night club singer of the late Forties who had brief film career at M-G-M.

Films: *Excuse My Dust, The Strip, Everything I Have Is Yours.*

**284  LIBERACE** (1919–    ). RN: Waldziu Valentino Liberace. Flamboyant pianist-entertainer, ex-child prodigy who became night club performer and made two minor film appearances. After television fame with his candelabra and sequined-suit trademarks, starred in *Sincerely Yours* (re-make of Leslie Arliss's *The Man Who Played God*) but it was not a success.

Films: *South Sea Sinner/East of Java* (ds), *Footlight Varieties, Sincerely Yours, When the Boys Meet the Girls.*

**285  LILLEY, EDWARD** (1896–    ). Prolific low-budget director at Universal able to turn out nine or ten pictures in one year. Had been New York stage director of several musicals inc. *Ziegfeld Follies of 1930.* At Universal from 1943.

Films: *Honeymoon Lodge, Larceny with Music, Moonlight in Vermont, Never a Dull Moment* (43), *Sing a Jingle/Lucky Days, Babes on Swing Street, Hi Good Lookin', My Gal Loves Music, Allergic to Love, Swing Out Sister.*

**286  LIVINGSTON, JAY** (1915–    ); Composer, and **EVANS, RAY**

(1915–   ), Lyricist. Song-writing team who attended college together and became cruise ship musicians, worked in radio before being signed by Paramount in 1944 to write title tunes, later complete scores. Also write for TV and Broadway.

Films: *Swing Hostess, On Stage Everybody* ("Stuff Like That There"), *Dream Girl* (cs), *Isn't It Romantic?, The Paleface* (cs, 48 Oscar "Buttons and Bows"), *Sorrowful Jones* (cs), *My Friend Irma* (cs), *Captain Carey USA/After Midnight* (ds, 50 Oscar "Mona Lisa"), *My Friend Irma Goes West* (cs), *Fancy Pants* (cs, inc. "Home Cookin'"), *The Lemon Drop Kid* (cs, inc. "Silver Bells"), *That's My Boy* (cs), *Here Comes the Groom, Aaron Slick from Pumkin Crick/ Marshmallow Moon, Son of Paleface* (cs, inc. "What a Night for a Wing Ding"), *The Stars Are Singing* (inc. "Haven't Got a Worry"), *Off Limits/Military Policeman* (cs), *Those Redheads from Seattle, Here Come the Girls, Red Garters* (inc. "Brave Man"), *The Man Who Knew Too Much* (ds, 56 Oscar "Que Sera Sera"), *Tammy and the Bachelor/Tammy* (cs), *The Big Beat* (inc. "As I Love You"), *Houseboat* (cs, inc. "Almost in Your Arms"), *A Private's Affair, The Blue Angel* (59), *All Hands on Deck* (cs).

**287 LOESSER, FRANK** (1910–1969). One of America's wittiest song-writers who started as studio lyricist until he discovered, when assigned to write soldier shows during Second World War, that he could write music as well. During long stay at Paramount wrote several hits for Dorothy Lamour and Betty Hutton (qq.v.).

Films: lyrics only: *Blossoms on Broadway, The Hurricane* ("Moon of Manakoora"), *Walter Wanger's Vogues of 1938, The Freshman Year, Swing That Cheer, College Swing/Swing Teacher Swing* (inc. "I Fall in Love with You Every Day"), *Cocoanut Grove, Sing You Sinners* ("Small Fry"), *Thanks for the Memory* ("Two Sleepy People"), *Cafe Society, Zaza* (ds), *Spawn of the North* (ds), *Destry Rides Again* (ws; inc. "See What the Boys in the Backroom Will Have"), *The Gracie Allen Murder Case, Hawaiian Nights, St. Louis Blues* (39), *Some Like It Hot* (39, inc. "The Lady's in Love with You"), *Man about Town, The Farmer's Daughter* (cs), *Johnny Apollo* (ds, inc. "Dancing for Nickels and Dimes"), *The Quarterback* (cs), *A Night at Earl Carroll's, Moon over Burma* (cs), *Youth Will Be Served, Buck Benny Rides Again, Typhoon* (ds), *Seven Sinners* (inc. "I've Been in Love Before [Haven't You?]"), *Dancing on a Dime, Las Vegas Nights, Manpower* (ds), *Mr. Bug Goes to Town/Hoppity Goes to Town, Aloma of the South Seas* (ds), *Glamour Boy/Hearts in Springtime, Kiss the Boys Goodbye, Sis Hopkins, Sailors on Leave* (cs), *Forest Rangers* (cs), *True to the Army, Priorities on Parade, Beyond the Blue Horizon* (ds), *Seven Days Leave* (inc. "I Get the Neck of the Chicken"), *Sweater Girl* (inc. "I Said No"), *This Gun for Hire* (ds), *Happy Go Lucky* (inc. "Murder He Says"), *Thank Your Lucky Stars* (inc. "They're Either Too Young or Too Old"), *See Here Private Hargrove* (cs, "In My Arms"), *Moon over Las Vegas, Something for the Boys.* Music and lyrics: *Christmas Holiday* (ds, "Spring Will Be a Little Late This Year"), *The Perils of Pauline* (inc. "I Wish I Didn't Love You So," "The Sewing Machine," "Poppa Don't Preach to Me"), *Variety Girl* (inc. "Tallahassee"), *Neptune's Daughter* (inc. 49 Oscar "Baby It's Cold Outside"), *Red Hot and Blue* (also acted, as gangster), *Let's Dance* (inc. "Why Fight the Feeling?"), *Where's Charley?, Hans Christian Andersen* (inc. "No Two People"), *Guys and Dolls* (inc. "Adelaide," "A Woman in Love"), *How to Succeed in Business without Really Trying.*

**288  LOEWE, FREDERICK** (1901– ). Vienna-born composer, at thirteen the youngest pianist ever to solo with Berlin Symphony Orchestra. In U.S.A. worked as riding instructor and boxer till able to break into theatre. Partnership with Alan Jay Lerner (q.v.) led to Broadway hits and subsequent films.

Films: *Life of the Party* (30); *Brigadoon, Gigi* (only Loewe-Lerner score written directly for screen, inc. 58 Oscar for title tune, also "I'm Glad I'm Not Young Anymore," "Thank Heaven for Little Girls," and "Say a Prayer for Me Tonight," a song which had been cut from stage musical *My Fair Lady*), *My Fair Lady, Camelot, Paint Your Wagon.*

**289  LOGAN, ELLA** (1903–1969). Glasgow-born singer in occasional films. Greatest success in stage production *Finian's Rainbow* (47). Stage *début* when three, U.S.A. 1932 for Broadway shows.
Films: *Top of the Town, Fifty-Second Street, Goldwyn Follies.*

**290  LOGAN, JOSHUA** (1908– ). Distinguished Broadway director who has had mixed success in cinema.

Films: *Bus Stop* (ds), *Sayonara* (ds), *South Pacific, Camelot, Paint Your Wagon.* Acted in *Main Street to Broadway* (ds).

**LOOS, MARY.** See **SALE, RICHARD.**

**291  LORD, DEL** (1895– ). Canadian-born director of light B films. Started as double and actor in Keystone comedies, later directed for Sennett.
Films: *Kansas City Kitty, Let's Go Steady, She's a Sweetheart, Singin' in the Corn, Blonde from Brooklyn, Memory for Two, Hit the Hay, I Love a Bandleader.*

**292  LORING, EUGENE** (1914– ). RN: LeRoy Kerpestein. Stage, film and ballet choreographer.
Films: *Ziegfeld Follies* ("La Traviata" number), *Yolanda and the Thief, The Toast of New Orleans, The Five Thousand Fingers of Doctor T, Deep in My Heart, Meet Me in Las Vegas/Viva Las Vegas, Funny Face, Silk Stockings* (co.), *Pepe.* Acted in *Torch Song* (ds).

**293  LOVE, BESSIE** (1898– ). RN: Juanita Horton. Texas-born star, in many silents before starring in M-G-M's first big musical. Now acts in England.
Films: *Broadway Melody, Hollywood Revue, Chasing Rainbows, Good News* (30), *They Learned about Women.*

**294  LUBITSCH, ERNST** (1892–1947). German director noted for elegantly sophisticated sex comedies. Started as low comedian in Berlin, film *début* as comic actor 1913. Director a year later, Hollywood 1922.
Films: *The Love Parade, Paramount on Parade* (excerpt), *Monte Carlo, The Smiling Lieutenant, One Hour with You* (co-dir. w. Cukor q.v.), *The Merry Widow* (34); *That Lady in Ermine* (died during

*Jeanette MacDonald with Nelson Eddy in GIRL OF THE GOLDEN WEST*

filming, work finished by Otto Preminger q.v.).

**295  LUDWIG, WILLIAM** (1912– ). Writer of Andy Hardy films and many others at M-G-M. Former lawyer.
Films: sc. *Love Finds Andy Hardy.* Co-sc. *The Sun Comes Up, The Great Caruso, The Merry Widow* (52), *The Student Prince, Athena, Hit the Deck* (55), *Interrupted Melody* (also st.), *Oklahoma, Ten Thousand Bedrooms.*

**296  LUPINO, IDA** (1918– ). British-born actress, primarily in drama, whose husky intoning of torch songs in *Road House* had considerable impact.

Films: *Paris in the Spring, The Gay Desperado, Anything Goes* (36), *Artists and Models* (37), *The Hard Way* (ds), *Thank Your Lucky Stars, Hollywood Canteen, The Man I Love* (ds), *Road House* (ds).

**297  LYNN, DIANA** (1924– ). RN: Delores Loehr. Accomplished child pianist under contract to Paramount in Forties, she also had a splendid way with a wicked comedy line and excelled in kid sister roles. Adult career suffered from poor material, now retired.

Films: *There's Magic in Music* (début), *Star Spangled Rhythm, And the Angels Sing, Out of This World* (played Chopin's

98

"Minute Waltz" while a clock on the piano timed her!), *Variety Girl, My Friend Irma* (cs), *My Friend Irma Goes West* (cs), *Meet Me at the Fair, You're Never Too Young* (cs).

**298  MacDONALD, JEANETTE** (1901–1965). Singing star of the Thirties and Forties whose career began in musical comedy chorus 1920. Playing leading roles when Ernst Lubitsch (q.v.) saw a screen test and chose her to star in *The Love Parade*. Sophisticated musicals at Paramount preceded M-G-M contract in 1933 and teaming with Nelson Eddy (q.v.), most successful singing partnership in screen history.

Films: *The Love Parade* (début, intro. "Dream Lover"), *The Vagabond King* (30), *Monte Carlo* (intro. "Beyond the Blue Horizon"), *Let's Go Native, The Lottery Bride, Oh for a Man* (cs), *One Hour with You, Love Me Tonight* (intro. "Lover"), *The Cat and the Fiddle, The Merry Widow* (34), *Naughty Marietta, Rose Marie* (36), *San Francisco,* (ds), *Maytime, The Firefly, Girl of the Golden West, Sweethearts, Broadway Serenade, New Moon, Bitter Sweet Smilin' Through* (ds), *I Married an Angel, Cairo, Follow the Boys* (44, as herself); *Three Daring Daughters/The Birds and the Bees, The Sun Comes Up* (ds).

**299  MacLAINE, SHIRLEY** (1934– ). RN: Shirley Maclean Beatty. Although discovered by Hollywood while dancing on Broadway, has made few film musicals. Studied dancing as child, professional *début* at four. Chorus work, TV and modelling led to chorus role in *The Pajama Game* on Broadway. Understudied Carol Haney (q.v.) as Gladys and on third night went on stage. Seen by producer Hal Wallis and given contract. Films: *Artists and Models* (cs, 56),

*"There's Gotta Be Something Better Than This" : Shirley MacLaine in SWEET CHARITY*

*Oceans 11* (cs, guest), *Can Can, What a Way to Go* (cs), *Sweet Charity*.

**300  MacMURRAY, FRED** (1908– ). Actor with particular flair for comedy whose light baritone singing voice was heard in several of his earlier films. Was saxophonist and dance band singer at Hollywood theatre when signed for movies.

Films: *Champagne Waltz, Swing High Swing Low, Cocoanut Grove, Sing You Sinners, Cafe Society, New York Town, Little Old New York* (ds), *The Lady Is Willing* (cs), *Forest Rangers* (cs), *And the Angels Sing* (intro. "My Heart's Wrapped Up in Gingham"), *Where Do We Go from Here?, Callaway Went Thataway/The Star Said No* (cs); *The Happiest Millionaire.*

**301 MacRAE, GORDON** (1921– ). Virile singing star signed by Warners after success as band vocalist and radio singer. Often co-starred with Doris Day (q.v.). Career received boost with leading roles in *Oklahoma* and (replacing Sinatra, q.v.) in *Carousel.*

Films: *Look for the Silver Lining, The Daughter of Rosie O'Grady, Return of the Frontiersman* (ws), *Tea for Two, West Point Story/Fine and Dandy, On Moonlight Bay, Starlift, About Face, By the Light of the Silvery Moon, The Desert Song* (53), *Three Sailors and a Girl* (intro.

"Face to Face"), *Oklahoma, Carousel, The Best Things in Life Are Free* (as Buddy DeSylva q.v.).

**302 MAMOULIAN, ROUBEN** (1897– ). Russian-born director, a great innovator in early days of talkies. Stage director from 1918, given Hollywood contract by Paramount, who were impressed by his use of clever photographic angles. Dir. original stage productions *Porgy and Bess, Oklahoma, Carousel.* Use of rhyming dialogue in film *Love Me Tonight* original and effective.

Films: *Applause, Love Me Tonight, Song of Songs* (ds), *The Gay Desperado, High Wide and Handsome; Summer Holiday* (rhyming dialogue partly used again but film an undeserved commercial disaster); *Silk Stockings.*

**303 MANCINI, HENRY** (1924– ). Probably best known film composer of Sixties, though most of his songs were theme tunes and not written for musicals. Worked at Universal as arranger for some years, having been dance band arranger and pianist (notably with Glenn Miller).

*Gordon MacRae (centre) with Dan Dailey and Sheree North in*
THE BEST THINGS IN LIFE ARE FREE

Films: orch. and comp. additional music: *The Glenn Miller Story, The Benny Goodman Story, Rock Pretty Baby, The Big Beat, Summer Love, High Time.* Orch. and comp. *Breakfast at Tiffany's* (cs, inc. 61 Oscar "Moon River"), *Days of Wine and Roses* (non-musical, but 62 Oscar for title song), *The Great Race* (cs), *Me Natalie* (ds), *Gaily Gaily/ Chicago Chicago* (cs), *Darling Lili.*

**304 MANN, ANTHONY** (1906–1967). Musicals form small part of this director's output, but *The Glenn Miller Story* is one of most successful screen biographies. Was stage actor and director, talent scout for David Selznick. First film 1942.

Films: *Moonlight in Havana, My Best Gal, Sing Your Way Home, The Bamboo Blonde; The Glenn Miller Story, Serenade.*

**305 MANNING, IRENE** (1917–     ). RN: Inez Harvuot. Regal singer of the Forties who enjoyed brief spell as leading lady.

Films: *Yankee Doodle Dandy, The Desert Song* (44), *Hollywood Canteen, Shine On Harvest Moon.*

**306 MARIN, EDWARD L.** (1901–     ). Director of medium-budget films, whose musicals were usually pleasantly sentimental.

Films: *Sweetheart of Sigma Chi* (33), *Everybody Sing, Listen Darling, Society Lawyer, Maisie* (cs), *Hullabaloo, Ringside Maisie* (cs), *Miss Annie Rooney, Show Business, Johnny Angel* (ds), *Abilene Town* (ws), *Nocturne* (ds), *Race Street* (ds).

**307 MARSHALL, GEORGE** (1891–     ). Reliable veteran director whose best films have pace and humour. Started as extra and stunt-man, spent six years with Sennett and once headed Fox's two-reel comedy department. Early films included Laurel and Hardy comedies for Hal Roach.

Films: *Three Hundred and Sixty-five Nights in Hollywood, Wild Gold* (ds), *She Learned about Sailors, Music Is Magic, Can This Be Dixie?, Battle of Broadway, Hold That Co-Ed, Goldwyn Follies, Destry Rides Again* (ws), *Pot O'Gold, Forest Rangers* (cs), *Star Spangled Rhythm, Riding High/Melody Inn, True to Life, And the Angels Sing, Incendiary Blonde, The Perils of Pauline, Variety Girl* (also acted), *My Friend Irma* (cs), *Fancy Pants* (cs), *Never a Dull Moment* (50), *Off Limits/Military Policeman* (cs), *Scared Stiff* (cs), *Money from Home* (cs), *Red Garters, The Second Greatest Sex, The Gazebo* (cs), *How the West Was Won* (ws, co-dir.), *Papa's Delicate Condition* (cs).

**308 MARTIN, DEAN** (1917–     ). RN: Dino Crocetti. Singer-actor with casual style. Started as straight half of comedy team with Jerry Lewis, singing a few songs in each of their films. Since going solo has varied parts, with particular success in series as private eye Matt Helm.

Films, with Lewis: *My Friend Irma, My Friend Irma Goes West, At War with the Army, The Stooge, That's My Boy, Sailor Beware, Jumping Jacks, Road to Bali* (guests) *Scared Stiff, The Caddy, Money from Home, Living It Up* (their closest film to pure musical), *Three Ring Circus, Artists and Models* (55), *You're Never Too Young, Pardners, Hollywood or Bust.* Solo: *Ten Thousand Bedrooms, Bells Are Ringing, Ocean's 11* (ds), *Road to Hong Kong* (guest), *What a Way to Go* (cs), *Robin and the Seven Hoods, Kiss Me Stupid* (cs).

**309 MARTIN, HUGH.** Composer who with Ralph Blane (q.v.) scored Broadway success with *Best Foot Forward*, signed by M-G-M to write new songs for film version and create new film scores.

Films: *Best Foot Forward* (inc. "Wish I May"), *Broadway Rhythm, Thousands Cheer, Meet Me in St. Louis* ("The Trolley Song," "The Boy Next Door," "Skip to My Lou," "Have Yourself a Merry Little Christmas"), *In Hollywood, Ziegfeld Follies* ("Love"), *Good News* (47, "Pass That Peace Pipe"), *Athena* (inc. "Love Can Change the Stars"), *The Girl Rush* (55, inc. "Birmingham," "An Occasional Man"), *The Girl Most Likely* (inc. "Balboa").

**310 MARTIN, MARY** (1913–    ). Singer who became overnight Broadway star singing "My Heart Belongs to Daddy" in 1938. Though starred in several films by Paramount, she never achieved on screen tremendous success of stage roles.

Films: *The Great Victor Herbert* (début), *Love Thy Neighbour, Rhythm on the River* (intro. "I Don't Want to Cry Anymore"), *Birth of the Blues, Kiss the Boys Goodbye, New York Town, Star Spangled Rhythm, Happy Go Lucky, True to Life, Night and Day* (as herself), *Main Street to Broadway* (ds, as herself).

**311 MARTIN, SKIP.** Arranger who scored music for dance bands, notably Charlie Barnet, prior to Hollywood.

Films: co-orch. *Singin' in the Rain, Dangerous When Wet* (solo), *Kiss Me Kate, A Star Is Born, Funny Face, April Love*.

**312 MARTIN, TONY** (1912–    ). RN: Alvin Morris. Romantic singing lead, former dance band singer-saxophonist. Married to Cyd Charisse (q.v.).

Films: *Follow the Fleet* (bit), *Banjo on My Knee* (ds), *Sing Baby Sing, Life Begins in College, The Holy Terror, Ali Baba Goes to Town, You Can't Have Everything, Sing and Be Happy, Kentucky Moonshine, Thanks for Everything, Sally Irene and Mary, Music in My Heart, Ziegfeld Girl, The Big Store, Till the Clouds Roll By, Casbah, Two Tickets to Broadway, Here Come the Girls, Easy to Love, Deep in My Heart, Hit the Deck* (55), *Let's Be Happy* (Brit.), *Party Girl* (voice only).

**313 MASSEY, ILONA** (1912–    ). RN: Ilona Hajmassy. Hungarian-born singing star, ex-seamstress who sang in opera chorus to help support family. Took over lead in *Tosca*. M-G-M scout heard her sing in Budapest.

Films: *Rosalie* (début), *Balalaika, Holiday in Mexico, Northwest Outpost/End of the Rainbow, Love Happy*.

**314 MAXWELL, MARILYN** (1921–    ). RN: Marvell Maxwell. Actress-singer who rarely got parts she deserved. Child dancer, band vocalist at sixteen. Seen in musical short by Buddy DeSylva (q.v.) and asked to make screen test.

Films: *Presenting Lily Mars, DuBarry Was a Lady, Thousands Cheer, Swing Fever, Lost in a Harem; Summer Holiday* (her best musical role), *Race Street* (ds), *The Lemon Drop Kid* (cs), *Off Limits/Military Policeman* (cs); *The Lively Set*.

**315 MAYO, ARCHIE** (1898–1968). Director, former musical comedy actor, extra, gag-man. First feature 1927.

Films: *Is Everybody Happy?* (29), *My Man, Oh Sailor Behave; Go into Your Dance; Youth Takes a Fling, They Shall Have Music/Melody of Youth, The Great

*Marilyn Maxwell with Mickey Rooney in SUMMER HOLIDAY*

*American Broadcast, Orchestra Wives, Sweet and Low Down.*

**316 MAYO, VIRGINIA** (1922– ). RN: Virginia Jones. Musical and dramatic actress, equally convincing as chorus girl or gangster's moll. Part of vaudeville act, then became Hollywood dancer, Goldwyn Girl. Now does theatre, night club work.

Films: *Sweet Rosie O'Grady, Pin Up Girl, Up in Arms, Seven Days Ashore* (first featured role), *Wonder Man, The Princess and the Pirate* (cs), *The Kid from Brooklyn, The Best Years of Our Lives* (ds), *The Secret Life of Walter Mitty* (cs), *A Song Is Born, Always Leave Them Laughing, West Point Story/Fine and Dandy, Painting the Clouds with Sunshine, Starlift, She's Working Her Way through College, She's Back on Broadway.*

**317 McCAREY, LEO** (1898–1969). Director noted for excellent comedies in Thirties, later became more sentimental. His *Going My Way,* with Bing Crosby (q.v.) as singing priest, won best film, actor, director and story Oscars.

Films: *Red Hot Rhythm, Let's Go Native, The Kid from Spain, Duck Soup, Belle of the Nineties, The Awful Truth* (cs), *Love Affair* (ds, also prod., co-st.), *Going My Way* (also prod., st.), *The Bells of St. Mary's* (ds, also prod., st.).

**318 McCORD, TED** (1912– ). Photographer, active in Hollywood since 1933.

Films: *Young Man with a Horn/Young Man of Music, Young at Heart; The Sound of Music.*

**319 McDONALD, FRANK** (1899– ). Second-feature director who worked in all *genres*. Was stage actor, director, author, then dialogue director for Warners. First film 1935.

Films: *Smart Blonde* (ds), *The Freshman Year; Swing Your Partner, Take It Big, Sing Neighbour Sing, Tell It to a Star, Hit Parade of 1947, When a Girl's Beautiful, Linda Be Good.*

**320 McDONALD, RAY** (1920–1959). Engaging young singer-dancer who had dancing act with sister on Broadway. Given part in Andy Hardy film by M-G-M, then contract.

Films: *Life Begins for Andy Hardy* (cs, début), *Babes on Broadway, Born to Sing, Presenting Lily Mars, Till the Clouds Roll By* (performed title number with June Allyson q.v.), *Good News* (47); *All Ashore.*

**321 McGUIRE, MARCY.** RN: Marilyn McGuire. Peppy 'teenager who symbolised the youth of an era when she sang "I Saw You First" to Frank Sinatra

*Ray McDonald dancing the title tune of TILL THE CLOUDS ROLL BY with June Allyson*

(q.v.) in *Higher and Higher.* Former cabaret singer.

Films: *Seven Days Leave, Around the World, Higher and Higher, Seven Days Ashore, Sing Your Way Home, Melody Maker, It Happened in Brooklyn; Mary Poppins.*

**322  McHUGH, JIMMY** (1894–1969). Irish-American composer of many hits and over fifty film scores. Ex-song plugger for Irving Berlin's (q.v.) publishing firm. Broadway success *Blackbirds of 1928* preceded Hollywood. Helped launch Duke Ellington's career, wrote "South American Way" for Carmen Miranda's (q.v.) Broadway *début*, wrote score for Frank Sinatra's (q.v.) first starring film. Two principal lyricists Dorothy Fields and Harold Adamson (qq.v.).

Films: *Love in the Rough, Flying High, Dance Fools Dance, Cuban Love Song, Dancing Lady, Meet the Baron* (cs), *Dinner at Eight* (ds, inc. "Don't Blame Me"), *Have a Heart, I Dream Too Much, Every Night at Eight* (inc. "I'm in the Mood for Love"), *King of Burlesque, Nitwits, Hooray for Love, Banjo on My Knee* (ds), *Dimples, The First Baby, Roberta* ("Lovely to Look At," co-credited to Jerome Kern q.v.), *Let's Sing Again, When Love Is Young, Hitting a New High, Breezing Home, You're a Sweetheart, Top of the Town* (inc. "Where Are You?"), *Merry-go-round of 1938, Road to Reno, Mad about Music, That Certain Age* (inc. "My Own"), *Youth Takes a Fling, Buck Benny Rides Again* (inc. "Say It"), *You'll Find Out, You're the One, Seven Days Leave* (inc. "Can't Get Out of This Mood"), *Higher and*

*Higher* (inc. "A Lovely Way to Spend an Evening"), *Happy Go Lucky* (inc. "Let's Get Lost"), *Hers to Hold* ("Say a Prayer for the Boys over There"), *Around the World, Four Jills in a Jeep, Moon over Las Vegas, Two Girls and a Sailor, The Princess and the Pirate* (cs), *Something for the Boys, Bring on the Girls* (inc. "You Moved Right In"), *Nob Hill* (inc. "I Don't Care Who Knows It"), *Doll Face/ Come Back to Me, Do You Love Me?, No Leave No Love, Calendar Girl, Hit Parade of 1947, Smash Up/A Woman Destroyed* (ds), *If You knew Susie* (inc. "My How the Time Goes By"), *A Date with Judy* ("It's a Most Unusual Day"); *His Kind of Woman* (ds); *A Private's Affair.* Played himself in *The Helen Morgan Story/Both Ends of the Candle.*

**323 McLEOD, NORMAN Z.** (1898–1964). Comedy and musical director, former cartoonist and writer. Co-dir: *Along Came Youth.* Dir: *Monkey Business, Horse Feathers, Many Happy Returns, Melody in Spring, Coronado, Red Heads on Parade, Pennies from Heaven,*

*Lady Be Good, Panama Hattie, The Powers Girl, The Kid from Brooklyn, The Secret Life of Walter Mitty* (cs), *Road to Rio, Isn't It Romantic?, The Paleface* (cs), *Let's Dance, My Favourite Spy* (51, cs), *Public Pigeon No. 1* (cs), *Alias Jesse James* (cs).

**324 McLERIE, ALLYN** (1926–    ). Canadian-born dancer, on stage from fifteen in many Broadway shows. Best film role recreating her stage performance as Amy in *Where's Charley?*

Films: *Words and Music* (début), *Where's Charley?, The Desert Song* (53), *Calamity Jane.*

**325 MELCHIOR, LAURITZ.** Operatic tenor noted for Wagnerian roles, given screen parts at M-G-M by Joe Pasternak (q.v.). Won fame in Copenhagen, made Covent Garden *début* 1919, Metropolitan 1926.

Films: *Thrill of a Romance* (début), *Two Sisters from Boston, This Time for Keeps, Luxury Liner; The Stars Are Singing.*

**326 MERCER, JOHNNY** (1909–    ). Fine lyricist, and occasional composer, actor, singer. Singing with Paul Whiteman's band when met Hoagy Carmichael (q.v.) and wrote "Lazy Bones," first hit. Joined Benny Goodman as vocalist till more hits led to Hollywood contract. Co-founder of Capitol Records.

Films as lyricist only unless otherwise stated: *College Coach, Old Man Rhythm* (also acted), *To Beat the Band* (also acted), *Varsity Show, Ready Willing and Able* (inc. "Too Marvellous for Words"), *Hollywood Hotel* (inc. "Hooray for Hollywood"), *The Singing Marine, Cowboy from Brooklyn, Garden of the Moon, Hard to Get* (inc. "You Must Have Been a Beautiful Baby"), *Going Places* (inc.

"Jeepers Creepers"), *Naughty but Nice, You'll Find Out, Second Chorus, You're the One, Blues in the Night* (inc. "This Time the Dream's on Me"), *Navy Blues, The Fleet's In* (inc. "Tangerine," "I Remember You"), *Star Spangled Rhythm* (inc. "That Old Black Magic," "Hit the Road to Dreamland"), *You Were Never Lovelier* (inc. "I'm Old Fashioned"), *True to Life, The Sky's the Limit* (inc. "One for My Baby," "My Shining Hour"), *To Have and Have Not* (ds, "How Little We Know"), *Here Come the Waves* (inc. "Accentuate the Positive"), *Out of This World, Her Highness and the Bellboy* (ds, "Dream," music also), *The Harvey Girls* (inc. 46 Oscar "On the Atchison, Topeka and Santa Fe"); *Always Leave Them Laughing, The Petty Girl/Girl of the Year, Here Comes the Groom* (51 Oscar "In the Cool Cool Cool of the Evening"), *Belle of New York* (inc. "Bachelor Dinner Song," "Naughty but Nice," "Baby Doll"), *Everything I Have Is Yours, Dangerous When Wet* (inc. "I Got out of Bed on the Right Side"), *Those Redheads from Seattle, Top Banana* (music also), *Seven Brides for Seven Brothers* (inc. "Sobbin' Women," "Lonesome Polecat," "Bless Yore Beautiful Hide"), *Daddy Long Legs* (music also, inc. "Something's Gotta Give"), *You Can't Run Away from It* (inc. "Temporarily"), *Timberjack* (ds), *Bernadine* (music also, inc. "Technique"), *Li'l Abner, Breakfast at Tiffany's* (cs, 61 Oscar "Moon River"), *Days of Wine and Roses* (non-musical, 62 Oscar title song), *The Great Race* (cs), *Darling Lili*.

**327 MERKEL, UNA** (1903–    ). Veteran character actress, musically memorable as Ginger Rogers's (q.v.) "Shuffle Off to Buffalo" partner in *Forty-Second Street* and Sid Silvers's

girl friend in *Born to Dance*. Played in many silents for Griffith and was Lillian Gish's double. After gaining prominence on stage returned to Hollywood.

Films: *Red-Headed Woman, Forty-Second Street, Broadway to Hollywood, The Merry Widow* (34), *Have a Heart, The Night Is Young, Broadway Melody of 1936, Born to Dance, Destry Rides Again* (ws), *Road to Zanzibar, This Is the Army, Sweethearts of the USA/Sweethearts on Parade; My Blue Heaven, Rich Young and Pretty, Golden Girl, The Merry Widow* (52), *With a Song in My Heart, I Love Melvin, Bundle of Joy; Spinout/California Holiday*.

**328 MERMAN, ETHEL** (1909–    ). RN: Ethel Zimmerman. Broadway's First Lady of Musical Comedy, a magnificent belter of song with neon personality. Stage musicals *Anything Goes, Annie Get Your Gun* and *Gypsy* were all created for her, but with exception of film version *Call Me Madam* Hollywood has never given her material or treatment that fully convey her quality.

Films: *Follow the Leader, Kid Millions, We're Not Dressing, The Big Broadcast of 1936, Anything Goes* (36), *Strike Me Pink, Alexander's Ragtime Band, Happy Landing, Straight Place and Show/They're Off, Stage Door Canteen; Call Me Madam, There's No Business like Show Business*.

**329 MILLER, ANN** (1919–    ). RN: Lucy Ann Collier. Screen's outstanding tap-dancer, a tall dark-haired beauty whose skill as a comedienne equals her dexterity and precision as a whirlwind tapper. Stage *début* when five, dancing in Hollywood night club when spotted for movies.

Films: *New Faces of 1937* (début), *Life*

of the Party (37), *Radio City Revels,*
*Tarnished Angel* (cs), *Having a Wonderful*
*Time, It's the Doctor's Orders, Hit Parade*
*of 1941, Too Many Girls, Melody Ranch,*
*Go West Young Lady, Time Out for*
*Rhythm, Priorities on Parade, True to the*
*Army, What's Buzzin' Cousin?, Reveille*
*with Beverley, Hey Rookie, Jam Session,*
*Carolina Blues, Eadie Was a Lady, Eve*
*Knew Her Apples, Thrill of Brazil, Easter*
*Parade, The Kissing Bandit* (guest), *On*
*the Town* (intro. "Prehistoric Man"),
*Texas Carnival, Two Tickets to Broad-*
*way, Lovely to Look At, Small Town Girl,*
*Kiss Me Kate, Deep in My Heart, Hit the*
*Deck, The Opposite Sex.*

**330 MILLER, MARILYN** (1900–
1936). RN: Marilyn Reynolds. Broadway
musical star of Twenties who re-created
her original roles in Jerome Kern's (q.v.)
*Sunny* and *Sally* in early talkies.

Films: *Sally, Sunny, Her Majesty*
*Love.*

**331 MINNELLI, VINCENTE** (1910–
). Outstanding director of musicals
whose films, particularly during his first
decade (1943–53) maintained a consistently high level. Born to family of
travelling actors, made stage *début* at

*Ann Miller whirlwind tapping for the*
*"Worry Bird" number in TWO TICKETS*
*TO BROADWAY*

three touring America's middle-west. Studied drawing and after work in photographic studio became designer of costumes and scenery for vaudeville and revues. Started directing, and had big success when he conceived, staged and designed Broadway revue *The Show Is On* 1936. (He used an old Gershwin number in this, "By Strauss," that he was to revive again for *An American in Paris*.) Other shows included *Ziegfeld Follies* and Jerome Kern's (q.v.) *Very Warm for May*. Brought to Hollywood and M-G-M by Arthur Freed (q.v.) and displayed immediate flair for film medium, his background in design being apparent in natural eye for effective use of colour, costume, and decor. Best work also has charm, vitality, humour and warmth. Although noted for several brilliant musicals, has had success also with drama and comedy. Supervised some numbers in *Strike Up the Band, Babes on Broadway, Panama Hattie*.

Films as dir: *Cabin in the Sky, I Dood It/By Hook or By Crook, Meet Me in St. Louis* (first of his films to star Judy Garland, q.v., whom he married 1945–51), *Yolanda and the Thief, Ziegfeld Follies* (parts only, inc. "Limehouse Blues," "This Heart of Mine," "The Babbitt and the Bromide," "Madam Crematon" and "La Traviata"), *Till the Clouds Roll By* (Garland sequences only), *The Pirate; An American in Paris, Lovely to Look At* (fashion-show sequence only), *The Story of Three Loves* (ds), *The Band Wagon, Brigadoon, Kismet* (55), *Designing Woman* (cs); *Gigi, Bells Are Ringing; On a Clear Day You Can See Forever*.

**332 MIRANDA, CARMEN** (1909–1955). RN: Maria de Carmo Miranda de Cunha. Volatile Latin-American performer, the Brazilian Bombshell. Her frenetic delivery and exotically flamboyant costumes, with heels nine inches high and headgear topped by piles of fruit, plus her sure musicianship and fractured-English humour, made her a top attraction. Radio and recording star and made four films native Rio de Janeiro 1934–38. Broadway hit 1939 singing "South American Way," performed same number in first Hollywood film.

Films: *Down Argentine Way* (début), *That Night in Rio* (intro. "I Yi Yi Yi Yi"), *Weekend in Havana* (intro. "When I Love I Love"), *Springtime in the Rockies, The Gang's All Here/The Girls He Left Behind, Four Jills in a Jeep* (guest), *Green-*

wich Village, Something for the Boys, Doll Face/Come Back to Me, If I'm Lucky, Copacabana, A Date with Judy, Nancy Goes to Rio; Scared Stiff (cs).

**333 MOHR, HAL** (1894–    ). Pioneer cameraman in Hollywood since 1915. Photographed first talkie, later the atmospheric colour photography for Universal's two horror-musicals of Forties.

Films: *The Jazz Singer, King of Jazz, Rio, Destry Rides Again* (ws); *Phantom of the Opera, The Climax* (ds), *Song of Scheherezade; Rancho Notorious* (ws). Dir. *When Love Is Young.*

**334 MONACO, JAMES** (1885–1945). Composer, known as Ragtime Jimmy in early part of century when bar-room pianist writing songs like "Row Row Row" and "You Made Me Love You" (both often featured in movies). Was fifty-one when signed by Hollywood, where he wrote hits for Bing Crosby (q.v.) and Betty Grable (q.v.).

Films: *Let's Go Places, Doctor Rhythm, Sing You Sinners* (inc. "I've Got a Pocketful of Dreams"), *The Star Maker* (inc. "An Apple for the Teacher"), *East Side of Heaven, Road to Singapore* (40, inc. "Too Romantic"), *If I Had My Way, Rhythm on the River* (inc. "Only Forever"), *Six Lessons from Madame LaZonga* (title tune, actually published preceding year), *Weekend in Havana* ("Romance and Rhumba"), *Stage Door Canteen, Pin Up Girl* (inc. "Time Alone Will Tell"), *Sweet and Low Down, The Dolly Sisters* (inc. "I Can't Begin To Tell You," his last song).

**335 MONROE, MARILYN** (1926–1962). RN: Norma Jean Baker. Blonde sex symbol of Fifties, former model whose combination of voluptuousness and innocence, together with an instinc-

tive flair for comedy and a touching vulnerability, have made her a screen legend.

Films: *Ladies of the Chorus, Love Happy, A Ticket to Tomahawk* (cs), *Niagara* (ds, intro. "Kiss"), *Gentlemen Prefer Blondes, River of No Return* (ds), *There's No Business like Show Business, Bus Stop* (ds), *Some Like It Hot* (cs, 59), *Let's Make Love.*

**336 MONTALBAN, RICARDO** (1920–    ). Latin leading man who made film *début* 1941 in native Mexico, signed by M-G-M in 1945 after winning Mexican equivalent of Oscar.

Films: *Fiesta, On an Island with You, The Kissing Bandit* (guest), *Neptune's Daughter, Two Weeks with Love, Mark of the Renegade* (ds), *Sombrero, Latin Lovers; Sayonara* (ds); *Let No Man Write My Epitaph* (ds); *Sweet Charity.*

**337 MOORE, CONSTANCE** (1919–    ). Singer and leading lady. Was singing on radio when signed by Universal in 1938. Starred in Broadway's *By Jupiter* 1942.

Films: *The Freshman Year, State Police, Swing That Cheer, Charley McCarthy Detective, Hawaiian Nights, Laugh It Off, Ma He's Making Eyes at Me, LaConga Nights, I'm Nobody's Sweetheart Now, Argentine Nights, Las Vegas Nights/The Gay City, Atlantic City, Show Business, Delightfully Dangerous, Earl Carroll's Vanities, Mexicana, In Old Sacramento* (ws), *Earl Carroll Sketchbook/Hats Off to Rhythm, Hit Parade of 1947; Spree.*

**338 MOORE, GRACE** (1901–1947). Soprano who had some film success in Thirties. Started as café singer. After musical comedy (*Hitchy-Koo* etc.) went to France to study voice, made Metropolitan *début* 1928. Acted in French film of opera *Louise* 1930, made first Hollywood film same year. Killed in airplane crash.

Films: *New Moon* (30), *A Lady's Morals* (as Jenny Lind), *One Night of Love, Love Me Forever, The King Steps Out, When You're in Love* (in which she let hair down to sing "Minnie the Moocher"), *I'll Take Romance.* Life story filmed 1953 with Kathryn Grayson (q.v.).

**339 MORENO, RITA** (1931–    ). Puerto-Rican actress-dancer whose best musical role was as the fiery Anita in *West Side Story.* Spanish dancer since childhood.

Films: *The Toast of New Orleans* (début, dancing "Tina Lina" with James Mitchell), *Pagan Love Song, Singin' in the Rain, The Fabulous Senorita, Latin Lovers, The King and I, The Vagabond King* (56); *West Side Story.*

**340 MORGAN, DENNIS** (1910–
   ). RN: Stanley Morner. Tenor, romantic lead who was radio announcer till opera star Mary Garden heard him sing and recommended him to M-G-M. Billed as Richard Stanley in early films.

Films: *The Great Ziegfeld* (sang "A Pretty Girl Is like a Melody"); *The Hard Way* (ds), *Thank Your Lucky Stars, The Desert Song* (44), *Shine On Harvest Moon, Hollywood Canteen, One More Tomorrow* (ds), *Two Guys from Milwaukee/Royal Flush, The Time the Place and the Girl, Cheyenne* (ws), *My Wild Irish Rose* (as Irish composer Chauncey Olcott), *One Sunday Afternoon, Two Guys from Texas, It's a Great Feeling, Painting the Clouds with Sunshine.*

**341 MORGAN, HELEN** (1900–1941). The woman for whom the phrase "torch

singer" was created, the original Julie of Broadway's *Show Boat* and night club star renowned for heart-rending ballads sung while perched on a grand piano. Made several notable film appearances, and her story was told in a 1957 biography.

Films: *Glorifying the American Girl,*

*Helen Morgan in APPLAUSE*

*Applause, Roadhouse Nights, You Belong to Me* (ds), *Marie Galante* (ds), *Frankie and Johnny* (35), *Go into Your Dance, Sweet Music, Show Boat* (36, re-creating her original performance and singing "Bill" and "Can't Help Loving That Man").

**342 MUNSHIN, JULES** (1913–1970). Comedian and dancer who starred in Broadway's *Call Me Mister* with Betty Garrett (q.v.) and like his co-star was signed by M-G-M.

Films: *Easter Parade, Take Me Out to the Ball Game/Everybody's Cheering, That Midnight Kiss, On the Town; Ten Thousand Bedrooms, Silk Stockings.*

**343 MURPHY, GEORGE** (1902– ). Dancer-actor who became California's Senator. A poor scholar, became dancer and made Broadway *début* in chorus *Good News*. Playing second lead in *Roberta* when signed by Goldwyn (q.v.) for film *Kid Millions*. Steady if unremarkable career followed. Has said "good guy" casting helped in later career as "dynamic conservative."

Films: *Kid Millions* (début), *After the Dance, Top of the Town, Broadway Melody of 1938, You're a Sweetheart, Hold That Co-Ed, Little Miss Broadway* (38), *Broadway Melody* (40), *Little Nelly Kelly, Two Girls on Broadway, Ringside Maisie* (cs), *Rise and Shine, Las Vegas Nights/The Gay City, Mayor of 44th Street, The Powers Girl, For Me and My Gal, This Is the Army, Broadway Rhythm, Show Business, Step Lively; Big City.*

**344 MURPHY, RALPH** (1895–1967). Director of generally minor films, in Hollywood since silents. Wrote, directed and acted on stage, co-sc. and co-dir. many movies before first solo direction 1941.

Films: *Girl without a Room, Collegiate, Florida Special, Top of the Town, You're the One, Glamour Boy/Hearts in Springtime, Salute for Three, Rainbow Island, Sunbonnet Sue.* Acted in *Star Spangled Rhythm.*

**345 MYROW, JOSEPH.** Composer, with Fox in late Forties, later freelanced.

Films: *Three Little Girls in Blue* (inc. "You Make Me Feel So Young"), *Mother Wore Tights* (inc. "Kokomo Indiana," "You Do"), *When My Baby Smiles at Me* (inc. "By the Way," "What Did I Do?"), *Beautiful Blonde from Bashful Bend* (cs), *Wabash Avenue* (inc. "Baby Won't You Say You Love Me?"), *The Girl Next Door, I Love Melvin* (inc. "A Lady Loves," "We Have Never Met as Yet"), *The French Line* (inc. "Lookin' for Trouble"), *Bundle of Joy* (inc. "All about Love," "Someday Soon," "Lullaby in Blue").

**346 NEAGLE, ANNA** (1904– ). RN: Florence Robertson. British actress-dancer, one-time gymnastics teacher who became chorus girl 1926, in films from 1930. Many British films, generally as famous women of history or modern upper-class ladies, and a few musicals in Hollywood.

Films: *Irene, No No Nanette* (40), *Sunny* (41).

**347 NELSON, GENE** (1920– ). RN: Gene Berg. Dancer, later director, formerly a skater with Sonja Henie (q.v.) ice show. Most of film acting career spent at Warners in early Fifties.

Films: *I Wonder Who's Kissing Her Now* (début); *The Daughter of Rosie O'Grady, Tea for Two, West Point Story/Fine and Dandy, Lullaby of Broadway* (first leading role), *Painting the Clouds*

111

with *Sunshine, Starlift, She's Working Her Way through College, She's Back on Broadway, Three Sailors and a Girl, So This Is Paris* (also co-ch.), *Oklahoma*. Dir. *Hootenanny Hoot, Kissin' Cousins, Your Cheating Heart, Harum Scarum/Harem Holiday.*

**348 NEWLEY, ANTHONY** (1931– ). London-born many-faceted entertainer. Started as child actor, later played character parts, did stage revue, became pop star. Co-wrote (with Leslie Bricusse) stage musical *Stop the World I Want to Get Off,* later filmed in Britain. Has individual singing style, and with Bricusse has probably written more standards than any composer of Sixties. Acted in *Doctor Dolittle*. Dir., sc., comp. and acted in *Can Heironymous Merkin Ever Forget Mercy Humppe and Find True Happiness?*

**349 NEWMAN, ALFRED** (1901–1970). Composer, conductor and arranger, a top name in Hollywood since early Thirties and for over twenty years head of Fox's musical department. As well as conducting and supervising the scoring of major musicals, also composed countless background scores for such non-musicals as *Street Scene, Captain from Castile, All about Eve* and *Airport*. Composed Fox's drum-roll trademark and later CinemaScope fanfare. A child piano prodigy at ten, conducted first Broadway show at fourteen. Conducted many Gershwin (q.v.) musicals on Broadway. Brought to Hollywood at suggestion of Irving Berlin (q.v.) and hired as composer-arranger by Sam Goldwyn (q.v.). Joined Fox 1940. Worked on all films in arranging capacity as well as conducting.

Films: *One Heavenly Night, Whoopee, Broadway through a Keyhole, Reaching for the Moon, Palmy Days, The Kid from Spain, Hallelujah I'm a Bum, Roman Scandals, Moulin Rouge, One Night of Love, Transatlantic Merry-go-round, Kid Millions, Folies Bergere/The Man from the Folies Bergere, Broadway Melody of 1936, Metropolitan, Strike Me Pink, The Gay Desperado, The Dancing Pirate, Ramona* (also comp.), *Born to Dance, Fifty-second Street, When You're in Love, Wee Willie Winkie* (ds), *The Hurricane* (ds, also comp. "Moon of Manakoora"), *They Shall Have Music/Melody of Youth* (also acted), *Goldwyn Follies, Alexander's Ragtime Band, The Star Maker, The Blue Bird* (also comp.), *Little Old New York* (ds), *Broadway Melody of 1940, Lillian Russell* (also comp.), *Johnny Apollo* (also comp.), *Young People, Moon over Her Shoulder* (also comp.), *Tin Pan Alley, That Night in Rio, The Great American Broadcast, A Yank in the RAF* (ds), *I Wake Up Screaming/Hot Spot* (ds, using Newman's popular "Street Scene" theme as background score), *Weekend in Havana, Song of the Islands, Ball of Fire* (cs), *My Gal Sal, Orchestra Wives, Springtime in the Rockies, Coney Island, Sweet Rosie O'Grady, Irish Eyes Are Smiling, Pin Up Girl, Diamond Horseshoe, State Fair* (45), *The Dolly Sisters, Three Little Girls in Blue, Centennial Summer, The Shocking Miss Pilgrim, Margie, Mother Wore Tights, I Wonder Who's Kissing Her Now, That Lady in Ermine, When My Baby Smiles at Me, Come to the Stable* (also comp. "Through a Long and Sleepless Night"), *Oh You Beautiful Doll, Dancing in the Dark, My Blue Heaven, On the Riviera, Wait Till the Sun Shines Nellie, With a Song in My Heart, You're My Everything, Call Me Mister, Stars and Stripes Forever/Marching Along, Call Me Madam, Tonight We Sing, There's No Business like Show Business, Daddy Long Legs, Carousel, Bus*

*Stop* (ds), *The King and I, South Pacific, Flower Drum Song, State Fair* (62), *How the West Was Won* (ws), *Camelot.*

**350  NORTH, SHEREE** (1933– ). RN: Dawn Bethel. Volatile dancer-actress who stopped show dancing in Broadway's *Hazel Flagg* (54). Dancing *début* when thirteen. Also plays dramatic roles.

Films: *Excuse My Dust; Living It Up* (film version of *Hazel Flagg*), *How to Be Very Very Popular, The Best Things in Life Are Free* (her best screen role), *Mardi Gras.*

**351  NOVARRO, RAMON** (1899–1969). RN: Ramon Samaniegoes. Mexican-born romantic lead of silent screen and early talkies. Singer in Hollywood restaurant when given spot in vaudeville. Film *début* 1923.

Films: *The Pagan* (ds), *Devil May Care, In Gay Madrid, Call of the Flesh, The Barbarian* (ds), *The Cat and the Fiddle, The Night Is Young, The Sheik Steps Out.*

**352  NUGENT, ELLIOTT** (1900– ). Director, former child vaudeville performer, actor (film *début* 1929), playwright and stage producer.

Films: *So This Is College* (acted only). As dir: *She Loves Me Not, Strictly Dynamite, Love in Bloom, Give Me a Sailor, Never Say Die* (cs); *Up In Arms, My Favourite Brunette* (cs), *Welcome Stranger; Just for You.*

**353  OAKIE, JACK** (1903– ). RN: Lewis D. Offield. Chubby comedian and musical performer who provided jovial support in scores of musicals and comedies in Thirties and Forties. Part of vaudeville double-act for many years, then film extra, silent star.

Films: *Sweetie, Fast Company, Close Harmony, The Street Girl, Hit the Deck* (30), *Let's Go Native, Paramount on Parade, The Sap from Syracuse, Sea Legs, Dude Ranch, June Moon, Million Dollar Legs* (cs), *From Hell to Heaven* (ds), *College Humour, Sitting Pretty, Too Much Harmony, Murder at the Vanities, College Rhythm, Shoot the Works, King of Burlesque, Big Broadcast of 1936, Collegiate, Colleen, Florida Special* (cs), *That Girl from Paris, The Champagne Waltz, Hitting a New High, Radio City Revels, Thanks for Everything, Young People, Tin Pan Alley, The Great American Broadcast, Rise and Shine, Navy Blues, Song of the Islands, Iceland, Hello Frisco Hello, Wintertime, Something to Shout About, Sweet and Low Down, The Merry Monahans, Bowery to Broadway, That's the Spirit, On Stage Everybody, When My Baby Smiles at Me.*

**354  O'BRIEN, MARGARET** (1937– ). RN: Angela Maxine O'Brien. Appealing child actress whose popularity in the Forties rivalled that of Shirley Temple (q.v.) in Thirties. Was a model at eighteen months. Though not the accomplished singer or dancer that her predecessor was, she was also less precocious and her duet with Judy Garland (q.v.) in *Meet Me in St. Louis* ("Under the Bamboo Tree") was an exquisite blend of charm and unpretentiousness.

Films: *Babes on Broadway* (début), *Thousands Cheer, Meet Me in St. Louis, Music for Millions, The Unfinished Dance, Big City; Glory* (cs).

**355  O'BRIEN, VIRGINIA** (1922– ). Droll singer-comedienne with distinctive sphinx-like style of singing. Is said to have been so terrified at an audition that she could not move facial muscles. Director coached her in style

*"Where Did You Learn to Dance?"* : Donald
O'Connor with Debbie Reynolds in
I LOVE MELVIN

and such success resulted that M-G-M
signed her.

Films: *Hullabaloo* (début), *The Big
Store, Lady Be Good, Ringside Maisie*
(cs), *Ship Ahoy, Panama Hattie, DuBarry
Was A Lady, Thousands Cheer, Meet the
People, Two Girls and a Sailor, The
Harvey Girls, Ziegfeld Follies, Till the
Clouds Roll By.*

### 356 O'CONNOR, DONALD (1925–

). Actor-dancer in show business
since childhood. Born to vaudeville
family, chosen by Paramount to play Bing
Crosby's (q.v.) kid brother in *Sing You
Sinners*. After several child roles returned
briefly to vaudeville. Became top 'teenage

star in series of lively musicals for
Universal, often teamed with Peggy
Ryan (q.v.). In early Fifties made series
of comedies with talking mule named
Francis. An excellent dancer and comic,
his adult career was given fresh impetus
by *Singin' in the Rain* and his show-
stopping "Make 'Em Laugh" number,
which led to major musical roles. Now
does night club act, occasional television.

Films: *Melody for Two* (début, in
speciality act with two brothers), *Sing
You Sinners, Million Dollar Legs, On
Your Toes; What's Cookin'?, Private
Buckaroo, Give Out Sisters, Get Hep to
Love/She's My Lovely, It Comes Up Love,
Strictly in the Groove, When Johnny
Comes Marching Home, Mr. Big, Top
Man, Chip Off the Old Block, Follow the
Boys* (44), *This Is the Life* (44), *The
Merry Monahans, Bowery to Broadway,
Patrick the Great; Something in the Wind,
Are You With It?, Feudin' Fussin' and
A-Fightin', Yes Sir That's My Baby,
Curtain Call at Cactus Creek/Take the
Stage, The Milkman* (cs), *Double Cross-
bones, Singin' in the Rain, I Love Melvin,
Call Me Madam, Walkin' My Baby
back Home, There's No Business like Show
Business, Anything Goes* (56).

### 357 PAIGE, JANIS (1922– ). RN:
Donna Mae Jaden. Sophisticated singer-

actress who was entertaining at Hollywood Canteen when spotted by M-G-M talent scout and given walk-on in *Bathing Beauty*. This led to Warner contract, but was used unimaginatively as heroine of medium-budget movies. In 1950 asked for release and turned to stage. Scored Broadway success in *The Pajama Game*, later returned to screen in character comedy roles.

Films: *Bathing Beauty, Hollywood Canteen, Her Kind of Man* (ds), *Two Guys from Milwaukee/Royal Flush, The Time the Place and the Girl, Love and Learn* (cs), *Cheyenne* (ws), *Wallflower* (cs), *Romance on the High Seas/It's Magic, One Sunday Afternoon, Two Gals and a Guy; Silk Stockings; Please Don't Eat the Daisies* (cs); *Follow the Boys* (63).

**358 PAIGE, ROBERT** (1910–    ). RN: John Arthur Page. Romantic singing lead in minor Universal musicals and comedies of Forties. A popular radio announcer before turning to acting, his best role was Deanna Durbin's (q.v.) leading man in *Can't Help Singing*. Now an executive in TV news.

Films: *Cain and Mabel* (début), *Dancing on a Dime, Melody Lane, Hellzapoppin', Almost Married, Don't Get Personal, What's Cooking?, Get Hep to Love/She's My Lovely, Pardon My Sarong, Cowboy in Manhattan, Crazy House* (guest), *Hi Buddy, How's About It?, Hi Ya Chum, Get Going, Mr. Big, Follow the Boys* (44), *Can't Help Singing, Shady Lady, Tangier* (ds); *Bye Bye Birdie*.

**359 PALMER, ERNEST.** Photographer active since 1919, mainly with Fox, whose Technicolor camerawork for Forties musicals was particularly impressive.

Films: *Sunny Side Up, Just Imagine, A Connecticut Yankee* (31), *Cavalcade* (ds), *Stand Up and Cheer, Star for a Night, Can This Be Dixie?, Banjo on My Knee* (ds), *Ali Baba Goes to Town, Straight Place and Show/They're Off, Hollywood Cavalcade, Shooting High* (ws), *Tall Dark and Handsome, Coney Island, Pin Up Girl, The Dolly Sisters, Centennial Summer, I Wonder Who's Kissing Her Now?*

**360 PAN, HERMES** (c. 1910–    ). Choreographer and dancer who has frequently worked with Fred Astaire (q.v.) inc. his TV shows.

Films: asst. ch. *Flying Down to Rio*. Ch. *The Gay Divorcee, Roberta, Old Man Rhythm, Top Hat, In Person, I Dream Too Much, Follow the Fleet, Swing Time, Shall We Dance?, Damsel in Distress, Radio City Revels, Second Chorus, That Night in Rio, Moon over Miami* (also danced), *My Gal Sal* (also danced), *Footlight Serenade, Song of the Islands, Springtime in the Rockies, Sweet Rosie O'Grady* (also danced), *Pin Up Girl* (also danced), *Irish Eyes Are Smiling, Diamond Horseshoe, Blue Skies, The Barkleys of Broadway* ("Shoes with Wings On" only), *Three Little Words, Let's Dance, Excuse My Dust, Texas Carnival, Lovely to Look At, Sombrero, Kiss Me Kate, The Student Prince, Jupiter's Darling, Hit the Deck* (55), *Meet Me in Las Vegas/Viva Las Vegas, Silk Stockings, Pal Joey, Porgy and Bess, The Blue Angel* (ds, 59), *Can Can, Flower Drum Song, My Fair Lady, Finian's Rainbow*.

**361 PARKS, LARRY** (1914–    ). Actor signed by Columbia in 1941 after stage experience, he played over a dozen minor roles before his sensational success as Al Jolson (q.v.) in *The Jolson Story*. Later quarrelled with studio over roles he was being given in routine swashbucklers, but it was the McCarthy hearings that virtually finished his Hollywood career.

Films: *You Were Never Lovelier, Blondie Goes to College* (cs), *Is Everybody Happy?* (43), *Hey Rookie, Stars on Parade, She's a Sweetheart, The Jolson Story, Down to Earth, Jolson Sings Again.*

**362  PASTERNAK, JOE** (1901–    ). Producer who delights in mixing highbrow music with popular. Responsible for the Deanna Durbin (q.v.) cycle at Universal, later helped promote the careers of Kathryn Grayson, Jane Powell and Mario Lanza (qq.v.) at M-G-M. Persuaded Stokowski to act in *One Hundred Men and a Girl*, let Dietrich

(q.v.) prove she was not just a static photographers' model by casting her in *Destry Rides Again* after she had been labelled "box-office poison" by exhibitors, and later made Lauritz Melchior and Jose Iturbi (qq.v.) actors. Hungarian-born, immigrated at seventeen, became dish-washer at studio canteen. Third asst. to Allan Dwan (q.v.), first asst. to Wesley Ruggles (q.v.) at Universal, then sent to Europe to supervise

studio's production there in early Thirties. Became influenced by French and German musicals, returned as producer to Hollywood, bringing director Henry Koster (q.v.) and made first Deanna Durbin feature.

Films: *Three Smart Girls, One Hundred Men and a Girl, Mad about Music, Three Smart Girls Grow Up, That Certain Age, First Love, Destry Rides Again* (ws), *It's a Date, Seven Sinners* (ds), *Spring Parade, The Flame of New Orleans* (cs), *Nice Girl?, It Started with Eve, Seven Sweethearts, Presenting Lily Mars, Thousands Cheer, Two Girls and a Sailor, Music for Millions, Thrill of a Romance, Anchors Aweigh, Her Highness and the Bellboy* (ds), *Two Sisters from Boston, Holiday in Mexico, No Leave No Love, The Unfinished Dance, This Time for Keeps, Three Daring Daughters/The Birds and the Bees, Big City, On an Island with You, A Date with Judy, Luxury Liner, The Kissing Bandit, In the Good Old Summertime, That Midnight Kiss, Nancy Goes to Rio, The Duchess of Idaho, Summer Stock/If You Feel like Singing, The Toast of New Orleans, The Great Caruso, Rich Young and Pretty, The Strip, Skirts Ahoy, The Merry Widow* (52), *Because You're Mine, Small Town Girl, Latin Lovers, Easy to Love, The Student Prince, Athena, Hit the Deck* (55), *Love Me or Leave Me, Meet Me in Las Vegas/Viva Las Vegas, The Opposite Sex, Ten Thousand Bedrooms, This Could Be the Night, Party Girl* (ds); *Where the Boys Are; Billy Rose's Jumbo; Girl Happy, Made in Paris* (cs).

**363  PAYNE, JOHN** (1912–    ). Romantic lead of Fox musicals who like Dick Powell (q.v.) later took tough roles. Worked as wrestler and 'phone operator to pay for dramatic lessons. Radio actor before film début 1936.

116

Films: *Hats Off, College Swing/Swing Teacher Swing, Love on Toast, Garden of the Moon, Kid Nightingale, Tin Pan Alley, Star Dust, The Great American Broadcast, Sun Valley Serenade, Weekend in Havana, Footlight Serenade, Iceland, Springtime in the Rockies, Hello Frisco Hello, The Dolly Sisters, Wake Up and Dream* (46).

*Alice Pearce with Gene Kelly in ON THE TOWN*

**364  PEARCE, ALICE** (1913–1966). Character comedienne, the memorable Lucy Schmeeler of *On the Town*, and perhaps even more appealing as the Salvation Army lady who with Vera-Ellen (q.v.) decides to be "Naughty but Nice" in *Belle of New York*.
Films: *On the Town; Belle of New York; How to Be Very Very Popular, The Opposite Sex.*

**365  PENNINGTON, ANN** (c. 1895– ). Broadway star whose dynamic dancing earned her title Shimmy Queen and who made a few early talkies. *Ziegfeld Follies début* 1913, introduced "Black Bottom" 1926.

Films: *Gold Diggers of Broadway, Is Everybody Happy?* (29), *Tanned Legs, Happy Days.*

**366  PINZA, EZIO** (1892–1957). RN: Fortunato Pinza. Italian opera star who after becoming Broadway matinée idol in *South Pacific* was starred by M-G-M in two movies.
Films: *Carnegie Hall* (début); *Strictly Dishonorable, Mr. Imperium/You Belong to My Heart; Tonight We Sing* (as Chaliapin).

**367  PLANCK, ROBERT** (c. 1910– ). Photographer, mainly with Fox and M-G-M, now active in TV.
Films: *This Is My Affair* (ds), *Life Begins in College, Love and Hisses, Thin Ice* (co.); *It Happened in Brooklyn, Luxury Liner, Summer Stock/If You Feel Like Singing, Royal Wedding/Wedding Bells, Texas Carnival, Torch Song* (ds), *Rhapsody* (ds), *The Girl Most Likely.*

**368  PLATT, MARC** (c. 1923– ). Athletic though slightly built dancer who came to Hollywood from Russian ballet and Broadway musical. Made few films at Columbia in Forties, brief comeback in *Seven Brides for Seven Brothers*, then spent several years as dance director of Radio City Music Hall ballet company.
Films: *Tonight and Every Night* (début), *Tars and Spars, Down to Earth, When a Girl's Beautiful; Seven Brides for Seven Brothers.*

**369  POLITO, SOL** (1892–1960). Photographer of many Busby Berkeley (q.v.) musicals, who started with silents and spent most of career at Warners, where his sharply toned, highly contrasted black-and-white photography was typical of that studio during the Thirties and Forties.

117

Films: *The Hot Heiress, Forty-Second Street, Gold Diggers of 1933, Footlight Parade* (co.), *Wonder Bar, Flirtation Walk, Go into Your Dance, In Caliente, Shipmates Forever, Colleen* (co.), *Sons O'Guns, Ready Willing and Able, Varsity Show, Gold Diggers in Paris, On Your Toes* (co.); *Rhapsody in Blue, Cinderella Jones.*

**370 PONS, LILY** (1898–    ). RN: Alice Pons. French-born coloratura soprano who made few films late Thirties. Operatic *début Lakme* France 1928, Metropolitan 1931, Hollywood 1935.

Films: *I Dream Too Much* (début), *That Girl from Paris, Hitting a New High; Carnegie Hall* (as herself, singing "The Bell Song").

**371 PORTER, COLE** (1891–1964). Composer and lyricist, one of America's three most accomplished words-and-music men (with Irving Berlin and Frank Loesser, qq.v.). Sophisticated, witty, his lyrics spiced with cultural allusions and *risqué* phrases, his music dexterous,

sweeping and often rhythmically unorthodox, he contributed outstanding scores to stage and screen. Born to wealth and luxury, had first piano piece published when eleven. At Yale, wrote two of their best-known football songs. First Broadway musical 1916, after which joined French Foreign Legion. First major success Broadway musical *Paris* 1928. He and wife, known as "the Coleporteurs," had become noted for European travels and dazzling splendour of parties at Paris and Venice homes during Twenties. After Broadway hit, was kept steadily busy by Broadway and Hollywood, though work was frequently underrated at time of its appearance. In 1937 disastrous riding accident resulted in years of pain and operations on right leg, culminating in amputation 1958. Final score same year, for TV version of *Aladdin.*

Films: *The Battle of Paris, Fifty Million Frenchmen, Wake Up and Dream* (34), *The Gay Divorcee* (only "Night and Day" was retained for this film version of Porter's Broadway hit), *Born to Dance*

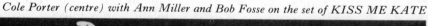
*Cole Porter (centre) with Ann Miller and Bob Fosse on the set of KISS ME KATE*

(first full-scale original film score inc. "Easy to Love," "I've Got You under My Skin," "Hey Babe," "Rap Tap on Wood," and, not used, "It's De-Lovely"), *Anything Goes* (36 and 56), *Rosalie* (inc. "In the Still of the Night"), *Broadway Melody* (40, inc. "I Concen-trate on You," "I've Got My Eyes on You"), *You'll Never Get Rich* (inc. "So Near and Yet So Far"), *Panama Hattie, Something to Shout About* ("You'd Be So Nice to Come Home To"), *DuBarry Was a Lady, Let's Face It, Hollywood Canteen* ("Don't Fence Me In," actually written 1934 for Fox film but not used), *Night and Day* (biography), *The Pirate* ("Be a Clown," "Mack the Black," "Nina," "Love of My Life," "You Can Do No Wrong"), *Adam's Rib* (cs, "Farewell Amanda"), *Stage Fright* (ds, "The Laziest Gal in Town," actually written 1927, now re-introduced by Marlene Dietrich q.v.), *Kiss Me Kate* ("From This Moment On," written for another stage musical and dropped, was added to film version of this show and became a hit), *High Society* (inc. "I Love You Samantha," "You're Sensational," "Who Wants to Be a Millionaire?," "True Love"), *Silk Stockings* ("Fated to Be Mated" and "Ritz Rock and Roll" were added to stage score), *Les Girls* (inc. "You're Just Too Too"), *Can Can, Star/Those Were the Happy Times* (fea-tured "The Physician" and "Solomon" from 1933 stage musical *Nymph Errant*).

**372 PORTER, JEAN** (1924– ). Small, cheerful red-haired dancer-actress who played 'teenage roles in Forties. Vaudeville as child, then Little Theatre groups and radio.

Films: *Babes on Broadway* (début, as dancer), *Bathing Beauty, San Fernando Valley* (ws), *In Hollywood, Easy To Wed, Betty Co-Ed, Little Miss Broadway* (47),

*Sweet Genevieve, Two Blondes and a Redhead; G.I. Jane.*

**373 POTTER, H. C.** (1904– ). Director, mainly comedy, who started in theatre. Films since 1935.

Films: *Romance in the Dark, The Story of Vernon and Irene Castle, Second Chorus, Hellzapoppin'; Three for the Show.*

**374 POWELL, DICK** (1904–1963). Actor-singer, wide-eyed, wide-grinned romantic lead of Warner musicals in Thirties who later switched to tough roles with success. Occasionally produced, directed and one of first stars to realise potential of television, forming Four Star Productions. Started as singer and MC, and at one time did vaudeville act with Ginger Rogers (q.v.). Married Joan Blondell, June Allyson (qq.v.). Often teamed with Ruby Keeler (q.v.) in early career.

Films: *Blessed Event* (début), *College Coach, Forty-Second Street, Footlight Parade, Gold Diggers of 1933, Twenty Million Sweethearts* (intro. "I'll String Along with You"), *Dames* (intro. "I Only Have Eyes for You"), *Flirtation Walk, Happiness Ahead, Wonder Bar, Broadway Gondolier* (intro. "Lulu's Back in Town"), *Gold Diggers of Broadway* (35), *Shipmates Forever, Thanks a Million* (intro. "Sitting High on a Hilltop"), *Colleen, Hearts Divided* (ds), *Gold Diggers of 1937* (intro. "With Plenty of Money and You"), *Stage Struck* (cs), *Hollywood Hotel, On the Avenue* (intro. "I've Got My Love to Keep Me Warm," "The Girl on the Police Gazette"), *The Singing Marine, Varsity Show, Going Places, Cowboy from Brooklyn* (intro. "Ride Tenderfoot Ride"), *Hard to Get* (intro. "You Must Have Been a Beautiful Baby"), *Naughty but Nice, In the Navy, Star Spangled Rhythm, Riding High/*

*Eleanor Powell with George Murphy in*
*BROADWAY MELODY OF 1940*

Melody Inn, Happy Go Lucky, True to Life (intro. "Old Music Master"), Meet the People; Susan Slept Here (cs). Prod. and dir. You Can't Run Away from It.

**375 POWELL, ELEANOR** (1912– ). M-G-M's tap-dancing star of late Thirties who developed her own distinctive heel-and-toe movement. Athletically built, started dancing at eleven, *début* Miami night club when thirteen, three years later on Broadway. After many years retirement made brief night club comeback in early Sixties.

Films: *George White's Scandals of 1935* (début), *Broadway Melody of 1936, Born to Dance, Broadway Melody of 1938, Rosalie, Honolulu, Broadway Melody* (40), *Lady Be Good, Ship Ahoy, I Dood It/By Hook or by Crook, Thousands Cheer, Sensations of 1945 ; The Duchess of Idaho* (guest, last film role to date).

**376 POWELL, JANE** (1928– ). RN: Suzanne Burce. Soprano who could also perform bluesy jazz-tinged numbers, she was a top 'teenage star at M-G-M for several years. Was a child singing star on radio when her parents took her from home-town Oregon to Los Angeles where, after two films for United Artists, she was given M-G-M contract. Still sings in night clubs and theatres.

Films: *Song of the Open Road* (début), *Delightfully Dangerous, Holiday in Mexico, Three Daring Daughters/The Birds and the Bees, A Date with Judy* (intro. "It's a Most Unusual Day"), *Luxury Liner, Nancy Goes to Rio, Two Weeks with Love* (revived one of first examples of ragtime, the 1911 "Oceana Roll"), *Royal Wedding/Wedding Bells* (intro. "Too Late Now"), *Rich Young and Pretty* (intro. "Wonder Why"), *Small Town Girl, Three Sailors and a Girl, Seven Brides for Seven Brothers*

*Jane Powell with Vic Damone
in RICH YOUNG AND PRETTY*

(intro. "Wonderful Wonderful Day," "Goin' Courtin'"), *Athena, Deep in My Heart, Hit the Deck* (55), *The Girl Most Likely.*

**377  PREISSER, JUNE** (c. 1920–    ). New Orleans-born dancer-actress with a twinkling sense of humour and unique style of acrobatic stomach-role which she frequently incorporated into her numbers. Stage *début* at two, when nine did dancing act with sister Cherry, appearing in *Ziegfeld Follies.* Dancing in show with Lupe Velez (q.v.) when tested for role of ex-child star Baby Rosalie (a parody of Shirley Temple q.v.) in *Babes in Arms.*

Films: *Babes in Arms* (début), *Strike Up the Band, Sweater Girl, Babes on Swing Street, Murder in the Blue Room, Let's Go Steady, I'll Tell the World, Junior Prom, Freddie Steps Out, High School Hero, Vacation Days, Sarge Goes to*

*June Preisser with Mickey Rooney
in STRIKE UP THE BAND*

*College, Two Blondes and a Redhead, Campus Sleuth, The Music Man* (49).

**378  PREMINGER, OTTO** (1906–    ). Austrian director who also acted in Hollywood until his success with *Laura* (non-musical). Films, including his musicals, have varied in quality, often lacking in warmth.

Films: Dir. *Under Your Spell; Danger Love at Work* (cs), *Centennial Summer, That Lady in Ermine* (completed after death of Ernst Lubitsch q.v.); *River of No Return* (ds), *Carmen Jones; Porgy and*

121

*Bess ; Skidoo* (cs). As actor: *They Got Me Covered* (cs).

**379 PRESLEY, ELVIS** (1935– ). Foremost singer of "rock-and-roll" era whose pop career and steady stream of mild musical films have lasted through subsequent changes of musical style. Mississippi-born, worked as lorry driver before hit recording "Heartbreak Hotel" 1956, shortly followed by films.

Films: *Love Me Tender* (ws, début), *Loving You, Jailhouse Rock, King Creole* (ds), *GI Blues, Flaming Star* (ws), *Wild in the Country* (ds), *Blue Hawaii, Follow That Dream, Kid Galahad, Girls Girls Girls, It Happened at the World's Fair, Fun in Acapulco, Kissin' Cousins, Viva Las Vegas/Love in Las Vegas, Roustabout, Girl Happy, Tickle Me, HarumScarum/ Harem Holiday, Frankie and Johnny* (66), *Paradise Hawaiian Style, Spinout/ California Holiday, Easy Come Easy Go, Double Trouble, Speedway, Stay Away Joe, Live a Little Love a Little, Charro, The Trouble with Girls, Change of Habit.*

**380 PRESNELL, HARVE** (1934– ). Former opera singer signed by M-G-M to recreate his Broadway role in *The Unsinkable Molly Brown*. Toured Europe in opera, was singing at Holly-

*Robert Preston in THE MUSIC MAN*

wood Bowl when spotted for Broadway.
Films: *The Unsinkable Molly Brown* (début), *When the Boys Meet the Girls ; Paint Your Wagon.*

**381 PRESTON, ROBERT** (1917– ). RN: Robert Preston Meservy. Broadway and Hollywood's "Music Man" was straight actor on stage and screen for many years before triumph as fast-talking, live-wire salesman Harold Hill.
Films: *Typhoon* (ds), *Moon over Burma* (cs), *New York Town ; Variety Girl, Big City ; The Music Man* (61).

**382 PREVIN, ANDRE** (1929– ). Conductor, composer, arranger and pianist active in all forms of music. Son of German conductor and music teacher who fled to U.S.A. from Nazis 1939, he continued musical study and was still in 'teens when signed by M-G-M as staff arranger, then conductor. Left Hollywood to become resident conductor with London Symphony Orchestra. Later collaborated with Alan Jay Lerner (q.v.)

122

on scores for Hollywood and Broadway (*Coco*).

Films as MD: *The Sun Comes Up* (also comp.), *Three Little Words, Small Town Girl, Kiss Me Kate, Give a Girl a Break, It's Always Fair Weather* (also comp., inc. "I Like Myself"), *Kismet, Invitation to the Dance, Silk Stockings, Designing Woman* (cs), *Gigi, Porgy and Bess, Bells Are Ringing, The Subterraneans* (also comp., acted), *My Fair Lady, Kiss Me Stupid* (cs), *Inside Daisy Clover* (also comp., inc. "You're Gonna Hear from Me"), *The Swinger* (cs, comp. title song), *Thoroughly Modern Millie.* Comp. *Pepe* (inc. "The Faraway Part of Town," also acted), *Valley of the Dolls* (ds), *Paint Your Wagon* (inc. "Gold Fever").

**383 PRINZ, LEROY** (1895– ). Choreographer, occasional director, who after exciting early life became chief dance director at Warners, staging all their dances from 1942 to 1953. Ran away from home as youth to join French Foreign Legion, staged dances at Folies Bergère, returned to U.S.A. as a flyer, went to Hollywood 1931 to choreograph for Cecil B. DeMille's biblical epics.

Films: ch. *Big Broadcast of 1936, All the King's Horses, Waikiki Wedding, Road to Singapore* (40), *Too Many Girls, Road to Zanzibar, All-American Co-Ed* (also dir., prod., co-st.), *Fiesta* (41, also dir., prod.), *Yankee Doodle Dandy* (w. Seymour Felix q.v.), *The Desert Song* (44), *This Is the Army, Thank Your Lucky Stars, Shine on Harvest Moon, Hollywood Canteen, Rhapsody in Blue, Night and Day, The Time the Place and the Girl, My Wild Irish Rose, April Showers, Romance on the High Seas/It's Magic, Two Guys from Texas, My Dream Is Yours, Look for the Silver Lining, It's a Great Feeling, Always Leave Them Laughing, Tea for Two, West Point Story/Fine and Dandy, Lullaby of Broadway, On Moonlight Bay, Painting the Clouds with Sunshine, Starlift, I'll See You in My Dreams, About Face, She's Working Her Way through College, April in Paris, The Eddie Cantor Story, The Jazz Singer* (53), *She's back on Broadway, By the Light of the Silvery Moon, Calamity Jane, Lucky Me, The Helen Morgan Story/Both Ends of the Candle, Sayonara* (ds), *South Pacific.*

**384 PROWSE, JULIET** (1937– ). Tall, technically superb dancer born in Bombay. Started in ballet, switched to modern dancing because of her height. Sporadic film career mingled with television, summer stock and London stage leads.

Films: *Gentlemen Marry Brunettes; Can Can, G.I. Blues; Spree.*

**385 QUINE, RICHARD** (1920– ). Director of unpretentious and enjoyable musicals who reached his peak with *My Sister Eileen* but has since ignored the musical. Was dancer in vaudeville and musical comedy, actor-dancer at M-G-M before becoming director at Columbia.

Films as actor: *Babes on Broadway, For Me and My Gal; Words and Music.* As dir: *Sunny Side of the Street, Purple Heart Diary/No Time for Tears, Sound Off, Rainbow Round My Shoulder* (also co-sc.), *All Ashore* (also co-sc.), *Cruisin' Down the River, So This Is Paris, My Sister Eileen; It Happened to Jane* (cs), *Paris when It Sizzles* (cs, also co-prod.).

**386 RAFT, GEORGE** (1895– ). Though an excellent ballroom dancer— he once danced in Texas Guinan's night club and Valentino asked him to be his double—it was his role in *Scarface* (non-musical) that brought stardom and he is best known as a screen gangster.

Films: *Palmy Days, Bolero, The Trum-*

*pet Blows, Rumba, Stolen Harmony, Every Night at Eight, You and Me* (ds); *Broadway* (42), *Follow the Boys* (44), *Johnny Angel* (ds), *Nob Hill, Nocturne* (ds), *Race Street* (ds); *Some Like It Hot* (cs, 59), *Ocean's 11* (ds, guest).

**387 RAINGER, RALPH** (1901–1942). RN: Ralph Reichenthal. Composer who wrote mainly for Paramount musicals, forming with Leo Robin (q.v.) one of Hollywood's best song-writing teams of Thirties. A New Yorker, left law firm to play and compose music. Played in orchestra for musical comedy, accompanied actor-singer Clifton Webb in vaudeville, became his rehearsal pianist for *The First Little Show* (29) in which Webb used one of his songs "Moanin' Low." Its success led to Hollywood. Died in air crash.

Films, with Billy Rose: *Be Yourself* ("When a Woman Loves a Man"). With George Marion Jnr.: *Along Came Youth.* All others with Leo Robin: *The Big Broadcast* ("Please"), *Torch Singer, A Bedtime Story, She Done Him Wrong* (inc. "A Guy Who Takes His Time"), *International House, The Way to Love, She Loves Me Not* ("Love in Bloom"), *Kiss and Make Up, The Trumpet Blows, Here Is My Heart* (inc. "June in January"), *Little Miss Marker/Girl in Pawn, Shoot the Works, Rumba, The Devil Is a Woman* (ds, inc. "If It Isn't Pain It Isn't Love"), *The Big Broadcast of 1936* (one of Rainger's numbers "I Wished on the Moon" had lyrics by Dorothy Parker), *Rose of the Rancho, Palm Springs* (inc. "I Don't Want to Make History"), *Big Broadcast of 1937, Three Cheers for Love, College Holiday, Swing High Swing Low, Artists and Models* (37), *Waikiki Wedding* (inc. "Blue Hawaii"), *Blossoms on Broadway, Easy Living* (non-musical, title song), *Give Me a Sailor, Big Broadcast of 1938* (inc. "Thanks for the Memory"), *Artists and Models Abroad, Romance in the Dark, Tropic Holiday, Her Jungle Love* (ds), *Never Say Die* (cs), *Paris Honeymoon, One Thousand Dollars a Touchdown* (cs), *Gulliver's Travels* (inc. "Faithful Forever"), *Rise and Shine, A Yank in the RAF* (ds), *Cadet Girl, Tall Dark and Handsome, Moon over Miami* (inc. "You Started Something"), *Footlight Serenade, My Gal Sal* (inc. "On the Gay White Way," "Oh The Pity of It All"), *Tales of Manhattan* (ds), *Coney Island* (inc. "Take It from There"), *Riding High/Melody Inn.*

**388 RALL, TOMMY** (1929–      ). Dancer who played second-leads in Fifties. Started as part of tap and tumbling act 1938, danced in musicals at Universal. Joined Ballet Theatre 1944, and has also sung in opera.

Films: *What's Cooking?, Private Buckaroo, Give Out Sisters, Get Hep to Love/She's My Lovely, Mr. Big; Kiss Me Kate, Invitation to the Dance, My Sister Eileen, The Second Greatest Sex, Seven Brides for Seven Brothers, Merry Andrew; Funny Girl.*

*Tommy Rall with Ann Miller in KISS ME KATE*

**389 RATOFF, GREGORY** (1897–1961). Russian-born director-actor, a graduate of the Moscow Arts Theatre and member of Yiddish Players of New York. Started in silents.

Films as actor: *Broadway through a Keyhole, Sitting Pretty, Girl without a Room, George White's Scandals* (34), *Let's Fall in Love, King of Burlesque, Sing Baby Sing, Sally Irene and Mary.* As dir: *Barricade* (ds), *Rose of Washington Square, I Was an Adventuress* (ds), *Footlight Serenade, The Heat's On/Tropicana, Something to Shout About, Song of Russia* (ds), *Irish Eyes Are Smiling, Where Do We Go from Here?, Do You Love Me?, Carnival in Costa Rica.*

**390 RAYE, MARTHA** (1916–    ). RN: Margie Yvonne Reed. Comedienne, a mistress of zany knockabout humour who also handles a song well and sings ballads with feeling. Daughter of song-and-dance act, stage *début* at three. In 1936 Norman Taurog (q.v.) gave her lead in *Rhythm on the Range* in which her rendition of "Mr. Paganini" brought stardom. Has been particularly energetic in efforts to entertain troops.

Films: *Rhythm on the Range* (début), *Big Broadcast of 1937, College Holiday, Artists and Models* (37), *Double or Nothing, Waikiki Wedding, Mountain Music, Hideaway Girl, College Swing/Swing Teacher Swing, Give Me a Sailor, Big Broadcast of 1938, Never Say Die* (cs), *One Thousand Dollars a Touchdown* (cs), *The Farmer's Daughter* (cs), *The Boys from Syracuse, Keep 'Em Flying, Hellzapoppin', Navy Blues, Four Jills in a Jeep, Pin Up Girl; Billy Rose's Jumbo; Pufnstuf.*

**391 REGAN, PHIL** (1906–    ). Irish-American tenor, former clerk, who had a lengthy but undistinguished career in movies. More successful on radio and TV.

Films: *Dames, Student Tour, Sweet Adeline, Broadway Hostess, Stars over Broadway, We're in the Money* (cs), *In Caliente, Happy Go Lucky* (36), *Laughing Irish Eyes, Hit Parade* (37), *Manhattan Merry-go-round/Manhattan Music Box, Outside of Paradise, She Married a Cop, Las Vegas Nights; Sweet Rosie O'Grady, Sunbonnet Sue, Swing Parade of 1946, Sweetheart of Sigma Chi* (46); *Three Little Words.*

**392 REISNER, CHARLES** (1887–1962). Director who started with silents and spent most of career with M-G-M, directing their all-star follow-up to *Broadway Melody, Hollywood Revue,* which included colour sequences.

Films: *Hollywood Revue, Chasing Rainbows* (this 1930 musical also had one number "Happy Days Are Here Again" filmed in colour), *Love in the Rough, Stepping Out, Flying High, Student Tour; Manhattan Merry-go-round/Manhattan Music Box; The Big Store, Meet the People, Lost in a Harem; The Travelling Saleswoman* (cs).

**393 RENNAHAN, RAY** (1898–    ). Photographer who has specialised in colour since 1921, pioneering with early systems and cameraman on the first three-stripe Technicolor feature *Becky Sharp* (non-musical). Since 1950 has worked mainly on Westerns.

Films: *Walter Wanger's Vogues of 1938, Goldwyn Follies* (co.), *Her Jungle Love* (ds), *Down Argentine Way* (co.), *That Night in Rio* (co.), *Belle of the Yukon, Lady in the Dark, Three Caballeros, Up in Arms, It's a Pleasure, Incendiary Blonde, The Perils of Pauline, The Paleface* (cs), *A Connecticut Yankee in King Arthur's Court* (49).

**394 REVEL, HARRY** (1905–1958). London-born composer who wrote scores for Berlin, London and New York musicals before Hollywood contract 1933.

Films: *Sitting Pretty* (inc. "Did You Ever See a Dream Walking?," also acted in film with lyricist Mack Gordon q.v.), *Broadway through a Keyhole, The Gay Divorcee* (inc. "Don't Let It Bother You"), *We're Not Dressing* (inc. "Love Thy Neighbour"), *She Loves Me Not, Shoot the Works* (inc. "With My Eyes Wide Open I'm Dreaming"), *College Rhythm* (inc. "Stay as Sweet as You Are"), *Love in Bloom, Stolen Harmony, Paris in the Spring, Two for Tonight* (inc. "Without a Word of Warning"), *Collegiate* (inc. "I Feel like a Feather in the Breeze"), *Poor Little Rich Girl, Florida Special* (cs), *Stowaway* (inc. "Goodnight My Love"), *Head over Heels* (Brit.), *This Is My Affair* (ds), *Wake Up and Live* (inc. "There's a Lull in My Life," "Never in a Million Years"), *Danger Love at Work* (cs), *You Can't Have Everything, Ali Baba Goes to Town, Love and Hisses, Hold That Co-Ed, Josette, Love Finds Andy Hardy* (cs, inc. "Meet the Beat of My Heart"), *Sally Irene and Mary, My Lucky Star* (inc. "I've Got a Date with a Dream"), *Thanks for Everything, Rebecca of Sunnybrook Farm* ("An Old Straw Hat"), *Rose of Washington Square* ("I Never Knew Heaven Could Speak"), *Young People* (inc. "Fifth Avenue," "Tra-la-la"), *Tin Pan Alley* ("You Say the Sweetest Things"), *Moon over Burma* (cs), *Four Jacks and a Jill, Call Out the Marines, Beyond the Blue Horizon* (ds), *Sing Your Worries Away, The Big Street* (ds), *Joan of Ozarks, The Mayor of 44th Street* (inc. "A Million Miles from Manhattan"), *Here We Go Again, Hit the Ice, Ghost Catchers, Minstrel Man, I'll Tell the World* (re-prised "Slap Polka," written for *Hit the Ice*), *The Stork Club* ("If I Had a Dozen Hearts"), *It Happened on Fifth Avenue* (cs).

**395 REYNOLDS, DEBBIE** (1932– ). RN: Mary Frances Reynolds. Actress who sings with charm and dances with vivacity. Her fresh high spirits and ingenuousness made her an appealing 'teenage star. Won "Miss Burbank of 1948" contest with imitation of Betty Hutton (q.v.) and signed by Warners, who named her Debbie. Dropped after small parts, signed by M-G-M to play Helen Kane (q.v.) in *Three Little Words*. Success in this and subsequent roles led to lead in *Singin' in the Rain*. Later had trouble shaking wholesome image and some parts tended towards saccharine.

Films: *The Daughter of Rosie O'Grady* (début), *Three Little Words, Two Weeks with Love* (had particular success reviving with Carleton Carpenter the 1914 novelty "Aba Daba Honeymoon" as well as the 1912 "Row Row Row"), *Mr. Imperium/You Belong to My Heart, Singin' in the Rain, Skirts Ahoy* (sang the 1919 "Oh By Jingo" in guest spot with Bobby Van, q.v.), *I Love Melvin* (intro. "A Lady Loves"), *The Affairs of Dobie Gillis, Give a Girl a Break* (intro. "Applause, Applause" with Gower Champion, q.v., "In Our United State" with Bob Fosse, q.v.), *Susan Slept Here* (cs), *Athena* (intro. "I Never Felt Better"), *Hit the Deck* (55), *The Tender Trap* (cs), *Meet Me in Las Vegas/Viva Las Vegas* (guest), *Bundle of Joy, Tammy and the Bachelor/Tammy* (cs, intro. "Tammy"), *Say One for Me, The Gazebo* (cs), *How the West Was Won* (ws), *The Unsinkable Molly Brown, The Singing Nun*.

**396 REYNOLDS, MARJORIE** (1921– ). RN: Marjorie Goodspeed. Actress and dancer, former child star, who danced well and made a pleasant impression as leading lady in Forties.

Films: *Wine Women and Song* (début), *College Humour ; Top Sergeant Mulligan, Holiday Inn, Star Spangled Rhythm, Dixie, Bring On the Girls, Duffy's Tavern, Meet Me on Broadway ; That Midnight Kiss ; Juke Box Rhythm.*

**397  RICHMAN, HARRY** (1895– ). Debonair singer, actor, composer and pianist, a major star of the *Scandals* and *Ziegfeld Follies* on Broadway, but never achieved equal success in films.

Films: *Puttin' On the Ritz* (intro. title song in routine similar to one used sixteen years later by Astaire, q.v.); *The Music Goes Round* (also lyrics).

**398  RITZ BROTHERS, THE (AL,** 1901–1965, **JIM** 1903– , **HARRY** 1906– ). Crazy comedy team who clowned, sang and danced. As well as frequent guest appearances in Thirties, had several musicals built around their talents.

Films: *Sing Baby Sing, One in a Million, On the Avenue, Life Begins in College, You Can't Have Everything, Kentucky Moonshine, Goldwyn Follies, Straight Place and Show/They're Off, Three Musketeers, Pack Up Your Troubles/We're in the Army Now, Argentine Nights, Behind the Eight Ball, Never a Dull Moment* (43), *Hi Ya Chum.*

**399  ROBBINS, GALE** (1924– ). Glamorous red-headed singer, former model and band vocalist who became typecast as gold-digging other woman. *Début* 1944.

Films: *Race Street* (ds), *The Barkleys of Broadway, Oh You Beautiful Doll, Three Little Words, Strictly Dishonour-able, The Belle of New York, Calamity Jane.*

**400  ROBBINS, JEROME** (1918– ). Choreographer who conceived, directed and choreographed Broadway's *West Side Story,* later co-directing film version. Studied with Eugene Loring (q.v.), danced in Broadway chorus, member of Ballet Theatre 1940, soloist 1941, created own ballets. His *Fancy Free* (44) was genesis of Broadway's *On the Town* (45), later filmed. Ballets and Broadway musicals have taken precedence over film work.

Films: ch. *The King and I* (re-creating his ballet "The Small House of Uncle Thomas"). Ch., co-dir. *West Side Story.* His choreography for Broadway's *Gypsy* was re-created for film by Robert Tucker.

**401  ROBERTI, LYDA** (c. 1909–1938). Polish-born blonde singer-comedienne with piquant Hungarian accent. Daughter of famous clown, toured Europe with him during childhood, playing Chicago when given first film role *Dancers in the Dark* 1932.

Films: *The Kid from Spain, Million Dollar Legs* (cs), *College Rhythm, George White's Scandals* (35), *Pick a Star, Nobody's Baby.*

**402  ROBERTS, ALLAN** (1905–1966). Lyricist under contract to Columbia from mid-Forties, usually working with either Doris Fisher or Lester Lee as composer.

Films: *Gilda* (ds, inc. "Put the Blame on Mame"), *Thrill of Brazil, Sing while You Dance, Betty Co-Ed, Singin' in the Corn, Cigarette Girl, Little Miss Broadway* (47), *When a Girl's Beautiful, Sweet Genevieve, Down to Earth* (inc. "This Can't Be Legal," "Let's Stay Young Forever," "They Can't Convince Me"), *Two Blondes and a Redhead, Glamour*

*Girl, Mary Lou, Lulu Belle, I Surrender Dear, Slightly French, Ladies of the Chorus, Make Believe Ballroom, Holiday in Havana, The Travelling Saleswoman* (cs), *Purple Heart Diary/No Time for Tears* ("Bread and Butter Woman"), *Miss Sadie Thompson* ("Marine Song").

**403 ROBESON, PAUL** (1898–     ). Negro actor and singer who left law firm to go on stage. Occasional films, mainly in Britain.

Films: *Show Boat* (36, intro. "I Still Suits Me"); *Tales of Manhattan* (ds).

**404 ROBIN, LEO** (1899–     ). Lyricist who worked as actor, newspaperman and publicist before first hit stage score *Hit the Deck* with Vincent Youmans (q.v.). Hollywood 1929 where he worked with several top composers.

Films: *Why Bring That Up?, Innocents of Paris* (inc. "Louise"), *Dance of Life, Hit the Deck* (30, 55), *Paramount on Parade, Dangerous Nan McGrew, Morocco* (ds), *Playboy of Paris, Monte Carlo* (inc. "Beyond the Blue Horizon"), *Along Came Youth, Dude Ranch, One Hour with You, Blonde Venus* (ds), *The Big Broadcast* (inc. "Please"), *You Belong to Me* (ds), *My Weakness, Here Comes Cookie, Preview Murder Mystery, The Jungle Princess* (ds), *Desire* (ds), *The*

*Leo Robin with Tony Martin on the set of HIT THE DECK*

*Champagne Waltz ;* for other films 1933–43 see RAINGER, RALPH; then: *Wintertime, The Gang's All Here/The Girls He Left Behind,* (inc. "No Love No Nothin'," "The Lady in the Tutti-Frutti Hat"), *Greenwich Village, Centennial Summer* (inc. "In Love in Vain," "Up with the Lark"), *The Time the Place and the Girl* (inc. "On a Rainy Night in Rio," "A Gal in Calico"), *Something in the Wind* (inc. "I Love a Mystery"), *Casbah* (inc. "For Every Man There's a Woman," "Hooray for Love," "What's Good about Good-bye?"), *Meet Me after the Show, Two Tickets to Broadway, Macao* (ds), *Just for You* (inc. "I'll Si Si Ya in Bahia," "Zing a Little Zong"), *Small Town Girl, Gentlemen Prefer Blondes, Latin Lovers, My Sister Eileen* (inc. "A Band and My Baby," "There's Nothing like Love").

**405 ROBINSON, BILL** (1878–1949). Negro tap dancer known as "Bojangles," famous for variety of his steps and as originator of stair tap routine. Star of vaudeville, night clubs and musical comedy in early part of century. Films from 1930, best remembered for his dances with Shirley Temple (q.v.).

Films: *Hooray for Love, Big Broadcast of 1936, The Little Colonel, The Littlest Rebel, Rebecca of Sunnybrook Farm, Just around the Corner, Stormy Weather.* Ch. *Dimples.*

**406 RODGERS, RICHARD** (1901–     ). Composer who with Lorenz Hart (q.v.) wrote some of richest scores for Broadway and Hollywood. From 1943 collaborated with Oscar Hammerstein (q.v.) and after Hammerstein's death sometimes wrote own lyrics. Had written score for varsity show when librettist Herbert Fields suggested his collaboration with Hart 1920. Though tempera-

*Richard Rodgers with Oscar Hammerstein*

mentally completely opposed, their songs were perfect unison of words and music. First hit show 1925 *Garrick Gaieties* which included first song hit "Manhattan."

Films, with Lorenz HART: *Spring Is Here, Follow Through, Heads Up, A Connecticut Yankee* (31), *The Hot Heiress* (first score written directly for screen), *Love Me Tonight* ("Isn't It Romantic?," "Lover," "Love Me Tonight," "The Poor Apache," and "Mimi"), *The Phantom President, Dancing Lady* ("Rhythm of the Day"), *Hallelujah I'm a Bum* (inc. "You Are Too Beautiful," also brief appearance by composers in bank scene), *Hollywood Party* (inc. "Reincarnation"), *Evergreen* (Brit. inc. "Dancing on the Ceiling"), *Mississippi* ("Easy to Remember," "Soon," "Down by the River"), *Dancing Pirate, Fools for Scandal* (inc. "How Can You Forget?"), *On Your Toes* (only ballet sequences retained from stage score), *Babes in Arms* (only title song and "Where or When" retained), *The Boys from Syracuse* ("Who Are You?" added to stage score), *Too Many Girls* ("You're Nearer" added to stage score), *They Met in Argentina, I Married an Angel, Yankee Doodle Dandy* ("Off the Record" from stage prod. *I'd Rather Be Right)*, *Stage Door Canteen, Higher and Higher* (retained "Disgustingly Rich" only), *Meet the People* (used "I Like to Recognise the Tune" from stage score *Too Many Girls)*; *Words and Music* (biography); *Gaby* (ds, "Where or When" used as theme), *Pal Joey; Billy Rose's Jumbo*. With Oscar HAMMERSTEIN: *State Fair* (45 Oscar "It Might as Well Be Spring," also "That's For Me," "It's a Grand Night for Singing," "All I Owe I Owe Ioway," "Isn't It Kinda Fun?" and "Our State Fair"); *Main Street to Broadway* (ds, also acted); *Oklahoma, Carousel, The King and I, South Pacific* (inc. "My Girl Back Home," cut from stage version but restored for film); *Flower Drum Song, State Fair* (62, inc. new songs with both words and music by Rodgers inc. "More Than Just a Friend," "This Isn't Heaven"); *The Sound of Music* (inc. new songs by Rodgers "I Have Confidence in Me" and "Something Good").

**407 ROGELL, ALBERT S.** (1901– ). Second-feature director who started in silents as apprentice cameraman.

Films: *Carnival Boat* (ds); *Start Cheering, Hawaiin Nights, Laugh It Off, I Can't Give You Anything but Love Baby, Argentine Nights, Sleepy Time Gal, Priorities on Parade, True to the Army* (re-make *She Loves Me Not)*, *Youth on Parade, Hit Parade of 1943, Earl Carroll Sketchbook/Hats off to Rhythm*.

*Ginger Rogers dances "The Yam" with Fred Astaire in CAREFREE*

**408 ROGERS, CHARLES "BUDDY"**
(1904–    ). Hollywood's All American boy of Twenties and Thirties, pleasant young hero of light musicals. Often teamed with Nancy Carroll (q.v.). Married Mary Pickford.

Films: *Close Harmony, Follow Through, Heads Up, Paramount on Parade, Safety in Numbers, Young Eagles, Along Came Youth, Take a Chance, Best of Enemies, Dance Band, Old Man Rhythm, This Way Please, The Road to Reno; Sing for Your Supper; The Reckless Age; Never a Dull Moment* (cs, 50).

**409 ROGERS, GINGER** (1911–    ). RN: Virginia Katherine McMath. Versatile actress-dancer whose legendary partnership with Fred Astaire (q.v.) in Thirties musicals established her as one of screen's best dancers. Went on to win Oscar for dramatic acting (*Kitty Foyle*) and acclaim for comedy performances (*The Major and the Minor, Roxie Hart*). Won Charleston contest 1925, toured vaudeville with two others as "Ginger and her Redheads." Small part in Broadway show led to Paramount contract 1930 and film *début* as flapper uttering famous line "Cigarette me, big boy." Returned to stage in *Girl Crazy*, introducing "Embraceable You." Minor films preceded *Forty-Second Street* (as "Anytime Annie") which led to better parts. RKO contract and teaming with Astaire in *Flying down to Rio* brought major stardom. Always varied roles, but decided 1939 to concentrate entirely on non-musicals. Reunited with Astaire when Judy Garland (q.v.) was unable to start *The Barkleys of Broadway.* Now works mainly in theatre.

Films: *Young Man of Manhattan* (début), *Queen High, The Sap from Syracuse, Follow the Leader, Carnival Boat* (ds), *Hat Check Girl, Forty-Second Street, Broadway Bad, Gold Diggers of 1933* (intro. "We're in the Money"), *Sitting Pretty, Flying down to Rio* (danced "The Carioca" in first teaming with Astaire), *Twenty Million Sweethearts, Change of Heart, The Gay Divorcee, Roberta, Top Hat* (intro. "The Piccolino"), *In Person, Follow the Fleet* (intro. "Let Yourself Go"), *Swing Time,*

130

few scores directly for screen.

Films: *The Desert Song* (29, 44, 53), *New Moon* (30, 40), *Viennese Nights* (inc. "Will You Remember Vienna?"), *Children of Dreams, The Night Is Young* (inc. "When I Grow Too Old to Dream"), *Maytime, Girl of the Golden West, Broadway Serenade, Balalaika, Let Freedom Ring, Up in Central Park, The Student Prince* (54, a 1928 version had also used the music as background score), *Deep in My Heart* (biography).

**411 ROONEY, MICKEY** (1920–    ). RN: Joe Yule Jnr. Diminutive and dynamic performer who in 1943 was America's number one box-office star, particularly popular in the Andy Hardy family series and in the musicals he made with Judy Garland (q.v.). Son of entertainers, made burlesque *début* at fifteen months, film *début* 1926 playing a midget. Starred in series of silent two-reelers as Mickey McGuire, taking character's name as his own. Re-christened Rooney by Universal, signed by M-G-M in 1935. Musician (plays five instruments), mimic, singer, dancer, comic and dramatic actor, he was top attraction for several years. After ill-written part of Lorenz Hart (q.v.) in *Words and Music* movie career faltered. Now more active in night clubs and TV.

Films: *Broadway to Hollywood, Beloved, I Like It That Way, Thoroughbreds Don't Cry, Love Finds Andy Hardy* (cs), *Babes in Arms, Andy Hardy Meets Debutante* (cs), *Strike Up the Band, Life Begins for Andy Hardy* (cs), *Babes on Broadway, Andy Hardy's Private Secretary* (cs), *Girl Crazy* (43), *Thousands Cheer; Killer McCoy* (ds), *Summer Holiday, Words and Music; The Strip, Sound Off, All Ashore, Off Limits/Military Policeman* (cs); *Breakfast at Tiffany's* (cs); *How to Stuff a Wild Bikini/How to*

*Shall We Dance?, Having a Wonderful Time, Vivacious Lady* (cs), *Carefree* (intro. "The Yam"), *The Story of Vernon and Irene Castle; Tales of Manhattan* (ds), *Lady in the Dark, Weekend at the Waldorf* (ds); *The Barkleys of Broadway; The First Travelling Saleslady* (cs).

**410 ROMBERG, SIGMUND** (1887–1951). Hungarian-born composer of light operettas, the more popular of which have been filmed by Hollywood. Only a

*Mickey Rooney watched by Judy Garland in GIRL CRAZY*

*Fill a Wild Bikini, Skidoo* (cs), *Eighty Steps to Jonah* (ds).

**412 ROSHER, CHARLES.** British-born photographer who went to U.S.A. in 1911, joined United Artists 1919 and has been leading cameraman since Thirties, mainly with M-G-M.

Films: *Dance Fools Dance, Moulin Rouge, Broadway Melody of 1936, Hollywood Hotel, Kismet* (ds, 44), *Yolanda and the Thief, Ziegfeld Follies* (co.), *Fiesta* (47), *Song of the Thin Man* (cs), *On an Island with You, Words and Music* (co.), *Neptune's Daughter, Annie Get Your Gun, Pagan Love Song, Show Boat* (51), *The Story of Three Loves* (ds, co.), *Kiss Me Kate, Jupiter's Darling*.

**413 ROSS, HERBERT.** Broadway choreographer now active as film director and choreographer.

Films: ch. two British musicals with pop star Cliff Richard. Ch. *Carmen Jones, Doctor Dolittle*. Ch. and dir. musical sequences: *Funny Girl*. Ch. and dir. *Goodbye Mr. Chips*.

**414 ROSS, SHIRLEY** (1909–    ). RN: Bernice Gaunt. Red-headed singer-actress best remembered for her duets with Bob Hope (q.v.). Raised in Hollywood, was singing with band when offered screen test.

Films: *Hollywood Party, San Francisco* (ds), *Blossoms on Broadway, Waikiki Wedding, Hideaway Girl, Big Broadcast of 1938* (intro. "Thanks for the Memory" with Hope), *Thanks for the Memory* (cs, intro. "Two Sleepy People" with Hope), *Paris Honeymoon, Some Like It Hot* (39), *Café Society, Sailors on Leave* (cs); *A Song for Miss Julie*.

**415 ROSSON, HAROLD** (1895–    ). Photographer, active in Hollywood since 1919. Spent most of career at M-G-M, and at one time married to actress Jean Harlow.

Films: *Madam Satan* (ds), *Cuban Love Song, The Barbarian* (ds), *The Cat and the Fiddle; The Wizard of Oz; No Leave No Love, Living in a Big Way, On the Town, Singin' in the Rain, I Love Melvin,*

132

*The Story of Three Loves* (ds, co.), *Dangerous When Wet, Pete Kelly's Blues*.

**416 ROTH, LILLIAN** (1910–    ). Musical performer whose life story was told in *I'll Cry Tomorrow*. Silent film *début* when five. Returned to screen after becoming star in theatre, talkie *début* 1929.

Films: *The Love Parade, The Vagabond King* (30), *Paramount on Parade, Animal Crackers, Madam Satan* (ds), *Sea Legs, Take a Chance*.

**417 ROWLAND, ROY** (1910–    ). Director with M-G-M from early Thirties. Started as script clerk, assistant dir. on Tarzan pictures, dir. shorts inc. Pete Smith Specialties. Recently active in Italy.

Films: *Hollywood Party* (included Disney cartoon sequence); *Killer McCoy* (ds), *Two Weeks with Love, Excuse My Dust, The Five Thousand Fingers of Dr. T, Hit the Deck* (55), *Meet Me in Las Vegas/ Viva Las Vegas, The Seven Hills of Rome*.

**418 RUBY, HARRY** (1895–    ). Composer who wrote both songs and scenarios in Hollywood. Started as publishers' pianist, toured vaudeville as member of musical trio. Became staff pianist at Bert Kalmar's (q.v.) publishing firm, later teamed with him to write hit scores, including several for the Marx Brothers.

Films, with Bert KALMAR: *Animal Crackers, Check and Double Check* (inc. "Three Little Words"), *The Cuckoos* (inc. "I Love You So Much"), *Top Speed, Horse Feathers* (inc. "Everyone Says I Love You," also co-sc.), *The Kid from Spain* (inc. "What a Perfect Combination"), *Duck Soup* (also sc.), *Kentucky Kernels* (cs), *Hips Hips Hooray, Happiness Ahead, Bright Lights* (35, "She Was an Acrobat's Daughter"),

*Walking on Air, Everybody Sing; Three Little Words* (biography). With other lyricists: *Wake Up and Dream* (46, inc. "Give Me the Simple Life"), *Do You Love Me?* (title song, lyrics also), *Carnival in Costa Rica, Copacabana* ("Go West Young Man"). Co-sc. *Lovely to Look At*.

**419 RUGGLES, WESLEY** (1889–    ). Director with long but generally undistinguished career, the 1930 *Cimarron* and Mae West's *I'm No Angel* notable exceptions. Former musical comedy actor, became one of original Keystone Kops 1914, then cameraman, director.

Films: *The Street Girl, Honey, I'm No Angel* (cs), *College Humour, Bolero, Shoot the Works; Sing You Sinners* (also prod.); *My Heart Goes Crazy/London Town* (Brit.).

**420 RUICK, BARBARA** (1930–    ). Charming singer-actress briefly under contract to M-G-M in Fifties, but most notable film role as Carrie in *Carousel*.

Films: *The Affairs of Dobie Gillis, I Love Melvin, Carousel*.

**421 RUSSELL, JANE** (1921–    ). RN: Ernestine Russell. Actress who came to films amid torrent of dubious

*Rosalind Russell in GYPSY*

publicity when Howard Hughes starred her in a film banned for three years, but proved to have fine comedy touch and attractively husky singing voice. Former photographers' model.

Films: *The Paleface* (cs, intro. "Buttons and Bows" with Bob Hope q.v.), *His Kind of Woman* (ds), *Double Dynamite/It's Only Money*, *Macao* (ds), *The Las Vegas Story* (ds), *Son of Paleface* (intro. "Am I in Love?" with Hope, "Wing Ding Tonight"), *Road to Bali* (guest), *Montana Belle* (ws), *Gentlemen Prefer Blondes* (intro. "Ain't There Anyone Here for Love?"), *The French Line* (intro. "Lookin' for Trouble"), *Gentlemen Marry Brunettes*, *The Revolt of Mamie Stover* (ds, intro. "Keep Your Eyes on the Hands"), *Fate Is the Hunter* (ds, as herself).

*Jane Russell in GENTLEMEN PREFER BLONDES*

**422 RUSSELL, ROSALIND** (1911– ). Actress-comedienne who made film *début* 1934 after stage experience but came to musicals late after Broadway success in *Wonderful Town*. Tremendous vitality and application compensate for technical shortcomings in song and dance.

Films: *The Night Is Young, Reckless; The Girl Rush* (ss); *Gypsy, Rosie* (cs).

**423 RYAN, PEGGY** (1924– ). RN: Margaret Orene Ryan. Lively teenage comedienne and dancer who teamed well with Donald O'Connor (q.v.) in Universal musicals of Forties. Child performer in vaudeville. On retiring from movies, ran dancing school.

Films: *Top of the Town, She Married a Cop, Miss Annie Rooney, Private Buckaroo, Give Out Sisters, Get Hep to Love/She's My Lovely, When Johnny Comes Marching Home, Mr. Big, Top Man, Chip off the Old Block, Babes on Swing Street, Follow the Boys* (44), *This Is the Life* (44), *The Merry Monahans, Patrick the Great, Here Come the Co-Eds, That's the Spirit, On Stage Everybody; There's a Girl in My Heart; All Ashore.*

**424 SALE, RICHARD** (1911– ). Writer, director, occasional composer of generally routine fare. Prolific short story writer prior to films. Often works in collaboration with wife Mary Anita Loos.

Films: co-sc. *Calendar Girl, Campus Honeymoon* (also comp.); *Let's Do It Again* (cs), *The French Line.* Dir., co-sc. *A Ticket to Tomahawk* (cs), *I'll Get By, Meet Me after the Show, The Girl Next Door, Gentlemen Marry Brunettes* (also co-prod., comp.).

**425 SALINGER, CONRAD** ( – 1962). Brilliant arranger, perhaps more responsible than anyone for the great sound of the M-G-M orchestra during the Forties, with the use of French horns, sweepingly sensual strings and exciting up-tempo brass. His work includes the bustling wheel-rhythms of "The Trolley Song" (*Meet Me in St. Louis*), the changing tempi leading to the ferocious Spanish climax of "Nina" (*The Pirate*), the yearning romanticism of "Little Girl Blue" (*Billy Rose's Jumbo*), the last piece of music he orchestrated before his suicide.

Films: co-orch. *Strike Up the Band, Ziegfeld Girl, Lady Be Good, Babes on Broadway, You Were Never Lovelier, For Me and My Gal, Panama Hattie, Best Foot Forward.* Orch. *Girl Crazy* (43), *Meet the People, Meet Me in St. Louis, Yolanda and the Thief, The Harvey Girls.* Co-orch. *Ziegfeld Follies.* Orch. *Till the Clouds Roll By, Good News* (47), *Summer Holiday, The Pirate.* Co-orch. *Easter Parade.* Orch. *Words and Music, The Barkleys of Broadway.* Co-orch. *On the Town, Show Boat* (51). Orch. *An American in Paris.* Co-orch. *Belle of New York, Singin' in the Rain, Kiss Me Kate, Seven Brides for Seven Brothers, Funny Face, Billy Rose's Jumbo.*

**426 SANDRICH, MARK** (1900– 1945). Director who started with Lupino Lane two-reelers, is now best remembered for his five Astaire–Rogers musicals.

Films: *Melody Cruise, Cockeyed Cavaliers, The Gay Divorcee, Hips Hips Hooray, Top Hat, Follow the Fleet, Shall We Dance?, Carefree, Man about Town, Buck Benny Rides Again, Love Thy Neighbour, Holiday Inn, Here Come the Waves.*

**427 SANDS, TOMMY** (1937– ). Pop star of late Fifties, former child singer and guitarist, who made a few films.

Films: *Sing Boy Sing* (début), *Mardi Gras, Love in a Goldfish Bowl* (cs), *Babes in Toyland* (61).

**428  SAN JUAN, OLGA** (1927–    ). Singer and dancer specialising in Spanish rhythms. Radio and night club star prior to films, later played lead in Broadway's *Paint Your Wagon* 1951.

Films: *Rainbow Island* (début), *Out of This World, Duffy's Tavern, Blue Skies, Variety Girl, Are You with It?, The Countess of Monte Cristo, The Beautiful Blonde from Bashful Bend* (cs), *One Touch of Venus*.

**429  SANTLEY, JOSEPH** (1889–    ). Veteran director of low-budget films, mainly for Republic. Former child actor in vaudeville, directed shorts before first feature 1930. Also directs TV musical shows.

Films: co-dir. *The Cocoanuts*. Dir. *Swing High, Loud Speaker, Million Dollar Baby, Laughing Irish Eyes, Dancing Feet, The Smartest Girl in Town, Walking on Air, Swing Sister Swing, Melody and Moonlight, Music in My Heart, Melody Ranch, Dancing on a Dime, Puddin' Head, Sis Hopkins, Ice-Capades, Rookies on Parade/Jamboree, Yokel Boy, Call of the Canyon* (ws), *Joan of Ozarks, Chatterbox, Here Comes Elmer/Hitchhike to Happiness, Sleepy Lagoon, Thumbs Up, Rosie the Riveter, Three Little Sisters, Brazil, Earl Carroll's Vanities, Make Believe Ballroom, When You're Smiling*.

**430  SCHERTZINGER, VICTOR** (1880–1941). Director and composer, former concert violinist and musical comedy conductor. Wrote first musical score ever composed directly to accompany a film (Ince's *Civilisation* 1916). Directed British film of *The Mikado* 1939 and composed songs for most of the musicals he directed. Films: dir. and comp. *Head Up*. Dir. *Paramount on Parade* (excerpt), *Safety in Numbers*. Dir., comp. *Cocktail Hour* (ds), *One Night of Love, Beloved, Let's Live Tonight, Love Me Forever, The Music Goes Round, Something to Sing About, Rhythm on the River* ("I Don't Want to Cry Anymore"), *Road to Singapore* (40, "Captain Custard," "The Moon and the Willow Tree"). Dir. *Birth of the Blues, Road to Zanzibar*. Dir., comp. *Kiss the Boys Goodbye* (inc. "Sand in My Shoes"), *The Fleet's In* (inc. "I Remember You," "Tangerine").

**431  SCHWARTZ, ARTHUR** (1900–    ). Composer, occasional producer, who worked as lawyer for several years before full-time song-writing with Howard Dietz (q.v.) for Broadway revues inc. *The Band Wagon*. Had several collaborators in Hollywood.

Films as comp: *Follow the Leader; She Loves Me Not* (one song only interpolated into each of these), *Under Your Spell, That Girl from Paris; Navy Blues, Cairo, Thank Your Lucky Stars* (inc. "Ice Cold Katy," "How Sweet You Are," "They're Either Too Young or Too Old," "The Dreamer," "Love Isn't Born," "I'm Riding for a Fall," "Goodnight Good Neighbour," also co-st.), *The Time the Place and the Girl* (inc. "A Gal in Calico," "A Rainy Night in Rio," "Oh but I Do"); *Dancing in the Dark* (utilised score of *The Band Wagon*); *Excuse My Dust, Dangerous When Wet* (inc. "Ain't Nature Grand?," "I Got Out of Bed on the Right Side"), *The Band Wagon, Torch Song* ("Two-Faced Woman"), *You're Never Too Young* (cs). Prod. *Cover Girl, Night and Day*.

**432  SEATON, GEORGE** (1911–    ). Writer-director, occasional producer, who started as stage actor, became writer at M-G-M, later Fox. Has made every type of film.

Films: co-sc. *A Day at the Races; That Night in Rio*. Orig. sc. *Coney Island*. Dir., sc. *Diamond Horseshoe, The Shocking Miss Pilgrim*. Co-prod. *Aaron Slick from Pumkin Crick/Marshmallow Moon, Somebody Loves Me*. Dir., sc. *Little Boy Lost* (ds), *The Country Girl* (ds).

**433 SEGAL, VIVIENNE** (c. 1898– ). Singer-actress, a Broadway star for thirty years who made occasional films. Original star of stage *Desert Song* (1926) and *Pal Joey* (1941). Played *Carmen* as sixteen-year-old student, heard by Sigmund Romberg (q.v.) who starred her in operetta.

Films: *Golden Dawn* (début), *Bride of the Regiment, Song of the West, Viennese Nights; The Cat and the Fiddle*.

**434 SEILER, LEWIS** (1891–1964). Director with long, varied, but generally undistinguished output. From assistant director and gagman became director of Tom Mix westerns (silent).

Films: *Paddy O'Day, Star for a Night, The First Baby, Turn Off the Moon, It All Came True* (ds), *You're in the Army Now, Something for the Boys, Doll Face/Come Back to Me, If I'm Lucky*.

**435 SEITER, WILLIAM A.** (1891–1964). Director, former artist and writer, who started with silents.

Films: *Smiling Irish Eyes, Sunny* (30), *Girl Crazy* (32), *Hello Everybody, Diplomaniacs* (cs), *Roberta, In Person, Dimples, Stowaway, Life of the Party* (37), *This Is My Affair* (ds), *Life Begins in College, Sally Irene and Mary, Thanks for Everything, It's a Date, Nice Girl?, Broadway* (42), *You Were Never Lovelier, Four Jills in a Jeep, Belle of the Yukon, It's a Pleasure, That Night with You, Lover Come Back, I'll Be Yours, Up in Central Park, One Touch of Venus*.

**436 SHAMROY, LEON** (1901– ). Photographer, former mechanical engineer. New York-born, in Hollywood from 1927 working mainly at Fox.

Films: *Kiss and Make Up, Blossoms on Broadway, Little Old New York* (ds), *Lillian Russell, I Was an Adventuress* (co.), *Down Argentine Way* (co.), *Tin Pan Alley, That Night in Rio* (co.), *The Great American Broadcast, Moon over Miami, A Yank in the RAF, Stormy Weather, Greenwich Village, State Fair* (45), *Where Do We Go from Here?, The Shocking Miss Pilgrim, That Lady in Ermine, Cheaper by the Dozen* (cs), *On the Riviera, With a Song in My Heart, Wait Till the Sun Shines Nellie, Tonight We Sing, Down among the Sheltering Palms, Call Me Madam, The Girl Next Door, There's No Business like Show Business, Daddy Long Legs, The King and I, The Best Things in Life Are Free, The Girl Can't Help It, South Pacific, Porgy and Bess, The Blue Angel* (59), *What a Way to Go* (cs), *Skidoo* (cs).

**437 SHAW, WINNIE** (1899– ). RN: Winifred Lei Momi. Singer who starred briefly at Warners in Thirties and was featured singer in celebrated "Lullaby of Broadway" number. Child performer in parents' vaudeville act, featured in Broadway shows before Hollywood *début* 1934.

Films: *Wild Gold* (début), *Million Dollar Ransom* (ds), *The Gift of Gab, Wake Up and Dream* (34), *Sweet Adeline, Gold Diggers of Broadway* (35, intro. "Lullaby of Broadway"), *In Caliente* (intro. "Lady in Red"), *Broadway Hostess, The Singing Kid, Sons O'Guns, Smart Blonde* (ds), *Ready Willing and Able* (intro. "Too Marvellous for Words"), *Melody for Two*.

137

**438 SHELDON, SIDNEY.** Writer, occasional producer and director.

Films: co-sc. *Easter Parade.* Sc. *Nancy Goes to Rio, Annie Get Your Gun, Rich Young and Pretty* (co.), *Remains to Be Seen* (cs), *You're Never Too Young* (cs), *Anything Goes* (56, also st.), *The Birds and the Bees* (cs); *Billy Rose's Jumbo.*

**439 SHERIDAN, ANN** (1915–1967). RN: Clara Lou Sheridan. Texas-born actress given title Oomph Girl in late Thirties. Paramount contract in 1933 after beauty contest, but became star at Warners. Beauty, intelligence and a distinctively throaty voice made her an asset to the few musicals she made.

Films: *Bolero, Murder at the Vanities, Shoot the Works, College Rhythm, Rumba, Mississippi, Sing Me a Love Song, San Quentin* (ds, first singing role), *Cowboy from Brooklyn, Broadway Musketeers, Naughty but Nice, It All Came True* (ds), *Torrid Zone* (ds), *Navy Blues, Juke Girl, Thank Your Lucky Stars* (intro. "Love Isn't Born (It's Made)"), *Shine On Harvest Moon* (as vaudeville star Nora Bayes), *One More Tomorrow* (ds), *Nora Prentiss* (ds), *Take Me to Town* (cs), *The Opposite Sex.*

**440 SHERMAN, RICHARD M.** (1928–    ) and **ROBERT B.** (1925–    ). Brother song-writing team signed by Walt Disney to write scores for his films in 1960, after success as pop composers.

Films: *The Parent Trap* (cs), *Summer Magic* (inc. "The Ugly Bug Ball"), *The Sword in the Stone, Mary Poppins* (inc. 64 Oscar "Chim Chim Cher-ee," also "A Spoonful of Sugar," "Feed the Birds," "Supercaliflagilisticexpialidocious"), *The Happiest Millionaire* (inc. "Fortuosity"), *The Jungle Book, Chitty Chitty Bang Bang* (in G.B.), *The One and Only*

*Original Genuine Family Band, Bedknob and Broomstick.*

**441 SHIRLEY, ANN** (1918–    ). RN: Dawn Paris. Pretty juvenile lead of Forties, a former child star in Twenties (as Dawn O'Day) who changed her name to that of heroine of *Anne of Green Gables* after starring in film version.

Films: *Four Jacks and a Jill, Mayor of 44th Street, The Powers Girl, Music in Manhattan, Make Mine Laughs.*

**442 SHORE, DINAH** (1917–    ). RN: Frances Rose Shore. Singer with limpid mellow contralto who had own radio show 1938, brief film career in Forties. Attributes its failure to fact "I'm not particularly photogenic," but since had big success on TV.

Films: *Thank Your Lucky Stars* (début, intro. "The Dreamer," "How Sweet You Are"), *Up in Arms* (intro. "Now I Know," "Tess's Torch Song"), *Follow the Boys* (44), *Belle of the Yukon, Make Mine Music* (voice only, intro. "Two Silhouettes"), *Till the Clouds Roll By, Fun and Fancy Free* (voice only), *Aaron Slick from Pumkin Crick/Marshmallow Moon.*

**443 SIDNEY, GEORGE** (1911–    ). Director who specialised in musicals at M-G-M. Son of performers, had vaudeville and musical background when signed by M-G-M in 1932. Directed many shorts, inc. several Our Gang comedies, features from 1941. While lacking visual flair of Minnelli (q.v.) was responsible for some outstanding achievements, though overall output variable.

Films: *Thousands Cheer, Bathing Beauty, Anchors Aweigh, The Harvey Girls, Ziegfeld Follies* ("Bring on the Beautiful Girls"), *Holiday in Mexico; Annie Get Your Gun, Show Boat* (51),

*Kiss Me Kate, Jupiter's Darling, The Eddy Duchin Story, Pal Joey, Pepe, Bye Bye Birdie, Viva Las Vegas/Love in Las Vegas, The Swinger* (cs), *Half a Sixpence.*

**444 SIEGEL, SOL C.** (1903– ). Producer since early days of talkies. Started as executive producer at Republic but musically most active at Paramount, Fox and M-G-M.

Films: *Glamour Boy/Hearts in Springtime, Blue Skies, Welcome Stranger, The Perils of Pauline, My Blue Heaven, On the Riviera, Call Me Madam, Gentlemen Prefer Blondes, There's No Business like Show Business, High Society, Man on Fire* (ds), *Les Girls, Merry Andrew.*

**445 SILVERS, PHIL** (1912– ). RN: Philip Silversmith. Fast-talking comedian, former child singer, vaudevillian and burlesque performer who became typecast as the hero's best friend in a series of Forties musicals, usually for Fox. Made two-reelers in early Thirties, prior to five-year spell with Minsky's. Biggest successes on Broadway and as TV's Sergeant Bilko.

Films: *Hit Parade of 1941* (feature début), *Footlight Serenade, You're in the Army Now* (cs), *My Gal Sal, Coney Island, Cover Girl, Something for the Boys, Four Jills in a Jeep, Take it or Leave It, Diamond Horseshoe, If I'm Lucky, Where Do We Go from Here?; Summer Stock/If You Feel like Singing, Top Banana* (a quickly shot transcription of his Broadway success), *Lucky Me; A Funny Thing Happened on the Way to the Forum.*

**446 SIMS, GINNY** (c. 1917– ). RN: Virginia Simms. Former band vocalist who made a few musicals in Forties, notably *Night and Day* in which she was cast as a composite of several

Broadway stars who had introduced Cole Porter's (q.v.) songs

Films: *Playmates, Here We Go Again, Hit the Ice, Broadway Rhythm, Shady Lady, Night and Day, Disc Jockey.*

**447 SINATRA, FRANK** (1915– ). Singer-actor, former band vocalist (with Tommy Dorsey, then Harry James) who went solo 1942 and became hit with swooning 'teenagers. After tentative roles in low-budget musicals signed by M-G-M and developed acting and dancing talents while voice matured and he became regarded as major interpreter of popular song. Career hit bad patch early Fifties, but Oscar-winning performance in *From Here to Eternity* (non-musical) and superb record albums "In the Wee Small Hours" and "Songs for Young Lovers" brought new authority as top recording and film star, straight actor and later producer.

Films: *Las Vegas Nights* (début, with

Dorsey's orchestra), *Ship Ahoy, Reveille with Beverley, Higher and Higher* (first acting role, intro. "I Couldn't Sleep a Wink Last Night," "A Lovely Way to Spend an Evening"), *The House I Live In* (short about racial intolerance), *Step Lively* (intro. "Come Out, Come Out Wherever You Are"), *Anchors Aweigh* (first dancing role, coached by Gene Kelly, q.v.), *Till the Clouds Roll By, It Happened in Brooklyn* (intro. "Time after Time"), *The Kissing Bandit, Take Me Out to the Ball Game/Everybody's Cheering, On the Town, Double Dynamite/It's Only Money, Meet Danny Wilson, Three Coins in the Fountain* (voice only), *Young at Heart, Guys and Dolls* (intro. "Adelaide"), *The Tender Trap* (cs), *Meet Me in Las Vegas/Viva Las Vegas* (bit), *High Society* (intro. "You're Sensational"), *The Joker Is Wild* (ds, as comedian Joe E. Lewis), *Pal Joey* (his version of the 1939 "Lady Is a Tramp" was highlight), *A Hole in the Head* (cs, intro. "High Hopes"), *Can Can, Pepe* (guest), *Ocean's 11* (cs), *Road to Hong Kong* (guest), *Robin and the Seven Hoods* (intro. "My Kind of Town").

**448 SKELTON, RED** (1910–    ). RN: Richard Skelton. Comedian given several starring vehicles by M-G-M. Left home when twelve to join travelling show. Vaudeville led to radio as MC, writer. Was MC at Roosevelt's Birthday Ball when he attracted attention of Mickey Rooney (q.v.) who got him test at M-G-M. Noted for comic mime routines (notably "Guzzler's Gin" sketch performed in *Ziegfeld Follies*) and a major attraction on TV.

Films: *Having a Wonderful Time* (début); *Lady Be Good, Ship Ahoy, Panama Hattie, Maisie Gets Her Man* (cs), *DuBarry Was a Lady, I Dood It/By Hook or By Crook, Thousands Cheer,*

*Bathing Beauty, Ziegfeld Follies, Neptune's Daughter, The Duchess of Idaho* (guest), *Three Little Words* (as Harry Ruby, q.v.), *Excuse My Dust, Texas Carnival, Lovely to Look At; Public Pigeon Number One* (cs); *Ocean's 11* (cs, guest).

**449 SONDHEIM, STEPHEN.** Lyricist, occasional composer, who made outstanding contributions to musical theatre during Sixties and whose three biggest stage hits have been filmed.

Films: *West Side Story* (lyrics), *Gypsy* (lyrics), *A Funny Thing Happened on the Way to the Forum* (music and lyrics).

**450 SOTHERN, ANN** (1909–    ). RN: Harriette Lake. Pert blonde actress with attractive singing voice and neat comedy style. Studied music before going on stage. Broadway *début* (as Harriet Lake) in Rodgers and Hart's (q.v.) *America's Sweetheart* 1931, Hollywood *début* three years later. Had great success in series of "Maisie" comedies 1939–46.

Films: *Let's Fall in Love* (début), *Kid Millions, Melody in Spring, The Girl Friend, Sweet Music, Hooray for Love, The Smartest Girl in Town, Walking on Air, Danger Love at Work* (cs), *Maisie* (cs), *Lady Be Good, Ringside Maisie* (cs), *Panama Hattie, Maisie Gets Her Man* (cs), *Thousands Cheer, Maisie Goes to*

*Reno* (cs), *April Showers, Words and Music* (sang 1926 "Where's That Rainbow?"), *Nancy Goes to Rio.*

**451 STEELE, TOMMY** (1936–   ). RN: Tommy Hicks. British product of rock-and-roll era who successfully broadened scope and appeal. Made several low-budget musicals in Britain prior to stage success in *Half a Sixpence* which led to Hollywood.

Films: *Half a Sixpence* (in G.B.), *The Happiest Millionaire, Finian's Rainbow.*

**452 STEVENS, GEORGE** (1904–   ). Respected drama director (*A Place in the Sun, Shane*) who made two musicals with Astaire (q.v.). In Hollywood since silent days.

Films: *Kentucky Kernels* (cs), *Nitwits, Swing Time, Damsel in Distress, Vivacious Lady* (cs).

**453 STEVENS, RISE** (1915–   ). Opera singer who starred with Nelson Eddy (q.v.) in *The Chocolate Soldier*, but teaming failed to generate interest shown in Eddy's teamings with Jeanette MacDonald (q.v.).

Films: *The Chocolate Soldier, Going My Way, Carnegie Hall* (as herself).

**454 STEWART, MARTHA** (1922–   ). RN: Martha Haworth. Singer, former band vocalist, who had brief film career in Forties.

Films: *Doll Face/Come Back to Me* (début), *I Wonder Who's Kissing Her Now?, Are You with It?, Aaron Slick from Pumkin Crick/Marshmallow Moon.*

**455 STOLL, GEORGE** (1905–   ). One of M-G-M's chief conductors and music supervisors from mid-Thirties to mid-Fifties. Former violin soloist, radio music director.

Films as MD: *Broadway Melody of 1938, Listen Darling, Honolulu, Ice Follies of 1939* (w. Franz Waxman), *Babes in Arms, Andy Hardy Meets Debutante* (cs), *Go West, Strike Up the Band, Little Nelly Kelly, Two Girls on Broadway, Ziegfeld Girl, Lady Be Good, Life Begins for Andy Hardy* (cs), *The Big Store, Babes on Broadway, Ship Ahoy, Panama Hattie, For Me and My Gal, DuBarry Was a Lady, Presenting Lily Mars, Cabin in the Sky, Best Foot Forward, Girl Crazy* (43), *I Dood It/By Hook or By Crook, Swing Fever, Two Girls and a Sailor, Meet Me in St. Louis, Music for Millions, Thrill of a Romance, Anchors Aweigh, Holiday in Mexico, No Leave No Love, This Time for Keeps, Big City, On an Island with You, A Date with Judy, The Kissing Bandit, Neptune's Daughter, In the Good Old Summertime, Nancy Goes to Rio, The Duchess of Idaho, The Toast of New Orleans, Two Weeks with Love, The Strip, Skirts Ahoy, I Love Melvin, Dangerous When Wet, Easy to Love, Rose Marie* (54), *The Student Prince, Athena, Hit the Deck* (55), *Love Me or Leave Me, Meet Me in Las Vegas/Viva Las Vegas, This Could Be the Night, The Seven Hills of Rome, For the First Time, Where the Boys Are, Billy Rose's Jumbo.*

**456 STOLOFF, MORRIS** (1893–   ). Conductor and arranger with Columbia since 1936. Violinist with Los Angeles Philharmonic before joining Paramount 1928 as chorus master. Won Oscars for scoring of *Cover Girl, The Jolson Story* and *Song without End.*

Films as MD: *The Awful Truth* (cs), *I'll Take Romance, Start Cheering, Music in My Heart, Go West Young Lady, Blondie Goes Latin, You'll Never Get Rich, Blondie Goes to College* (cs), *You Were Never Lovelier, Footlight Glamour, Beautiful but Broke, Cover Girl, Carolina*

*Blues, Eadie Was a Lady, Tonight and Every Night, A Song to Remember, Gilda* (ds), *The Jolson Story, Down to Earth, Jolson Sings Again, Affair in Trinidad* (ds), *All Ashore, The Five Thousand Fingers of Doctor T, Miss Sadie Thompson, Three for the Show, My Sister Eileen, The Eddy Duchin Story, You Can't Run Away from It, Pal Joey, Song without End.*

**457  STONE, ANDREW** (1902–   ). Director-producer-writer best known for his thrillers shot entirely on location.

Films as dir: *The Great Victor Herbert* (also prod., co-st.), *There's Magic in Music, Stormy Weather, Sensations of 1945, The Bachelor's Daughters* (ds); *Song of Norway.*

**458  STORM, GALE** (1922–   ). RN: Josephine Cottle. Fresh-faced singer-actress, popular in low-budget musicals of Forties. Later TV star.

Films: *Rhythm Parade, Campus Rhythm, Nearly Eighteen, They Shall Have Faith, Sunbonnet Sue, Swing Parade of 1946, It Happened on Fifth Avenue* (cs), *Curtain Call at Cactus Creek/Take the Stage.*

**459  STRADLING, HARRY** (1901–1970). Expert photographer, British-born, who worked in Hollywood from early Forties and won Oscars for both black-and-white and colour cinematography.

Films: *Thrill of a Romance, Easy to Wed, Holiday in Mexico, Till the Clouds Roll By* (co.), *The Pirate, Easter Parade, Words and Music* (co.), *The Barkleys of Broadway, In the Good Old Summertime; Hans Christian Andersen; Guys and Dolls, The Eddy Duchin Story, The Pajama Game; Gypsy, My Fair Lady; Funny Girl, Hello Dolly!, On a Clear Day You Can See Forever.*

142

**460  STREISAND, BARBRA** (1942–   ). RN: Barbara Streisand. Singer-actress, biggest musical star to emerge during Sixties. Brooklyn-born, won talent contest in Greenwich Village bar. Night club engagements led to TV, small

but acclaimed role in Broadway show. Role of Fanny Brice (q.v.) in Broadway's *Funny Girl* set seal on stardom, film version following.

Films: *Funny Girl* (début), *Hello Dolly!, On a Clear Day You Can See Forever.*

**461  STYNE, JULE** (1905–   ). RN: Jules Stein. London-born composer in States since childhood. Concert pianist at nine, later led own dance band, did musical arrangements. Vocal coach at Fox mid-Thirties, working with Alice

Faye and Shirley Temple (qq.v.). Started composing songs for insertion into Fox musicals and comedies, then worked on minor films at Republic, including several Roy Rogers Westerns. First hit 1942 "I Don't Want to Walk without You" (lyrics by Frank Loesser, q.v.), but first long-term collaborator Sammy Cahn (q.v.). Other lyricists include Comden and Green, Leo Robin and Stephen Sondheim (qq.v.) for tuneful and literate stage and film scores.

Films: *Hold That Co-Ed, Kentucky Moonshine, Pack Up Your Troubles/We're in the Army Now, Barnyard Follies, Melody Ranch, Melody and Moonlight, Sing Dance and Plenty Hot, Puddin' Head, Angels with Broken Wings, Rookies on Parade/Jamboree* (title song only), *Sis Hopkins, Ice-Capades, Sailors on Leave, Call of the Canyon* (ws, one of several Westerns during this period), *Hi Neighbour, Sleepy Time Gal, Ice-Capades Revue, Beyond the Blue Horizon* (ds), *Johnny Doughboy, Sweater Girl* (inc. "I Don't Want to Walk without You"), *The Powers Girl, Priorities on Parade, Youth on Parade* (inc. "I've Heard That Song Before"), *Hit Parade of 1943, Salute for Three, Here Comes Elmer/Hitchhike to Happiness, Let's Face It, Swing Your Partner, Thumbs Up, Step Lively* (inc. "Come Out Come Out Wherever You Are"), *Knickerbocker Holiday, Rosie the Riveter, Jam Session* ("Victory Polka"), *Follow the Boys* (44, inc. "I'll Walk Alone"), *Janie* (cs), *Carolina Blues* (inc. "There Goes That Song Again"), *Tonight and Every Night* (inc. "Anywhere"), *Anchors Aweigh* (inc. "I Begged Her," "What Makes the Sun Set?"), *The Stork Club* ("Love Me"), *Tars and Spars, Cinderella Jones, The Kid from Brooklyn, Earl Carroll Sketch Book/Hats Off to Rhythm, The Sweetheart of Sigma Chi* (46, "Five Minutes More"), *Ladies' Man* (47), *It Happened in Brooklyn* ("Time after Time," "It's the Same Old Dream," "I Believe," "Whose Baby Are You?," "Brooklyn Bridge," "The Song's Gotta Come from the Heart"), *Glamour Girl, Romance on the High Seas/It's Magic* (inc. "It's You or No-one," "Put 'Em in a Box, Tie 'Em with a Ribbon," "Run Run Run," "It's Magic"), *Two Guys from Texas, It's a Great Feeling* (inc. "There's Nothing Rougher than Love"), *I'll Get By* (reprised his 1944 hit "It's Been a Long Long Time"), *West Point Story/Fine and Dandy* (inc. "By the Kissing Rock," "You Love Me"), *Meet Me after the Show* (inc. "I Feel like Dancing"), *Two Tickets to Broadway* (inc. "Baby You'll Never Be Sorry"), *Double Dynamite/It's Only Money* (cs), *Macao* (ds), *Gentlemen Prefer Blondes, Three Coins in the Fountain* (non-musical, 54 Oscar title tune), *Living It Up* (inc. "Money Burns a Hole in My Pocket"), *My Sister Eileen* (inc. "There's Nothing like Love," "We're Great but No-one Knows It," "A Band and My Baby"); *Bells Are Ringing; Gypsy; Funny Girl.*

**462 SUTHERLAND, EDWARD** (1895– ). Veteran British-born director best remembered for Thirties comedies with W. C. Fields. Vaudeville performer, then silent actor in serials, juvenile lead in Keystone comedies. Assistant director to Chaplin prior to solo work.

Films as co-dir: *Dance of Life, Close Harmony.* As dir: *Pointed Heels, Fast Company, Paramount on Parade* (excerpt), *The Sap from Syracuse, Palmy Days, June Moon, International House, Too Much Harmony, Mississippi, Every Day's a Holiday, The Champagne Waltz, One Night in the Tropics, The Boys from Syracuse, Sing Your Worries Away, Dixie, Follow the Boys* (44).

143

**463 TAMBLYN, RUSS** (1934–     ).
Acrobatic dancer and actor, former child
radio, stage and film performer (as Rusty
Tamblyn).

Films: *Captain Carey USA/After
Midnight* (ds); *Seven Brides for Seven
Brothers, Hit the Deck* (55), *tom thumb,
West Side Story, The Wonderful World
of the Brothers Grimm, How the West Was
Won* (ws), *Follow the Boys* (63).

**464 TASHMAN, LILLYAN** (1899–
1934). Brooklyn-born blonde star of
silents and early talkies. Stage in *Ziegfeld
Follies*, film *début* 1924.

Films: *Gold Diggers of Broadway* (29),
*No No Nanette* (30), *One Heavenly Night,
Puttin' On the Ritz, On the Level, Too
Much Harmony, Wine Women and Song,
Frankie and Johnny* (35).

**465 TAUROG, NORMAN** (1899–
). Director of generally lightweight
fare, in Hollywood from 1913. Child
actor, later directed silent comedies for
Vitagraph. Most of career with Paramount or M-G-M

Films: *Lucky Boy, Follow the Leader,
The Phantom President, A Bedtime Story,
The Way to Love, We're Not Dressing,
College Rhythm, Big Broadcast of 1936,
Rhythm on the Range, Strike Me Pink,
You Can't Have Everything, Mad about
Music, Broadway Melody* (40), *Little*

*Nelly Kelly, Presenting Lily Mars* (43),
*Girl Crazy* (43); *Big City, Words and
Music, That Midnight Kiss, The Toast of
New Orleans, Rich Young and Pretty,
Jumping Jacks* (cs), *The Stooge* (cs), *The
Stars Are Singing, The Caddy* (cs), *Living
It Up, You're Never Too Young* (cs), *The
Birds and the Bees* (cs), *Pardners* (cs),
*Bundle of Joy; G.I. Blues, All Hands on
Deck, Blue Hawaii, Girls Girls Girls, It
Happened at the World's Fair, Palm
Springs Weekend* (cs), *Tickle Me, Spinout/
California Holiday, Double Trouble,
Speedway, Live a Little Love a Little*.

**466 TEMPLE, SHIRLEY** (1928–     ).
The movies' most celebrated child star, a
remarkable, dimpled little dancer, singer,
mimic and actress whose talents were
blended with an assurance and professionalism that disarmed even those who
shied at her precocity. Daughter of Los
Angeles bank clerk, enrolled in dancing
class when three, spotted by talent scout
for series of one-real comedies "Baby
Burlesks." Persistent mother made major
studios aware of daughter's talent, small
roles in features following. Public and
critical response to number "Baby Take
a Bow" in *Stand Up and Cheer* led to Fox
contract and star vehicles. Given special
Oscar 1934 for bringing "more happiness
to millions of children and millions of
grown-ups than any child of her years in
the history of the world." Less successful
as 'teenage star, retired but for occasional
TV hosting appearances. Active in Re-
publican politics.

Films: *Bottoms Up, Carolina* (both
unbilled bits), *Stand Up and Cheer,
Change of Heart* (ds), *Little Miss Marker/
Girl in Pawn, Baby Take a Bow* (ds),
*Now and Forever* (ds), *Bright Eyes* (intro.
"On the Good Ship Lollipop"), *The
Little Colonel* (ds), *Curly Top* (intro.
"Animal Crackers in My Soup," "When

*Shirley Temple with Bill Robinson in THE LITTLEST REBEL*

I Grow Up"), *The Littlest Rebel* (included her famous staircase dance with Bill Robinson, q.v.), *Captain January* (intro. "At the Codfish Ball," also sang Sextet from *Lucia di Lammermoor* with Guy Kibbee and Slim Summerville), *Poor Little Rich Girl* (intro. "But Definitely"), *Dimples* (intro. "Picture Me without You.'), *Stowaway* (included her solo impersonation of Fred Astaire and Ginger Rogers, qq.v.), *Wee Willie Winkie* (ds), *Heidi* (ds), *Rebecca of Sunnybrook Farm* (intro. "Come and Get Your Happiness"), *Little Miss Broadway, Just around the Corner* (intro. "I Love to Walk in the Rain"), *The Little Princess* (ds), *The Bluebird, Young People* (as well as new numbers, extracts from *Curly Top* and *Stand Up and Cheer* were used in this), *Kathleen* (ds—for her one song in

this, voice was dubbed), *Miss Annie Rooney* (cs).

**467  THOMAS, DANNY** (1914–    ). RN: Amos Jacobs. Actor-comedian, former burlesque, radio and night club comic, now popular television star.

Films: *The Unfinished Dance* (début), *Big City, Call Me Mister, I'll See You in My Dreams* (his best role, as lyricist Gus Kahn, q.v.), *The Jazz Singer* (53).

**468  THOMPSON, KAY** (1902–    ). Tall, sophisticated actress-singer-writer-composer-arranger, one-time vocal coach for Judy Garland (q.v.) at M-G-M. A piano prodigy with St Louis Symphony at sixteen, became dance band vocalist, went to California 1929 with Mills Brothers, became singer and arranger with Fred Waring's orchestra. Produced own radio show, joined M-G-M 1942, working closely with Robert Alton (q.v.) on several musicals. Formed own night club act 1947 (with Alton's assistance), published successful book *Eloise* 1955.

Films as actress: *Manhattan Merry-go-round/Manhattan Music Box, Stars over Broadway; The Kid from Brooklyn; Funny Face* (intro. "Think Pink"). Comp. *Ziegfeld Follies* ("Madame Crematon" w. Roger Edens, q.v.), *No Leave No Love.* Voc. arr. *Broadway Rhythm, The Harvey Girls, The Kid from Brooklyn, Ziegfeld Follies.*

**469  THORPE, RICHARD** (1896–    ). RN: Rollo Smolt Thorpe. Versatile veteran director, former musical comedy and vaudeville performer who became film actor 1921, director 1923 with scores of silent Westerns. Most of career with M-G-M.

Films: *Rainbow over Broadway; Two Girls and a Sailor, Thrill of a Romance, Her Highness and the Bellboy* (ds), *Fiesta*

(47), *This Time for Keeps, On an Island with You, A Date with Judy, The Sun Comes Up, Three Little Words, The Great Caruso ; The Student Prince, Athena ; Ten Thousand Bedrooms, Jailhouse Rock ; Follow the Boys* (63), *Fun in Acapulco.*

**470  TIBBETT, LAURENCE** (1896–1960). One of first grand opera stars to be heard in talkies. California-born, made Metropolitan *début* 1923, two years later stopped show as Ford in *Falstaff.* Baritone voice first heard on screen in *The Rogue Song,* for which he won Oscar nomination. After Hollywood experience he was regarded as one of best actors on operatic stage.

Films : *The Rogue Song, New Moon* (30), *The Prodigal, Cuban Love Song, Metropolitan, Under Your Spell.*

**471  TORME, MEL** (1925–    ). RN : Melvin Howard Tormé. Singer-actor-composer in occasional films. Stage *début* at four, drummer with Chico Marx's band 1942. Formed superb vocal group The Mel-tones, joined Artie Shaw band, went solo 1946.

Films : *Higher and Higher* (début), *Pardon My Rhythm, Let's Go Steady, Janie Gets Married* (cs), *Night and Day, Good News, Words and Music, The Duchess of Idaho.*

**472  TROTTI, LAMAR** (1900–1952). Writer, occasional producer, who spent most of career with Fox. His scripts for directors John Ford, Henry King (q.v.) and Walter Lang (q.v.) skilfully mixed elements of patriotism, sentiment and warm Americana while avoiding stickiness. Started as newspaper writer, magazine editor. Hollywood from 1933.

Films : co-sc. *Hold That Girl, Wild Gold* (ds), *Bachelor of Arts, This Is the Life* (35). St., sc. *The First Baby.* Sc.

*Ramona.* Sc., co-st. *Can This Be Dixie,* Co-st., co-sc. *This Is My Affair* (ds), *In Old Chicago* (ds), *Alexander's Ragtime Band, Tales of Manhattan* (sequence). Prod., sc. *Mother Wore Tights, When My Baby Smiles at Me.* Prod., co-sc. *You're My Everything.* Prod., sc. *Cheaper by the Dozen* (cs). Prod. co-sc. *My Blue Heaven.* Prod., st., sc. *With a Song in My Heart.* Prod., sc. *Stars and Stripes Forever/Marching Along.* St. *There's No Business like Show Business.*

**473  TUCKER, SOPHIE** (1884–1966). RN : Sophie Abuza. Stout, lovable vaudeville performer dubbed "Last of the Red-hot Mammas," ill-served by Hollywood. Started as black-face singer.

Films : *Honky Tonk* (début), *Broadway Melody of 1938, Thoroughbreds Don't Cry ; Follow the Boys* (44, sang her trademark, the 1910 "Some of These Days"), *Sensations of 1945.*

**474  TUTTLE, FRANK** (1892–1963). Director, former continuity writer at Paramount. Started with silents.

Films : *Sweetie, Paramount on Parade* (excerpt), *Love among the Millionaires, True to the Navy, Dude Ranch, The Big Broadcast* (32), *Roman Scandals, Here Is My Heart, All the King's Horses, Two for Tonight, College Holiday, Waikiki Wedding, Doctor Rhythm, Paris Honeymoon, Charlie McCarthy Detective ; This Gun for Hire* (ds); *Suspense* (ds).

**475  VALLEE, RUDY** (1901–    ). RN : Hubert Prior Vallee. Actor-singer, former saxophonist and band-leader, who in the Thirties rivalled Crosby (q.v.) in popularity. Dubbed "The Vagabond Lover," which gave title to first film, and noted for use of megaphone. Later excelled in playing stuffy millionaires. Made several two-reelers with

146

orchestra in early Thirties.

Films: *The Vagabond Lover* (début), *Glorifying the American Girl, International House, George White's Scandals* (34), *Sweet Music, Gold Diggers in Paris, Second Fiddle, Too Many Blondes, Time Out for Rhythm, Happy Go Lucky, People Are Funny, The Beautiful Blonde from Bashful Bend* (cs); *Ricochet Romance, Gentlemen Marry Brunettes, The Helen Morgan Story/Both Ends of the Candle* (as himself); *How to Succeed in Business without Really Trying, The Night They Raided Minsky's* (cs), *Live a Little Love a Little.*

**476  VAN, BOBBY** (c. 1930–    ). RN: Robert Jack Stein. Nimble dancer-actor-choreographer, former trumpeter, who starred in Broadway revival *On Your Toes* (54), made a few films.

Films: *Skirts Ahoy, Because You're Mine, Small Town Girl, The Affairs of Dobie Gillis, Kiss Me Kate.* Ch. *Ladies' Man* (cs, 61).

**477  VAN DYKE, DICK** (1925–    ). Tall, amiable comedian-dancer who sometimes fails to project in cinema the charm he conveyed in successful TV series. Started as night club entertainer in pantomime act. Success in Broadway's *Bye Bye Birdie* led to film *début.*

Films: *Bye Bye Birdie, What a Way to Go* (cs), *Mary Poppins* (intro. "Chim-Chim Cher-ee"), *Chitty Chitty Bang Bang* (in G.B.).

**478  VAN DYKE, W. S.** (1889–1944). Director, mainly with M-G-M where his few musicals were mostly with Jeanette MacDonald (q.v.). Vaudeville and theatre before films, Griffith's assistant on *Intolerance.*

Films: *The Pagan* (ds), *Cuban Love Song; Naughty Marietta, Rose Marie* (36), *After the Thin Man* (cs), *San Francisco* (ds), *Rosalie, Sweethearts, Bitter Sweet, I Married an Angel, Cairo.*

**479  VAN HEUSEN, JAMES** (1913–    ). Composer of many hits for Bing Crosby (q.v.) during a long association with Paramount. Started as pianist and singer, composed college shows with brother of Harold Arlen (q.v.) who advised him on musical career. Worked as elevator boy prior to first hit. Paramount contract 1940.

Films, with lyricist Johnny Burke (q.v.): *Love Thy Neighbour, Playmates, Road to Zanzibar, My Favourite Spy* (42), *Road to Morocco* (inc. "Moonlight Becomes You"), *Dixie* (inc. "Sunday Monday and Always"), *Lady in the Dark* ("Suddenly It's Spring"), *Going My Way* (inc. 44 Oscar "Swinging on a Star"), *And the Angels Sing* (inc. "It Could Happen to You," "His Rocking Horse Ran Away"), *Belle of the Yukon* (inc. "Like Someone in Love," "Sleighride in July"), *The Bells of St. Mary's* ("Aren't You Glad You're You?"), *Road to Utopia* (inc. "Personality"), *Cross My Heart, London Town/My Heart Goes Crazy* (Brit.), *Welcome Stranger* (inc. "Country Style"), *Road to Rio* (inc. "But Beautiful," "You Don't Have to Know the Language"), *Mystery in Mexico, The Emperor Waltz, A Connecticut Yankee in King Arthur's Court* (inc. "Busy Doing Nothing," "If You Stub Your Toe on the Moon"), *Top O' The Morning, Riding High* (50, inc. "Sunshine Cake"), *Mr. Music* (inc. "Accidents Will Happen," "Life Is So Peculiar"), *Road to Bali, Little Boy Lost* (ds). With Mack Gordon (q.v.): *Young at Heart* ("You My Love"). With Sammy Cahn (q.v.): *The Tender Trap* (cs), *Anything Goes* (56), *The Joker Is Wild* (ds, 57 Oscar "All the Way"), *Paris Holiday* (cs), *Say One for Me, A*

Hole in the Head (cs, 59 Oscar "High Hopes"), *High Time* (inc. "The Second Time Around"), *Pocketful of Miracles* (cs), *Papa's Delicate Condition* (cs, 63 Oscar "Call Me Irresponsible"), *Robin and the Seven Hoods* (inc. "My Kind of Town," "Style"), *The Pleasure Seekers* (cs), *Thoroughly Modern Millie* ("The Tapioca" and title tune), *Star/Those Were the Happy Times* ("Star").

**480 VELEZ, LUPE** (1909–1944). RN: Guadalupe Velez de Villalobos. Tempestuous Mexican star popular in B-pictures. Father killed in revolution, became Wampas Baby Star 1928, later dubbed Mexican Spitfire.

Films: *Lady of the Pavements* (ds), *The Wolf Song, Cuban Love Song, Hot Pepper, Hollywood Party, Palooka, Strictly Dynamite; The Girl from Mexico, Playmates, Six Lessons from Madame LaZonga, Honolulu Lu, Redhead from Manhattan.*

**481 VERA-ELLEN** (1926–    ). RN: Vera-Ellen Rohe. Delightful dancer, one of most versatile in Hollywood history. Adept in tap, toe, acrobatic and dramatic dancing, and among best partners of Fred Astaire (q.v.). Started dancing when ten, became Rockette then specialty dancer. Broadway musicals in steadily bigger roles (danced with Ray Bolger, q.v., in *By Jupiter*) led to contract with Sam Goldwyn (q.v.). Dissatisfied with progress, about to return to New York when M-G-M engaged her for "Slaughter on Tenth Avenue" ballet in *Words and Music. On the Town* followed, first in a series of superb dancing roles.

Films: *Wonder Man* (début), *The Kid from Brooklyn, Love Happy, Three Little Girls in Blue, Carnival in Costa Rica,*

*Vera-Ellen as "Miss Turnstiles" in ON THE TOWN*

*Words and Music, On the Town, Three Little Words, Happy Go Lovely* (Brit.), *Belle of New York, Call Me Madam, White Christmas, Let's Be Happy* (Brit.).

**482 VERDON, GWEN** (1925–    ). RN: Gwyneth Verdon. Red-headed dancer and choreographer who, after many years in Hollywood, became star on Broadway. At six billed in vaudeville as "the world's fastest tapper," later did modelling and chorus work then became assistant to Jack Cole (q.v.). In this capacity worked in Hollywood for five years, mainly at Fox, coaching stars including Betty Grable and Marilyn Monroe (qq.v.). Often danced herself, but part sometimes cut. In 1953 auditioned for stage *Can Can* and supporting part made her star overnight.

Films: danced in: *On the Riviera, Meet Me after the Show, David and Bathsheba* (non-musical), *The Merry Widow* (52), *The I Don't Care Girl, The Farmer Takes a Wife*. Ch. and danced "Voodoo" number in *Mississippi Gambler* (53, non-musical). In above films billed as Gwyneth Verdon. Re-created Broadway starring role in *Damn Yankees/What Lola Wants*.

**483 VIDOR, CHARLES** (1900–1959). Director of Hungarian descent who made films in Germany prior to Hollywood. First film 1932.

Films: *New York Town, Cover Girl, A Song to Remember, Gilda* (ds), *Loves of Carmen* (ds); *Hans Christian Andersen, Rhapsody, Love Me or Leave Me, The Joker Is Wild* (ds), *Song without End* (started, but died during filming).

**484 WALKER, NANCY** (1922– ). RN: Anna Myrtle Swoyer. Diminutive comedienne whose career has been hampered by poor material. Daughter of acrobat, became singer and auditioned for George Abbott (q.v.) who had role of determined co-ed "Blind Date" in Broadway's *Best Foot Forward* written for her. Signed by M-G-M for film version, but greatest successes have been on Broadway.

Films: *Best Foot Forward* (début), *Girl Crazy, Broadway Rhythm* (intro. "Milkman Keep Those Bottles Quiet"); *Lucky Me*.

**485 WALSH, RAOUL** (1892– ). Director, once playwright and actor who appeared in *Birth of a Nation*. Happier with action films than musicals.

Films: *The Cockeyed World, Hot for Paris, Going Hollywood, Sailor's Luck, Every Night at Eight, Under Pressure, Klondike Annie, Hitting a New High,* *Artists and Models* (37), *College Swing/ Swing Teacher Swing, St. Louis Blues* (39), *Manpower* (ds); *The Man I Love* (ds), *Cheyenne* (ws), *One Sunday After- noon; Glory Alley* (ds); *The Revolt of Mamie Stover* (ds); *A Private's Affair*.

**486 WALTERS, CHARLES** (1911– ). Dancer and choreographer who graduated at M-G-M to directing and maintained remarkably high standard for first half-dozen musicals. Started as stage and night club dancer, made Broadway hit dancing with Betty Grable (q.v.) in *DuBarry Was a Lady*. Choreographed several Broadway shows, inc. *Let's Face It, St. Louis Woman*. Hollywood from 1942.

Films: ch. *Seven Days Leave, Pre- senting Lily Mars* (co.), *Best Foot Forward, Girl Crazy* (43), *Meet Me in St. Louis, In Hollywood, Ziegfeld Follies* (Garland sequence), *Summer Holiday*. Dir. *Good News* (47, also ch.), *Easter Parade, The Barkleys of Broadway, Sum- mer Stock/If You Feel like Singing, Texas Carnival, Belle of New York, Dangerous When Wet* (also co-ch.), *Lili* (also ch. and danced), *Torch Song* (ds, also ch. and danced as Joan Crawford's partner), *Easy to Love, The Glass Slipper, The Tender Trap* (cs), *High Society, Please Don't Eat the Daisies* (cs), *Billy Rose's Jumbo, The Unsinkable Molly Brown*.

**487 WARREN, HARRY** (1893– ). Composer active in Hollywood since 1930, three-time Oscar winner who wrote hits for Dick Powell, Alice Faye, Glenn Miller, Betty Grable, Judy Garland (qq.v.) and many others. From drummer in carnival band worked as stagehand then property man at Vitagraph studios, where he was movie extra, assistant director, provided off-stage music and in spare time composed. First hit 1923,

Warner contract 1930.

Films: *Spring Is Here, The Crooner, Roman Scandals* (inc. "Keep Young and Beautiful"), *Forty-Second Street* ("Shuffle Off to Buffalo," "You're Getting to Be a Habit with Me," "Young and Healthy," and title song), *Gold Diggers of 1933* (inc. "We're in the Money"), *Footlight Parade, Moulin Rouge, Twenty Million Sweethearts* (inc. "I'll String along with You"), *Dames* (inc. "I Only Have Eyes for You"), *Wonder Bar, Go into Your Dance* (inc. "She's a Latin from Manhattan," "About a Quarter to Nine"), *In Caliente, Gold Diggers of Broadway* (35, inc. Oscar-winning "Lullaby of Broadway"), *Broadway Gondolier* (inc. "Lulu's Back in Town"), *Shipmates Forever, Stars over Broadway* (inc. "September in the Rain"), *Colleen, Sons O'Guns, Sing Me a Love Song, Hearts Divided, Cain and Mabel, Gold Diggers of 1937* (inc. "With Plenty of Money and You"), *The Singing Marine, Mr. Dodd Takes the Air* (inc. "Remember Me?"), *Melody for Two, San Quentin* (ds), *Cowboy from Brooklyn* (title song only), *Garden of the Moon, Gold Diggers in Paris, Hard to Get* (inc. "You Must Have Been a Beautiful Baby"), *Going Places* (inc. "Jeepers Creepers"), *Naughty but Nice, Honolulu, Young People, Down Argentine Way* (inc. "Two Dreams Met"), *Tin Pan Alley, The Great American Broadcast, That Night in Rio* (inc. "I Yi Yi Yi Yi Yi"), *Weekend in Havana, Sun Valley Serenade* (inc. "I Know Why," "Chatanooga Choo-Choo," "At Last," "It Happened in Sun Valley"), *Springtime in the Rockies, Orchestra Wives* (inc. "Serenade in Blue," "I've Got a Gal in Kalamazoo"), *Song of the Islands* (title song only), *Iceland* (inc. "There Will Never Be Another You"), *Hello Frisco Hello* (inc. 43 Oscar "You'll Never Know"), *Sweet Rosie O'Grady* (inc. "My

Heart Tells Me"), *The Gang's All Here/The Girls He Left Behind* (inc. "No Love No Nothin'," "A Journey to a Star"), *Diamond Horseshoe* (inc. "The More I See You," "In Acapulco," "I Wish I Knew"), *Yolanda and the Thief* (inc. "Coffee Time"), *The Harvey Girls* (inc. 46 Oscar "The Atchison, Topeka and Santa Fe"), *Ziegfeld Follies* ("This Heart of Mine"), *Summer Holiday, The Barkleys of Broadway* (inc. "Shoes with Wings On," "You'd Be Hard to Replace," "My One and Only Highland Fling"), *My Dream Is Yours, Summer Stock/If You Feel like Singing* (inc. "You Wonderful You"), *Texas Carnival, Belle of New York* (inc. "Baby Doll," "Bachelor Dinner Song," "Oops"), *Skirts Ahoy* (inc. "What Good Is a Gal without a Guy?"), *Just for You* (inc. "Zing a Little Zong"), *The Caddy* (cs, inc. "That's Amore"), *Artists and Models* (56), *The Birds and the Bees* (cs), *Rock-a-bye Baby* (cs), *Ladies' Man* (cs, 61).

**488 WATERS, ETHEL** (1900–    ). Negro entertainer who started by singing "blue" songs (as Mama Stringbean), became star of Broadway revues. Later had success in straight parts.

Films: *On with the Show* (intro. "Am I Blue?"), *Gift of Gab; Cairo, Tales of Manhattan* (ds), *Cabin in the Sky* (intro.

*Ethel Waters with Eddie "Rochester" Anderson in CABIN IN THE SKY*

"Happiness Is a Thing Called Joe"), *Stage Door Canteen, Stormy Weather ; Member of the Wedding* (ds, re-creating her Broadway performance, sang "His Eye Is On the Sparrow").

**489   WAYNE, DAVID** (1916–   ). RN: Wayne McKeekan. Actor-singer with amusingly impudent comic approach, the original Og of Broadway's *Finian's Rainbow.* Started acting with college dramatics, joined marionette show.

Films: *Adam's Rib* (cs, intro. "Farewell, Amanda"), *My Blue Heaven, With a Song in My Heart, Wait Till the Sun Shines Nellie, The I Don't Care Girl, Down among the Sheltering Palms, To-night We Sing* (as impresario Sol Hurok), *The Tender Trap* (cs).

**490   WEBSTER, PAUL FRANCIS** (c. 1910–   ). Lyricist, in Hollywood since Thirties, responsible for many title numbers in recent years, inc. 55 Oscar *Love Is a Many-Splendored Thing* (non-musical).

Films: *Rainbow on the River, Make a Wish, Walter Wanger's Vogues of 1938, Breaking the Ice, Fisherman's Wharf ; Seven Sweethearts, Presenting Lily Mars, Hit the Ice, Ghost Catchers, Minstrel Man, Johnny Angel* (ds, "Memphis in June"), *I'll Tell the World, The Stork Club* (inc. "Doctor Lawyer and Indian Chief"), *How Do You Do?, It Happened on Fifth Avenue* (cs); *The Great Caruso* ("The Loveliest Night of the Year"), *The Merry Widow* (52), *Calamity Jane* (inc. 53 Oscar "Secret Love"), *Lucky Me* (inc. "I Speak to the Stars," "Superstition Song"), *Timberjack* (ds), *April Love, Marjorie Morningstar* (ds), *A Certain Smile* (ds, title song), *The Alamo* (ws, inc. "The Green Leaves of Summer"), *Made in Paris* (cs).

**491   WEILL, KURT** (1900–1950). German composer who worked in early years with Bertolt Brecht, fled to U.S.A. from Nazis in Thirties. German *Die Dreigroschenoper (The Threepenny Opera)* filmed twice in Europe. U.S. work (mainly for Broadway) less harsh, more lyrical.

Films: *You and Me* (ds, "The Right Guy for Me"), *Lady in the Dark, Knickerbocker Holiday, Where Do We Go from Here?* (his only full-scale score written directly for screen, with music grouped into long sections like miniature operas), *One Touch of Venus.*

**492   WEST, MAE** (1892–   ). Legendary sex-symbol of early talkies, a buxom blonde with unique come-hither style and superbly casual delivery of outrageous *double entendres.* Stage *début* as child, first Broadway revue 1911. Her play *Sex* (1926) won her prison sentence. Further plays led to Paramount contract 1932, where her first two starring films saved studio from selling out to M-G-M. Wrote all own dialogue for films, rarely musicals in true sense but usually with a few songs in her seductive Brooklyn-accented tones.

Films: *She Done Him Wrong* (based on her play *Diamond Lil,* intro. "I Wonder Where My Easy Rider's Gone," "A Guy What Takes His Time"), *I'm No Angel* (intro. "They Call Me Sister Honky Tonk"), *Belle of the Nineties* (intro. "My Old Flame"), *Goin' to Town* (intro. "Now I'm a Lady"), *Klondike Annie* (intro. "I'm an Occidental Woman"), *Go West Young Man, Every Day's a Holiday ; My Little Chickadee* (cs); *The Heat's On/ Tropicana ; Myra Breckinridge* (cs).

**493   WHELAN, TIM** (1893–1957). Director who often worked in Britain (co-dir. *Thief of Bagdad*), made minor films in U.S.A.

Films: *A Perfect Gentleman; Seven Days Leave, Higher and Higher, Step Lively, Swing Fever.*

**494 WHITE, ONNA.** Broadway choreographer who occasionally works on films.

Films: *The Music Man* (61), *Bye Bye Birdie* (w. Tom Panko), *Oliver.*

**495 WHITING, RICHARD** (1891–1938). Composer, former pianist, whose early hits "Ain't We Got Fun," "Sleepy Time Gal" and "Till We Meet Again" have often been used by movies. In Hollywood from start of talkies.

Films: *Why Bring That Up? Innocents of Paris* (inc. "Louise"), *Dance of Life, Sweetie, Paramount on Parade, Dangerous Nan McGrew, Let's Go Native, Follow Through, Monte Carlo* (inc. "Beyond the Blue Horizon"), *Safety in Numbers* (inc. "My Future Just Passed"), *Playboy of Paris* (inc. "My Ideal"), *Monkey Business, Dude Ranch, Along Came Youth* (reprised two songs from *Playboy of Paris*), *One Hour with You, Red-headed Woman, Adorable, Take a Chance, My Weakness, Bottoms Up, Bright Eyes* ("On the Good Ship Lollipop"), *She Learned about Sailors, Transatlantic Merry-go-round, Three Hundred and Sixty-five Nights in Hollywood, Hold That Girl, Here Comes Cookie, Coronado, Big Broadcast of 1936, Sing Baby Sing* ("When Did You Leave Heaven?"), *The First Baby, Rhythm on the Range, Varsity Show* (inc. "Have You Got Any Castles Baby?"), *Ready Willing and Able* (inc. "Too Marvellous for Words"), *Hollywood Hotel* (inc. "Hooray for Hollywood"), *Cowboy from Brooklyn* (inc. "Ride Tenderfoot Ride").

**496 WHORF, RICHARD** (1906–1966). Actor-director who made Broad-

way *début* 1927; Hollywood 1941, where after several years of generally serious character parts became director of musicals and comedies. Later active in TV.

Films as actor: *Blues in the Night* (début), *Yankee Doodle Dandy, Juke Girl, Christmas Holiday* (ds). As dir: *Till the Clouds Roll By, It Happened in Brooklyn, Luxury Liner.*

**497 WILLIAMS, ESTHER** (1921– ). The screen's only major swimming star whose highly-coloured, extravagant pieces of escapist entertainment were sure-fire box-office during Forties. A swimming champion at fifteen, was appearing in Billy Rose's Aquacade when spotted by M-G-M, who wanted a rival to Fox's Sonja Henie (q.v.). Long grooming period, small roles in *Andy Hardy's Double Life* and *A Guy Named Joe* (non-

musicals) led to first starring film *Bathing Beauty* which set pattern for rest of career. Developed engaging personality and became adept with comedy lines but, after final M-G-M musical, career faltered with ill-chosen dramatic parts. Now retired.

Films: *Bathing Beauty, Thrill of a Romance, Till the Clouds Roll By* (bit, as herself), *Ziegfeld Follies, Easy to Wed, Fiesta* (47), *This Time for Keeps, On an Island with You, Take Me Out to the Ball Game/Everybody's Cheering, Neptune's Daughter* (intro. "Baby It's Cold Outside"), *Duchess of Idaho, Pagan Love Song, Texas Carnival, Callaway Went Thataway/The Star Said No* (cs, as herself), *Skirts Ahoy!, Million Dollar Mermaid/The One-Piece Bathing Suit* (as earlier swimming champion and silent star Annette Kellerman), *Dangerous When Wet, Easy to Love, Jupiter's Darling.*

**498  WILSON, MARIE** (1916–       ). RN: Kathleen Elizabeth White. Endearing dumb blonde, discovered while appearing with Beverly Hills drama group in mid-Thirties. Now in night clubs and TV.

Films: *Broadway Hostess, The Great Ziegfeld, Melody for Two, Fools for Scandal, Broadway Musketeers, Rookies on Parade/Jamboree, Broadway* (42), *Music for Millions, You Can't Ration Love, Shine on Harvest Moon* (intro. "So Dumb but So Beautiful" w. Jack Carson, q.v.), *No Leave No Love, Linda Be Good, My Friend Irma* (cs), *My Friend Irma Goes West* (cs).

**499  WINNINGER, CHARLES** (1884–196 ). Character actor, in theatre from childhood, who in Hollywood musicals became the embodiment of the older generation of performers—thoroughly professional, always ready with not always appreciated advice for the younger generation, but generally able to make a triumphant return to the boards. Started in family show as youngest tap drummer in theatre. Tent shows and melodramas led to Broadway 1909. Original Cap'n Andy in stage *Show Boat*, repeated role in 1936 film version.

Films: *Children of Dreams, Flying High; Show Boat* (36), *You Can't Have Everything, Every Day's a Holiday, Three Smart Girls, You're a Sweetheart, Three Smart Girls Grow Up, Destry Rides Again* (ws), *Babes in Arms, If I had My Way, Pot of Gold, Ziegfeld Girl; Coney Island, Hers to Hold, Broadway Rhythm, Belle of the Yukon, State Fair* (45), *Living in a Big Way, Something in the Wind, Give My Regards to Broadway.*

**500  WISE, ROBERT** (1914–       ). Director of biggest-grossing musical of all time, *The Sound of Music*, though he made his reputation with horror and strong drama. Started as editor (co-edited *The Story of Vernon and Irene Castle*, edited *Seven Days Leave*) then promoted to B-picture director by RKO.

Films as dir: *Mystery in Mexico; This Could Be the Night* (producer Joe Pasternak, q.v., planned this as colour film, but Wise thought black-and-white more suitable for its tawdry night club settings). Prod., co-dir. *West Side Story.* Prod., dir. *The Sound of Music, Star/Those Were the Happy Times.*

**501  WITHERS, JANE** (1926–       ). Freckle-faced tomboy child star, the antithesis of Shirley Temple (q.v.) at Fox, who was given lower budget vehicles but won large following with her natural high spirits and normalcy. Atlanta-born, had own radio show when four billed as "Dixie's Dainty Dewdrop" and displaying sharp gift for mimicry. Mother took

153

her to Hollywood in 1932, bit parts led to David Butler (q.v.) casting her as bully to Shirley in *Bright Eyes*. Now does TV commercials, charity work.

Films: *Bright Eyes, This Is the Life* (35), *Paddy O'Day, Can This Be Dixie?, The Holy Terror* (37), *Rascals, The Boy Friend, Pack Up Your Troubles/We're in the Army Now, Shooting High* (ws), *Johnny Doughboy, My Best Gal, The Affairs of Geraldine ; The Right Approach.*

**502  WOOD, NATALIE** (1937–    ). RN: Natasha Gurdin. Former child actress even more successful as adult. An extra at four, played many child parts. First grown-up role *Rebel without a Cause* (non-musical) after which beauty and sensitive acting led to plum parts.

Films: *Never a Dull Moment* (cs, 50), *Just for You* (child parts); *Marjorie Morningstar* (ds), *All the Fine Young Cannibals* (ds), *West Side Story, Gypsy* (as Gypsy Rose Lee q.v.), *The Great Race* (cs), *Inside Daisy Clover* (ds).

**503  WRUBEL, ALLIE** (1905–    ). Composer, former saxophonist with Paul Whiteman's orchestra, given Warner contract 1934.

Films: *Bright Lights* (31), *Happiness Ahead, Dames* ("Try to See It My Way"), *Flirtation Walk, Sweet Music, We're in the Money* (cs), *In Caliente* (inc. "The Lady in Red"), *Broadway Hostess, Bright Lights* (35), *I Live for Love ; Life of the Party* (37), *Music for Madame, Radio City Revels ; Private Buckaroo* (title song only); *Sing Your Way Home* (inc. "I'll Buy That Dream"), *Make Mine Music* ("Johnny Fedora and Alice Blue Bonnet"), *Swing Parade of 1946, Song of the South* (inc. 46 Oscar "Zip-a-Dee-Doo-Dah"), *The Fabulous Dorseys, Melody*

*Natalie Wood in GYPSY*

154

*Time, I Surrender Dear; Never Steal Anything Small.*

**504  WYMAN, JANE** (1914–    ). RN: Sarah Jane Fulks. Actress equally accomplished in drama or musical comedy. Former radio singer (as Jane Durrell), auditioned for Leroy Prinz (q.v.) in 1934 and given Warner contract. Decade of minor roles followed, usually as wise-cracking chorus girl or heroine's bestfriend. After Oscar for *Johnny Belinda* (non-musical) alternated between suffering ladies and musical comedy heroines.

Films: *King of Burlesque, Cain and Mabel, Smart Blonde* (ds), *Gold Diggers of 1937, The King and the Chorus Girl, Ready Willing and Able, The Singing Marine, Mr. Dodd Takes the Air, Fools for Scandal, Tail Spin* (ds), *Kid Nightingale, You're in the Army Now, My Favourite Spy* (42), *Footlight Serenade, Hollywood Canteen, One More Tomorrow* (ds), *Night and Day, Cheyenne* (ws), *It's a Great Feeling* (guest), *Starlift, Here Comes the Groom, Just for You, Let's Do It Again* (cs).

**505  WYMORE, PATRICE** (1926–   ). Tall dancer-comedienne, former child performer, model and Broadway understudy, signed by Warners 1950, but film career disappointingly brief despite captivating personality and dancing skill.

Films: *Tea for Two* (début), *Starlift, I'll See You in My Dreams, She's Working Her Way through College, She's Back on Broadway.*

**506  YARBOROUGH, JEAN** (1900–   ). Director, former prop man with Hal Roach, who spent entire career making second features, though often with acceptable musical sequences.

Films: *Top Sergeant Mulligan, Follow the Band, Hi Ya Sailor, Get Going, Weekend Pass, Moon over Las Vegas, South of Dixie, Twilight on the Prairie, In Society, Under Western Skies* (ws), *The Naughty Nineties* (cs), *On Stage Everybody, Cuban Pete; Holiday in Havana, Casa Manana, Jack and the Beanstalk, Lost in Alaska* (cs).

**507  YOUMANS, VINCENT** (1898–1946). Broadway composer who wrote rarely for screen though his *No No Nanette* and *Hit the Deck* have each been filmed twice, while *Tea for Two* utilised many songs from the former. Son of New York hatmaker, was an accomplished pianist who composed in spare time until John Philip Sousa helped to popularise a Youman's march that was to become "Hallelujah."

Films: *No No Nanette* (30, 40), *Hit the Deck* (30, 55), *Song of the West, Flying down to Rio* (inc. "The Carioca," "Music Makes Me," "Orchids in the Moonlight"), *Take a Chance.*

**508  YOUNG, ALAN.** RN: Angus Young. British-born radio and TV comedian occasionally in films. Formerly a cartoonist, he became comedian in Canada.

Films: *Margie* (début); *Aaron Slick from Pumkin Crick/Marshmallow Moon; Gentlemen Marry Brunettes; tom thumb; The Wonderful World of the Brothers Grimm.*

**509  ZORINA, VERA** (1917–   ). RN: Eva Brigitte Hartwig. Ballet dancer, German-born, who at fourteen partnered Anton Dolin in London. Musical comedy success led to films.

Films: *Goldwyn Follies, On Your Toes* (re-creating role she played in London stage version); *Louisiana Purchase* (re-creating Broadway role), *Star Spangled Rhythm, Follow the Boys* (44), *Lover Come Back* (46).

# Index

Because You're Mine (1952) 196; 51, 60, 190, 267, 362, 476.

Bedknob and Broomstick (Robert Stevenson 1970) 266, 440.

Bedtime Story, A (1933) 465, 74, 387, 404.

Behind the Eight Ball (William Morgan 1942) 116, 126, 398.

Belle of New York (1952) 486; 6, 16, 118, 139, 163, 177, 326, 364, 399, 425, 481, 487.

Belle of the Nineties (1934) 317; 24, 86, 232, 492.

Belle of the Yukon (1944) 435; 56, 222, 393, 442, 479, 499.

Belles on Their Toes (1952) 282; 63, 88, 144.

Bells Are Ringing (1960) 331; 80, 160, 163, 219, 308, 382, 461.

Bells of St. Mary's, The (1945) 317; 56, 90, 121, 479.

Beloved (1934) 430; 40, 411.

Benny Goodman Story, The (Valentine Davies 1956) 24, 104, 174, 303.

Bernadine (1957) 282; 42, 172, 326.

Best Foot Forward (1943) 58; 4, 15, 22, 24, 28, 37, 46, 113, 123, 124, 153, 163, 171, 209, 309, 425, 455, 484, 486.

Best of Enemies (Rian James 1933) 408.

Best Things in Life Are Free, The (1956) 95; 3, 52, 82, 96, 100, 117, 144, 214, 301, 350, 436.

Best Years of Our Lives, The (William Wyler 1946) 63, 316.

Betty Co-Ed (1946) 128; 241, 372, 402.

Beyond the Blue Horizon (Alfred Santell 1942) 195, 260, 287, 394, 461.

Be Yourself (1930) 165; 49, 387.

Big Beat, The (Will Cowan 1958) 24, 85, 286, 303.

Big Boy (1930) 91; 129, 234.

Big Broadcast, The (1932) 474; 44, 90, 387, 404.

Big Broadcast of 1936 (1935) 465; 90, 143, 328, 353, 383, 387, 404, 405, 495.

Big Broadcast of 1937 (1936) 273; 23, 387, 390, 404.

Big Broadcast of 1938 (1938) 273; 193, 220, 260, 387, 390, 404, 414.

Big City (1948) 465; 123, 170, 343, 354, 362, 381, 455, 467.

Big City Blues (1932) 278; 38.

Big Pond, The (Hobart Henley 1930) 74, 145.

Big Store, The (1941) 392; 15, 28, 312, 355, 455.

Big Street, The (Irving Reis 1942) 22, 177, 394.

Bikini Beach (William Asher 1964) 18, 167.

Billy Rose's Jumbo (1962) 486; 31, 104, 112, 133, 202, 362, 390, 406, 425, 438, 455.

Birds and the Bees, The (1948) See *Three Daring Daughters*.

Birds and the Bees, The (1956) 465; 68, 85, 173, 438, 487.

Birth of the Blues (1941) 430; 8, 24, 90, 117, 121, 310.

Bitter Sweet (1940) 478; 85, 105, 138, 238, 298.

Black Tights (Terence Young 1959) 23, 73, 74.

Blessed Event (1932) 115; 129, 374.

Blonde Crazy (1931) 115; 38, 59.

Blonde from Brooklyn (1945) 291.

Blonde Venus (Josef von Sternberg 1932) 119, 404.

Blondie Goes Latin (Frank B. Strayer 1941) 193, 456.

Blondie Goes to College (Frank B. Strayer 1942) 36, 60, 72, 361, 456.

Blondie of the Follies (1932) 185; 108, 133, 163.

Blondie's Blessed Event (Frank B. Strayer 1942) 60, 72.

Bloodhounds of Broadway (Harmon Jones 1952) 173, 191, 230.

Blossoms on Broadway (Richard Wallace 1937) 287, 387, 404, 414, 436.

Cruisin' Down the River (1953) 385; 126, 140,208.

Cuban Love Song (1931) 478; 133, 151, 322, 415, 470, 480.

Cuban Pete (1946) 506.

Cuckoos, The (Paul Sloane 1930) 239, 418.

Curly Top (1935) 93; 40, 124, 214, 253, 466.

Curtain Call at Cactus Creek/Take the Stage (1950) 259; 356, 458.


Daddy Long Legs (Jean Negulesco 1955) 16, 23, 24, 64, 144, 326, 349, 436.

Dames (1934) 142; 31, 38, 129, 145, 244, 374, 391, 487, 503.

Damn Yankees/What Lola Wants (1958) 1, 123; 158, 213, 482.

Damsel in Distress (1937) 452; 16, 28, 33, 175, 176, 360.

Dance Band (Marcell Barnell 1935) 408.

Dance Fools Dance (1931) 29; 89, 141, 151, 322, 412.

Dance Girl Dance (Dorothy Arzner 1940) 22.

Dance Hall (Irving Pichel 1941) 261.

Dance of Life (co-dir. John Cromwell 1929) 462 (co.); 66, 86, 280, 404, 495.

Dance Team (1932) 263; 131.

Dance With Me Henry (1956) 26.

Dancing Co-Ed (S. Sylvan Simon 1939) 24.

Dancing Feet (1936) 429.

Dancing in the Dark (Irving Reis 1949) 105, 120, 230, 349, 431.

Dancing Lady (1933) 276; 2, 16, 25, 89, 138, 151, 202, 262, 322, 406.

Dancing on a Dime (1941) 429; 98, 262, 287, 358.

Dancing Pirate, The (Lloyd Corrigan 1936) 202, 349, 406.

Dancing Sweeties (1930) 142; 129.

Danger Love at Work (1937) 378; 182, 195, 394, 450.

Dangerous Nan McGrew (Malcolm St.

Clair 1930) 145, 240, 404, 495.

Dangerous When Wet (1953) 486; 11, 67, 192, 252, 258, 311, 326, 415, 431, 455, 497.

Darling Lili (1970) 140; 9, 303, 326.

Date with Judy, A (1948) 469; 2, 15, 24, 116, 123, 252, 322, 332, 362, 376, 455.

Daughter of Rosie O'Grady, The (1950) 57; 27, 205, 301, 347, 395.

Day at the Races, A (Sam Wood 1937) 28, 102, 139, 184, 235, 261, 432.

Days of Glory (Jacques Tourneur 1944) 23.

Deep in My Heart (1954) 123; 73, 77, 82, 101, 118, 139, 243, 245, 292, 312, 329, 376, 410.

Delicious (1931) 57; 148, 172, 175, 176.

Delightfully Dangerous (Arthur Lubin 1945) 337, 376.

Demoiselles de Rochefort, Les/Young Girls of Rochefort (Jacques Demy 1966) 69, 97, 245.

Deputy Marshall (William Berke 1949) 265.

Desert Song, The (1929) 115; 40, 197, 410.

Desert Song, The (1944) 155; 197, 213, 305, 340, 383, 410.

Desert Song, The (1953) 223; 188, 197, 213, 301, 324, 410.

Designing Woman (1957) 331; 5, 78, 187, 382.

Desire (1936) 43; 119, 218, 404.

Destry Rides Again (1939) 307; 67, 119, 218, 287, 327, 333, 362, 499.

Devil Is a Woman, The (Josef von Sternberg 1935) 119, 387, 404.

Devil May Care (Sidney Franklin 1929) 351.

Diamond Horseshoe (1945) 432; 171, 183, 186, 208, 349, 360, 445, 487.

Dimples (1936) 435; 253, 322, 405, 466.

Dinner at Eight (1933) 92; 104, 151, 322.

Diplomaniacs (1933) 435.

Disc Jockey (Will Jason 1951) 24, 446.

Dixiana (Luther Reed 1930) 103.

163

Foreign Affair, A (Billy Wilder 1948) 119, 218.

Forest Rangers (1942) 307; 210, 218, 287, 300.

Forever Darling (1956) 196; 22, 60.

For Me and My Gal (1942) 31; 15, 28, 104, 139, 153, 163, 169, 245, 343, 385, 425, 455.

For the First Time (Rudolph Maté 1959) 267, 455.

For the Love of Mary (Frederick De-Cordova 1948) 104, 134.

Forty Little Mothers (1940) 31; 62.

Forty-Second Street (1933) 19; 31, 103, 129, 244, 327, 369, 374, 409, 487.

Four Jacks and a Jill (Jack Hively 1941) 41, 206, 394, 441.

Four Jills in a Jeep (1944) 435; 2, 24, 149, 186, 208, 230, 261, 322, 332, 390, 445.

Fox Movietone Follies (1929) 57; 84, 186.

Frankie and Johnny (1935) 17; 203, 341, 464.

Frankie and Johnny (Frederick De-Cordova 1966) 379.

Freddie Steps Out (1946) 128; 241, 377.

French Line, The (1954) 19; 37, 345, 421, 424.

Freshman Year, The (1938) 319; 287, 337.

Frisco Sal (George Waggner 1945) 159.

From Hell to Heaven (Earle C. Kenton 1933) 86, 232, 353.

Frontier Gal (1945) 259.

Fun and Fancy Free (Cartoon 1947) 11, 105, 141, 442.

Fun in Acapulco (1963) 469; 147, 379.

Funny Face (1957) 123; 16, 118, 139, 175, 176, 216, 237, 292, 311, 425, 468.

Funny Girl (William Wyler 1968) 143, 275, 388, 413, 459, 460, 461.

Funny Thing Happened on the Way to the Forum, A (Richard Lester 1966) 445, 449.

Gaby (Curtis Bernhardt 1956) 23, 64, 181, 406.

Gaily Gaily/Chicago Chicago (Norman Jewison 1969) 303.

Gals Incorporated (1943) 182; 217.

Gang's All Here, The/The Girls He Left Behind (1943) 31; 24, 88, 149, 192, 332, 404, 487.

Garden of the Moon (1938) 31; 326, 363, 487.

Gay City, The. See *Las Vegas Nights.*

Gay Desperado, The (1936) 302; 296, 349.

Gay Divorcee, The/The Gay Divorce (1934) 426; 16, 33, 84, 183, 184, 186, 360, 371, 394, 409.

Gay Purr-ee (Cartoon 1963) 11, 13, 169, 199.

Gay Ranchero, The (William Witney 1948) 162, 193.

Gay Senorita, The (1946) 128; 146.

Gazebo, The (1960) 307; 395.

Gene Krupa Story, The/Drum Crazy (Don Weis 1958) 24.

Gentlemen Marry Brunettes (1955) 424; 78, 88, 177, 384, 421, 475, 508.

Gentlemen Prefer Blondes (1953) 207; 2, 63, 69, 78, 177, 335, 404, 421, 444, 461.

George White's Scandals (1934) 165; 124, 133, 141, 149, 214, 389, 401, 475.

George White's Scandals of 1935 (George White 1935) 131, 141, 149, 375.

George White's Scandals of 1945 (Felix E. Feist 1945) 24, 109, 145, 195.

Geraldine (R. G. Springsteen 1954) 65.

Get Going (1943) 506; 358.

Get Hep to Love/She's My Lovely (1942) 259; 162, 228, 356, 358, 388, 423.

Ghost Catchers (1944) 76; 228, 394, 490.

G.I. Blues (1960) 465; 379, 384.

Gift of Gab (Karl Freund 1934) 84, 143, 437, 488.

Gigi (1958) 331; 64, 74, 163, 288, 382.

G.I. Jane (Reginald Le Borg 1951) 372.

Gilda (1946) 483; 78, 211, 402, 456.

Girl Can't Help It, The (Frank Tashlin 1956) 436.

Girl Crazy (1932) 435; 175, 176, 191.

Girl Crazy (1943) 465; 4, 24, 31, 124, 139, 153, 163, 169, 175, 176, 411, 425, 455, 484, 486.

Girl Friend, The (1935) 58; 195, 232, 238, 450.

Girl from Mexico (1939) 182; 480.

Girl from Missouri, The (Jack Conway 1934) 120, 122, 237.

Girl Happy (Boris Sagal 1965) 362, 379.

Girl in Pawn. See *Little Miss Marker*.

Girl Most Likely, The (1958) 273; 37, 70, 309, 367, 376.

Girl Next Door, The (1953) 424; 11, 96, 111, 183, 205, 275, 345, 436.

Girl of the Golden West, The (1938) 276; 105, 137, 138, 141, 238, 298, 410.

Girl of the Year. See *The Petty Girl*.

Girl Rush, The (1944) 125; 265.

Girl Rush, The (Robert Pirosh 1955) 6, 37, 69, 104, 113, 121, 258, 309, 422.

Girls Girls Girls (1962) 465; 379.

Girls He Left Behind, The. See *The Gang's All Here*.

Girl without a Room (1933) 344; 148, 389.

Give a Girl a Break (1954) 123; 70, 72, 94, 158, 176, 181, 382, 395.

Give Me a Sailor (1938) 352; 186, 220, 387, 390, 404.

Give My Regards to Broadway (1948) 19; 96, 499.

Give Out Sisters (1942) 76; 10, 96, 122, 356, 388, 423.

Give Us This Night (1936) 196; 197.

Glamour Boy/Hearts in Springtime (1941) 344; 147, 159, 287, 444.

Glamour Girl (1948) 128; 24, 60, 241, 402, 461.

Glass Slipper, The (1955) 486; 23, 64.

Glenn Miller Story, The (1954) 304; 4, 14, 24, 104, 174, 265, 303.

Glorifying the American Girl (Millard Webb 1929) 62, 122, 199, 341, 475.

Glory (1956) 57; 192, 354.

Glory Alley (1952) 485; 14, 64.

Going Highbrow (1935) 155; 61, 246.

Going Hollywood (1933) 485; 53, 90, 108, 156, 163, 246.

Going My Way (1944) 317; 90, 121, 453, 479.

Going Places (1938) 142; 14, 326, 374, 487.

Going Steady (Fred F. Sears 1958) 241.

Goin' to Town (1935) 196; 86, 145, 492.

Go into Your Dance (1935) 31, 315; 83, 129, 234, 244, 246, 341, 369, 487.

Gold Diggers in Paris (1938) 142; 31, 129, 261, 369, 475, 487.

Gold Diggers of Broadway (1929) 115; 129, 365, 464.

Gold Diggers of Broadway (1935) 31; 129, 374, 437, 487.

Gold Diggers of 1933 (1933) 278; 31, 38, 129, 244, 369, 374, 409, 487.

Gold Diggers of 1937 (1936) 19; 13, 31, 38, 129, 199, 213, 374, 487, 504.

Golden Dawn (1930) 142; 197, 433.

Golden Earrings (1947) 273; 119, 147.

Golden Girl (1951) 19; 27, 111, 150, 173, 230, 327.

Goldwyn Follies (1938) 307; 21, 23, 130, 175, 176, 180, 289, 349, 393, 398, 509.

Goodbye Mr. Chips (1969) 413; 75.

Good News (Nick Grinde & Edgar J. McGregor 1930) 52, 117, 141, 214, 293.

Good News (1947) 486; 4, 37, 52, 80, 117, 139, 163, 209, 214, 268, 309, 320, 425, 471.

Go West (1940) 58; 28, 46, 65, 94, 139, 238, 455.

Go West Young Lady (Frank B. Strayer 1941) 60, 72, 329, 456.

Go West Young Man (Henry Hathaway 1936) 56, 232, 492.

Grace Moore Story, The. See *So This Is Love*.

Gracie Allen Murder Case, The (1939) 189; 287.

He Laughed Last (1956) 140; 257.

Helen Morgan Story, The/Both Ends of the Candle (1957) 95; 39, 143, 213, 247, 322, 383, 475.

Hell Bound (1931) 264; 79.

Hello Dolly (1969) 245; 14, 139, 209, 249, 271, 459, 460.

Hello Everybody (1933) 435; 86, 232.

Hello Frisco Hello (1943) 223; 25, 149, 183, 206, 353, 363, 487.

Hellzapoppin' (1941) 373; 68, 116, 162, 358, 390.

Here Comes Cookie (William LeBaron 1935) 404, 495.

Here Comes Elmer/Hitchhike to Happiness (1943) 429; 60, 461.

Here Comes the Band (Paul Sloane 1935) 2, 54, 122, 262.

Here Comes the Groom (Frank Capra 1951) 14, 27, 63, 90, 99, 200, 260, 286, 326, 504.

Here Come the Co-Eds (Edgar Fairchild 1945) 423.

Here Come the Girls (Claude Binyon 1953) 68, 77, 220, 286, 312.

Here Come the Waves (1944) 426; 13, 90, 121, 225, 326.

Here Is My Heart (1934) 474; 90, 387, 404.

Here's to Romance (1935) 189; 84.

Here We Go Again (1942) 136; 394, 446.

Her Highness and the Bellboy (1945) 469; 4, 326, 362.

Her Jungle Love (George Archainbaud 1938) 260, 387, 393, 404.

Her Kind of Man (Frederick DeCordova 1946) 357.

Her Majesty Love (William Dieterle 1931) 330.

Hers to Hold (Frank Ryan 1943) 134, 322, 499.

He's My Guy (1943) 76; 109.

Hey Rookie (1944) 26; 123, 329, 361.

Hi Beautiful (1944) 182.

Hi Buddy (Harold Young 1943) 116, 358.

Hideaway Girl (George Archainbaud 1937) 86, 164, 262, 390, 414.

Hi Gaucho (Tommy Atkins 1936) 65.

Higher and Higher (1943) 493; 2, 105, 195, 202, 321, 322, 406, 447, 471.

High School Hero (1946) 128; 241, 377.

High Society (1957) 486; 14, 72, 90, 371, 444, 447.

High Society Blues (1930) 57; 148, 172.

High Time (1960) 140; 60, 90, 303, 479.

High Wide and Handsome (1937) 302; 132, 197, 247, 260.

Hi Good Lookin' (1944) 285; 24, 116, 217.

Hi Neighbour (1942) 259; 461.

Hips Hips Hooray (1934) 426; 184, 186, 239, 418.

His Butler's Sister (1943) 43; 85, 134.

His Kind of Woman (John Farrow 1951) 2, 86, 322, 421.

Hitchhike to Happiness. See *Here Comes Elmer*.

Hit Parade, The (Gus Meins 1937) 24, 265, 391.

Hit Parade of 1941, The (1940) 17; 21, 246, 265, 329, 445.

Hit Parade of 1943, The (1943) 407; 2, 24, 65, 210, 461.

Hit Parade of 1947, The (1947) 319; 2, 322, 337.

Hit Parade of 1951, The (1950) 17; 65.

Hit the Deck (Luther Reed 1930) 353, 404, 507.

Hit the Deck (1955) 417; 101, 177, 281, 295, 312, 329, 360, 362, 376, 395, 404, 455, 463, 507.

Hit the Hay (1945) 291; 61.

Hit the Ice (1943) 259; 394, 446, 490.

Hitting a New High (1937) 485; 2, 322, 353, 370.

Hi'Ya Chum (Harold Young 1943) 116, 162, 358, 398.

Hi'Ya Sailor (1943) 506.

Hold Everything (1930) 115; 129.

Hold On (Arthur Lubin 1966) 241.

It Happened at the World's Fair (1963) 465; 379.

It Happened in Brooklyn (1947) 496; 60, 94, 124, 133, 188, 190, 268, 275, 321, 367, 447, 461.

It Happened on Fifth Avenue (1947) 115; 394, 458, 490.

It Happened to Jane (1959) 385; 112, 274.

It's a Date (1940) 435; 134, 164, 362.

It's a Great Feeling (1949) 57; 60, 67, 89, 112, 213, 340, 383, 461, 504.

It's a Great Life (Sam Wood 1929) 145.

It's Always Fair Weather (1955) 123, 245; 73, 80, 96, 163, 187, 249, 382.

It's a Pleasure (1945) 435; 122, 215, 393.

It Should Happen to You (1954) 92; 219, 268, 274.

It's Magic. See *Romance on the High Seas*.

It's Only Money. See *Double Dynamite*.

It Started with Eve (1941) 255; 134, 224, 362.

I've Always Loved You. See *Concerto*.

I Wake Up Screaming/Hot Spot (1941) 223; 186, 261, 349.

I was an Adventuress (1940) 389; 23, 436.

I Wonder Who's Kissing Her Now? (1947) 19; 82, 205, 230, 347, 349, 359, 454.

Jack and the Beanstalk (1952) 506.

Jailhouse Rock (1957) 469; 379.

Jamboree (1944). See *Rookies on Parade*.

Jam Session (1944) 26; 14, 24, 60, 123, 329, 461.

Janie (1944) 95; 60, 461.

Janie Gets Married (Vincent Sherman 1946) 279, 471.

Jazz on a Summer's Day (Bert Stern 1959) 14, 24.

Jazz Singer, The (1927) 91; 32, 143, 234, 333.

Jazz Singer, The (1953) 95; 145, 213, 270, 383, 467.

Jet Set, The (William Asher 1965) 18.

Jimmy and Sallie (James Tinling 1933) 131.

Jitterbugs (Mal St. Slair 1943) 35.

Joan of Ozarks (1942) 429; 61, 160, 394.

Johnny Angel (1945) 306; 63, 386, 490.

Johnny Apollo (Henry Hathaway 1940) 182, 260, 287, 349.

Johnny Doughboy (1942) 17; 5, 47, 60, 461, 501.

Johnny Holiday (Willis Goldbeck 1950) 63.

Joker Is Wild, The (1957) 483; 60, 88, 143, 173, 447, 479.

Jolson Sings Again (1950) 282; 143, 234, 361, 456.

Jolson Story, The (1947) 189; 72, 78, 143, 234, 248, 361, 456.

Josette (1938) 136; 7, 109, 183, 256, 394.

Joy of Living (Tay Garnett 1938) 22, 132, 151, 247.

Jubilee Trail (Joseph Kane 1954) 279.

Juke Box Jennie (Harold Young 1942) 217.

Juke Box Rhythm (1959) 128; 85, 230, 241, 396.

Juke Girl (Curtis Bernhardt 1942) 439, 496.

Jumbo. See *Billy Rose's Jumbo*.

Jumping Jacks (1952) 465; 308.

June Moon (1931) 462; 353.

Jungle Book, The (Cartoon 1968) 11, 200, 440.

Jungle Princess, The (William Thiele 1936) 218, 260, 404.

Junior Prom (1946) 128; 377.

Jupiter's Darling (1955) 443; 70, 72, 243, 252, 360, 412, 497.

Just around the Corner (1938) 93; 109, 148, 256, 405, 466.

Just for You (1952) 352; 90, 404, 487, 502, 504.

Just Imagine (1930) 57; 52, 117, 214, 359.

Kansas City Kitty (1944) 291; 24, 72, 109, 123, 162.

Louisiana Hayride (1944) 26; 61, 72, 224.
Louisiana Purchase (1941) 93; 32, 121, 124, 127, 220, 509.
Love Affair (1939) 317; 13, 33, 132.
Love among the Millionaires (1930) 474; 191.
Love and Hisses (1937) 263; 24, 68, 109, 183, 256, 394.
Love and Learn (Frederick DeCordova 1947) 67, 357.
Love Comes Along (Rupert Julian 1930) 103, 280.
Love Finds Andy Hardy (George B. Seitz 1938) 139, 169, 183, 295, 394, 411.
Love Happy (David Miller 1949) 226, 313, 335, 481.
Love in a Goldfish Bowl (Jack Sher 1961) 427.
Love in Bloom (1935) 352; 183, 394.
Love in Las Vegas. See *Viva Las Vegas*.
Love in the Rough (1930) 392; 151, 322.
Love Live and Laugh (William K. Howard 1929) 230.
Lovely to Look at (1937). See *Thin Ice*.
Lovely to Look at (1952) 278; 15, 70, 72, 94, 156, 188, 243, 329, 331, 360, 418, 448.
Love Me Forever (1935) 430; 238, 338.
Love Me or Leave Me (1955) 483; 59, 60, 112, 143, 275, 362, 455.
Love Me Tender (Robert Webb 1956) 105, 379.
Love Me Tonight (1932) 302; 74, 202, 298, 406.
Love on Toast (E. A. Dupont 1938) 21, 86, 262, 363.
Love Parade, The (1929) 294; 54, 74, 298, 416.
Lover Come Back (1946) 435; 22, 509.
Lover Come Back (Delbert Mann 1962) 112.
Loves of Carmen, The (1948) 483; 211.
Love Thy Neighbour (1940) 426; 98, 310, 469.
Loving You (Hal Kanter 1957) 379.

Lucky Boy (co-dir. Charles C. Wilson 1929) 465 (co.); 230.
Lucky Days. See *Sing a Jingle*.
Lucky Legs (1943) 26; 146.
Lucky Me (1954) 124; 112, 145, 160, 213, 383, 445, 484, 490.
Lullaby of Broadway (1951) 57; 112, 213, 347, 383.
Lulu Belle (Leslie Fenton 1948) 260, 402.
Luxury Liner (1948) 496; 325, 362, 367, 376.

Macao (Josef von Sternberg 1952) 404, 421, 461.
Mad about Music (1938) 465; 2, 134, 322, 362.
Madam Satan (Cecil B. DeMille 1930) 415, 416.
Made in Paris (Boris Sagal 1966) 12, 145, 362, 490.
Magic Fire (William Dieterle 1956) 82.
Ma, He's Making Eyes at Me (Harold Schuster 1940) 337.
Main Attraction, The (Daniel Petrie 1962) 42.
Main Street to Broadway (Tay Garnett 1953) 197, 201, 290, 310, 406.
Maisie (1939) 306; 450.
Maisie Gets Her Man (1942) 115; 139, 209, 448, 450.
Maisie Goes to Reno (1944) 29; 145, 164, 168, 450.
Make a Wish (Kurt Neumann 1937) 47, 490.
Make Believe Ballroom (1949) 429; 24, 257, 402.
Make Mine Laughs (Richard Fleischer 1949) 41, 109, 111, 195, 265, 441.
Make Mine Music (Cartoon 1946) 10, 11, 24, 105, 138, 442, 503.
Mammy (1930) 95; 32, 232, 234.
Man about Town (1939) 426; 186, 200, 218, 260, 287.
Man Called Adam, A (Leo Penn 1968) 14, 110.

Man from the Folies Bergere. See *Folies Bergere.*

Manhattan Angel (1949) 128; 228.

Manhattan Heartbeat (David Burton 1943) 109.

Manhattan Merry-go-round/Manhattan Music Box (1937) 392; 135, 391, 468.

Manhattan Music Box. See *Manhattan Merry-go-round.*

Manhattan Parade (1932) 19; 13, 253.

Man I Love, The (1947) 485; 296.

Man on Fire (Ranald MacDougall 1957) 90, 444.

Manpower (1941) 485; 119, 218, 287.

Man Who Knew Too Much, The (Alfred Hitchcock 1956) 112, 286.

Many Happy Returns (1934) 323; 86, 232.

Marching Along. See *Stars and Stripes Forever.*

Mardi Gras (1958) 185; 42, 350, 427.

Margie (1946) 251; 25, 88, 349, 508.

Marianne (1929) 276; 53, 108, 141, 163.

Marie Galante (1934) 251; 341.

Marjorie Morningstar (Irving Rapper 1958) 145, 245, 490, 502.

Mark of the Renegade (Hugo Fregonese 1951) 73, 336.

Marshmallow Moon. See *Aaron Slick from Pumkin Crick.*

Mary Lou (1948) 128; 402.

Mary Poppins (Robert Stevenson 1965) 9, 11, 254, 321, 440, 477.

Masquerade in Mexico (1946) 273; 135, 260.

Mayor of Forty-fourth Street (1942) 189; 24, 68, 343, 394, 441.

Maytime (1937) 276; 138, 238, 298, 410.

Meet Danny Wilson (Joseph Pevney 1952) 447.

Meet Me after the Show (1951) 424; 78, 105, 186, 230, 404, 461, 482.

Meet Me at the Fair (Douglas Sirk 1953) 96, 297.

Meet Me in Las Vegas/Viva Las Vegas (1956) 417; 23, 60, 69, 73, 96, 101, 110, 221, 257, 275, 292, 360, 362, 395, 447, 455.

Meet Me in St. Louis (1944) 331; 37, 46, 48, 139, 153, 156, 163, 169, 309, 354, 425, 455, 486.

Meet Me on Broadway (Leigh Jason 1946) 72, 146, 396.

Meet Miss Bobbysox (Glenn Tryon 1944) 24.

Meet the Baron (1933) 264; 133, 151, 322.

Meet the People (1944) 392; 4, 22, 145, 164, 199, 202, 209, 256, 262, 355, 374, 406, 425.

Melody and Moonlight (1940) 429; 126, 162, 461.

Melody Cruise (1933) 426; 184, 200.

Melody for Three (Earle C. Kenton 1941) 5.

Melody for Two (Louis King 1937) 129, 356, 437, 487, 498.

Melody Girl. See *Sing Dance and Plenty Hot.*

Melody Inn. See *Riding High* (1943).

Melody in Spring (1934) 323; 450.

Melody Lane (1941) 259; 358.

Melody Maker (William Berke 1946) 321.

Melody Parade (1943) 128.

Melody Ranch (1940) 429; 133, 329, 461.

Melody Time (Cartoon 1948) 10, 11, 111, 265, 503.

Member of the Wedding (Fred Zinnemann 1953) 488.

Memory for Two (1945) 291; 200.

Me Natalie (Fred Coe 1969) 303.

Merry Andrew (1958) 249; 72, 242, 275, 388, 444.

Merry-go-round of 1938 (1937) 93; 2, 256, 322.

Merry Monahans, The (1944) 259; 39, 353, 356, 423.

Merry Widow, The (1934) 294; 74, 202, 238, 298, 327.

Merry Widow, The (Curtis Bernhardt 1952) 78, 258, 281, 295, 327, 362, 482, 490.

My Best Girl (1944) 304; 501.

My Blue Heaven (1950) 255; 13, 37, 96, 105, 173, 186, 327, 349, 444, 472, 489.

My Dream Is Yours (1949) 95; 24, 37, 67, 112, 164, 213, 383, 487.

My Fair Lady (1964) 92; 9, 177, 201, 216, 288, 360, 382, 459.

My Favourite Brunette (1947) 352; 106, 220, 260.

My Favourite Spy (Tay Garnett 1942) 479, 504.

My Favourite Spy (1951) 323; 220.

My Friend Irma (1949) 307; 85, 286, 297, 308, 498.

My Friend Irma Goes West (Hal Walker 1950) 286, 297, 308, 498.

My Gal Loves Music (1944) 285; 24.

My Gal Sal (1942) 93; 82, 211, 261, 349, 360, 387, 404, 445.

My Heart Goes Crazy. See *London Town*.

My Lips Betray (John Blystone 1933) 40, 204.

My Little Chickadee (1940) 76; 492.

My Lucky Star (1938) 115; 109, 137, 183, 215, 222, 394.

My Man (1929) 315; 49.

Myra Breckinridge (Michael Sarne 1970) 145, 492.

My Sister Eileen (1955) 385; 140, 158, 170, 272, 274, 388, 404, 456, 461.

Mystery in Mexico (1948) 500; 479.

My Weakness (1933) 57; 204, 404, 495.

My Wild Irish Rose (1947) 57; 82, 213, 340, 383.


Nancy Goes to Rio (1950) 276; 68, 85, 237, 332, 362, 376, 438, 450, 455.

Naughty But Nice (1939) 142; 326, 374, 439, 487.

Naughty Marietta (1935) 478; 104, 138, 181, 298.

Naughty Nineties, The (1945) 506.

Navy Blues (1941) 19; 67, 195, 326, 353, 390, 431, 439.

Nearly Eighteen (1943) 128; 458.

Neptune's Daughter (1949) 58; 24, 94, 170, 252, 287, 336, 412, 448, 455, 497.

Never a Dull Moment (1943) 285; 265, 398.

Never a Dull Moment (1950) 307; 132, 408, 502.

Never Give a Sucker an Even Break/ What a Man (1941) 76; 228.

Never Say Die (1939) 352; 220, 387, 390, 404.

Never Steal Anything Small (Charles Lederer 1959) 59, 174, 236, 503.

New Faces of 1937 (Leigh Jason 1937) 52, 145, 217, 329.

New Moon, The (John Cromwell 1930) 197, 338, 410, 470.

New Moon (1940) 276; 105, 138, 197, 298, 410.

New Movietone Follies of 1930 (Benjamin Stoloff 1930) 84.

New Orleans (Arthur Lubin 1947) 14, 24.

New York Town (1941) 483; 300, 310, 381.

Niagara (Henry Hathaway 1953) 335.

Nice Girl? (1941) 435; 134, 362.

Night and Day (1946) 95; 82, 213, 310, 371, 383, 431, 446, 471, 504.

Night at Earl Carroll's, A (Kurt Neumann 1940) 218, 287.

Night at the Opera, A (Sam Wood 1935) 53, 163, 235.

Night Club Girl (1945) 76; 116.

Night Is Young, The (Dudley Murphy 1935) 197, 327, 351, 410, 422.

Night Song (John Cromwell 1947) 63.

Night They Raided Minsky's, The (William Friedkin 1969) 256, 475.

Nitwits, The (1935) 452; 151, 186, 322.

Nob Hill (Henry Hathaway 1945) 2, 35, 68, 322, 386.

Nobody's Baby (Gus Meins 1937) 246, 401.

Nocturne (1946) 306; 25, 386.

No Leave No Love (Charles Martin 1946) 24, 37, 123, 145, 164, 231, 322, 362, 415, 455, 468, 498.

Romeo and Juliet (Paul Czinner 1965) 23.

Rookies. See *Buck Privates*.

Rookies on Parade/Jamboree (1941) 429; 24, 60, 72, 461, 498.

Rosalie (1937) 478; 41, 138, 139, 313, 371, 375.

Rose Marie (1936) 478; 104, 138, 166, 181, 197, 235, 298.

Rose Marie (1954) 278; 15, 31, 39, 166, 197, 243, 256, 258, 455.

Rose of the Rancho (Marion Gering 1936) 40, 387, 404.

Rose of Washington Square (1939) 389; 143, 149, 150, 183, 234, 394.

Rosie (David Lowell Rich 1967) 422.

Rosie the Riveter (1944) 429; 162, 461.

Roustabout (John Rich 1964) 379.

Royal Flush. See *Two Guys from Milwaukee*.

Royal Wedding/Wedding Bells (1951) 123; 16, 68, 139, 163, 190, 262, 268, 367, 376.

Rumba (Marion Gering 1935) 386, 387, 404, 439.

Sadie McKee (Clarence Brown 1934) 53, 89, 163.

Safety in Numbers (1930) 430; 54, 408, 495.

Sailor Beware (Hal Walker 1952) 225, 308.

Sailor's Luck (1933) 485; 131.

Sailors on Leave (Herbert Dalmass 1941) 287, 414, 461.

St. Benny the Dip (Harry Lee Danziger 1951) 208.

St. Louis Blues (1939) 485; 193, 260, 262, 287.

St. Louis Blues (Allen Reisner 1958) 20, 82, 154.

Sally (John Francis Dillon 1929) 129, 247, 330.

Sally Irene and Mary (1938) 435; 24, 109, 133, 149, 183, 222, 312, 389, 394.

Salome (William Dieterle 1953) 211.

Salt and Pepper (Richard Donner 1968) 110, 268.

Saludos Amigos (Norman Ferguson 1943) 11.

Salute for Three (1943) 344; 127, 141, 461.

San Antonio Rose (1941) 259; 116, 162.

San Fernando Valley (John English 1944) 372.

San Francisco (1936) 478; 53, 139, 163, 298, 414.

San Quentin (1937) 19; 129, 439, 487.

Sap from Syracuse, The (1930) 462; 190, 199, 353, 409.

Sarge Goes to College (Will Jason 1947) 377.

Sarong Girl (1943) 128.

Say It With Songs (1929) 19; 52, 117, 214, 234.

Sayonara (1957) 290; 32, 336, 383.

Say One for Me (Frank Tashlin 1959) 60, 90, 395, 479.

Scared Stiff (1953) 307; 308, 332.

Scatterbrain (Gus Meins 1940) 61, 160.

Sea Legs (Victor Heerman 1930) 353, 416.

Second Chorus (1940) 373; 16, 24, 326, 360.

Second Fiddle (1939) 263; 32, 212, 215, 475.

Second Greatest Sex, The (1955) 307; 88, 179, 256, 388.

Secret Life of Walter Mitty, The (1947) 323; 152, 180, 242, 316.

See Here Private Hargrove (George Blair 1944) 287.

See My Lawyer (1945) 76.

Senorita from the West (Frank Strayer 1945) 235.

Sensations of 1945 (1944) 457; 24, 375, 473.

Serenade (1956) 304; 267.

Seven Brides for Seven Brothers (1954) 123; 15, 72, 94, 100, 116, 118, 156, 178, 181, 243, 249, 252, 326, 368, 376, 388, 425.

Seven Days Ashore (1944) 17; 316, 321.

Seven Days Leave (1942) 493; 22, 24, 287, 321, 322, 486, 500.

Seven Hills of Rome, The (1958) 417; 267, 455.

Seven Little Foys, The (Melville Shavelson 1955) 59, 68, 220.

Seven Sinners (Tay Garnett 1940) 119, 218, 287, 362.

Seven Sweethearts (1942) 43; 164, 188, 262, 362, 490.

Shady Lady (George Waggner 1945) 358, 446.

Shall We Dance? (1937) 426; 16, 33, 175, 176, 360, 409.

She Couldn't Say No (1930) 19; 129, 192.

She Done Him Wrong (Lowell Sherman 1933) 387, 404, 492.

She Has What It Takes (1943) 26; 146.

Sheik Steps Out, The (Irving Pichel 1937) 351.

She Learned about Sailors (1934) 307; 149, 495.

She Loves Me Not (1934) 352; 90, 183, 387, 394, 404, 431.

She Married a Cop (Sidney Salkow 1939) 164, 262, 391, 423.

She's a Sweetheart (1944) 291; 72, 162, 224, 361.

She's Back on Broadway (1953) 125; 178, 213, 316, 347, 383, 505.

She's My Lovely. See *Get Hep to Love*.

She's Working Her Way through College (1952) 223; 60, 130, 178, 213, 316, 347, 383, 505.

Shine On Harvest Moon (1944) 57; 67, 143, 305, 340, 383, 439, 498.

Ship Ahoy (1942) 58; 15, 24, 94, 199, 256, 262, 355, 375, 447, 448, 455.

Ship Cafe (1935) 155; 50.

Shipmates (Harry Pollard 1930) 141.

Shipmates Forever (1935) 43; 129, 244, 369, 487.

Shocking Miss Pilgrim, The (1947) 432; 175, 176, 186, 208, 349, 436.

Shooting High (1940) 189; 359, 501.

Shoot the Works (1934) 419; 183, 353, 387, 394, 404, 439.

Show Boat (Harry Pollard 1929) 197, 247.

Show Boat (James Whale 1936) 132, 197, 235, 247, 341, 403, 499.

Show Boat (1951) 443; 6, 70, 118, 139, 163, 168, 177, 188, 197, 229, 243, 247, 412, 425.

Show Business (1944) 306; 62, 109, 337, 343.

Show Girl in Hollywood (1930) 278; 234, 244.

Show of Shows, The (John Adolfi 1929) 55.

Silk Stockings (1957) 302; 16, 30, 73, 163, 177, 292, 342, 357, 360, 371, 382.

Silver Skates (1943) 182; 21, 30.

Sincerely Yours (1955) 125; 284.

Sing a Jingle/Lucky Days (1944) 285; 235.

Sing and Be Happy (James Tinling 1937) 109, 312.

Sing Another Chorus (1941) 259; 126, 162.

Sing Baby Sing (1936) 263; 149, 246, 312, 389, 398, 495.

Sing Boy Sing (1958) 144; 427.

Sing Dance and Plenty Hot/Melody Girl (Lew Landers 1940) 52, 126, 461.

Sing for Your Supper (1941) 26; 60, 72, 146, 408.

Singing Fool, The (1929) 19; 52, 117, 214, 234.

Singing in the Corn (1946) 291; 61, 402.

Singing Kid, The (William Keighley 1936) 13, 83, 199, 213, 234, 437.

Singing Marine, The (1937) 142; 31, 129, 326, 374, 487, 504.

Singing Nun, The (1966) 255; 395.

Singing Sheriff, The (1944) 182; 24, 116.

Singin' in the Rain (1952) 123, 245; 23, 53, 73, 80, 139, 163, 177, 194, 198, 209, 311, 339, 356, 395, 415, 425.

Sing Me a Love Song (1936) 142; 129, 439, 487.

Sing Neighbour Sing (1944) 319.

Sing while You Dance (D. Ross Lederman 1946) 402.

Sing Your Way Home (1945) 304; 195, 321, 503.

Sing Your Worries Away (1942) 462; 137, 206, 246, 256, 394.

Sing You Sinners (1938) 419; 56, 63, 90, 248, 287, 300, 334, 356.

Sis Hopkins (1941) 429; 24, 61, 210, 287, 461.

Sitting Pretty (Harry Joe Brown 1933) 183, 195, 353, 389, 394, 409.

Six Lessons from Madame LaZonga (John Rawlins 1941) 334, 480.

Skidoo (1969) 378; 18, 71, 411, 436.

Skirts Ahoy! (1952) 263; 35, 37, 68, 275, 362, 395, 455, 476, 487, 497.

Sky's the Limit, The (Edward H. Griffith 1943) 13, 16, 279, 326.

Sleeping Beauty (Cartoon 1959) 11.

Sleepy Lagoon (1943) 429; 61, 111.

Sleepy Time Gal (1942) 407; 61, 461.

Slightly French (Douglas Sirk 1949) 7, 229, 260, 402.

Slightly Terrific (1944) 76.

Small Town Girl (Leslie Kardos 1953) 31, 51, 252, 329, 362, 376, 382, 404, 476.

Smart Blonde (1936) 319; 437, 504.

Smartest Girl in Town, The (1936) 429; 151, 280, 450.

Smart Politics. See *Campus Sleuth.*

Smash Up/A Woman Destroyed (Stuart Heisler 1947) 2, 177, 210, 322.

Smiling Irish Eyes (1929) 435.

Smiling Lieutenant, The (1931) 294; 74, 156.

Smilin' Through (1941) 43; 298.

Snow White and the Seven Dwarfs (Cartoon 1937) 11, 70.

Society Lawyer (1939) 306; 54, 139, 181.

So Dear to My Heart (Harold Schuster 1948) 105.

So Long Letty (1929) 19; 192.

Sombrero (Norman Foster 1953) 73, 94, 237, 336, 360.

Somebody Loves Me (1952) 46; 143, 225, 229, 432.

Some Like It Hot (George Archainbaud 1939) 24, 220, 262, 287, 414.

Some Like It Hot (Billy Wilder 1959) 78, 118, 274, 335, 386.

Something for the Boys (1944) 434; 2, 35, 68, 81, 219, 287, 322, 332, 445.

Something in the Wind (Irving Pichel 1947) 134, 190, 356, 404, 499.

Something to Shout About (1943) 389; 7, 36, 73, 171, 353, 371.

Something to Sing About (1937) 430; 59.

Song and Dance Man (1936) 136.

Song for Miss Julie, A (William Rowland 1945) 23, 414.

Song Is Born, A (1948) 207; 14, 24, 63, 116, 180, 242, 316.

Song of Love (Clarence Brown 1947) 69, 82.

Song of My Heart (Benjamin Glazer 1948) 82.

Song of Norway (1970) 457.

Song of Russia (1944) 389.

Song of Scheherazade (Walter Reisch 1947) 82.

Song of Songs (1933) 302; 119, 218.

Song of the Buckaroo (Al Herman 1939) 146.

Song of the Flame (1930) 91; 175, 197.

Song of the Islands (1942) 264; 183, 186, 349, 353, 360, 487.

Song of the Open Road (S. Sylvan Simon 1944) 376.

Song of the Sarong (Harold Young 1945) 116.

Song of the South (Harve Foster 1946) 11, 86, 105, 232, 503.

Song of the Thin Man (1947) 58; 412.

Song of the West (1930) 142; 40, 197, 433, 507.

Song O' My Heart (1930) 43.

Song to Remember, A (1945) 483; 82, 227, 456.

Song without End (1960) 92, 483; 82, 456.

Son of Paleface (Frank Tashlin 1952) 220, 286, 421.

Sons O'Guns (1936) 19; 38, 83, 129, 369, 437, 487.

Sorrowful Jones (1949) 263; 22, 220, 286.

So This Is College (Sam Wood 1929) 141, 352.

So This Is Love/The Grace Moore Story (1953) 125; 143, 188.

So This Is Paris (1955) 385; 113, 174, 179, 347.

Sound Off (1952) 385; 140, 411.

Sound of Music, The (1964) 500; 9, 72, 139, 177, 197, 254, 271, 318, 406.

South of Dixie (1944) 506.

South Pacific (1958) 290; 105, 173, 177, 197, 349, 383, 406, 436.

South Sea Sinner/East of Java (1950) 223; 284.

Spawn of the North (Henry Hathaway 1938) 260, 262, 287.

Speedway (1968) 465; 379.

Spinout/California Holiday (1967) 465; 327, 379.

Spree (1967) 273; 101, 337, 384.

Spring Is Here (John Francis Dillon 1930) 202, 406, 487.

Spring Parade (1942) 255; 134, 362.

Spring Reunion (Robert Pirosh 1957) 225.

Springtime in the Rockies (1942) 93; 24, 183, 186, 192, 332, 349, 360, 363, 487.

Stage Door Canteen (1943) 43; 21, 24, 41, 129, 202, 222, 230, 270, 328, 334, 406, 488.

Stage Fright (Alfred Hitchcock 1950) 119, 371.

Stage Mother (Charles Brabin 1933) 53, 163.

Stage Struck (1936) 31; 13, 199, 213, 374.

Stand Up and Cheer (Hamilton Mac-Fadden 1934) 25, 40, 52, 131, 359, 466.

Star!/Those Were the Happy Times (1968) 500; 9, 60, 72, 143, 209, 249, 371, 479.

Star Dust (1940) 264; 183, 192, 212, 363.

Star for a Night (1936) 434; 359.

Star Is Born, A (1954) 92; 13, 67, 139, 169 176, 203, 213, 269, 311.

Starlift (1951) 115; 59, 112, 178, 200, 213, 301, 316, 347, 383, 504, 505.

Star Maker, The (1939) 115; 56, 82, 90, 334, 349.

Star Said No, The. See *Callaway Went Thataway*.

Stars and Stripes Forever/Marching Along (1952) 255; 15, 82, 349, 472.

Stars Are Singing, The (1953) 465; 77, 286, 325.

Stars on Parade (Lew Landers 1944) 361.

Stars over Broadway (William Keighley 1935) 31, 83, 129, 391, 468, 487.

Star Spangled Rhythm (1942) 307; 8, 13, 23, 45, 90, 99, 106, 121, 127, 177, 210, 220, 225, 233, 260, 297, 310, 326, 344, 374, 396, 509.

Start Cheering (1938) 407; 98, 106, 133, 456.

State Fair (1945) 264; 35, 88, 177, 197, 208, 349, 406, 436, 499.

State Fair (Jose Ferrer 1962) 12, 42, 68, 105, 107, 149, 197, 349, 406.

State Police (John Rawlins 1938) 337.

Stay Away Joe (Peter Tewkesbury 1968) 379.

Step Lively (1944) 493; 60, 105, 113, 343, 447, 461.

Stepping Out (1930) 392; 141, 192.

Stepping Sisters (1932) 150.

Stingaree (William Wellman 1934) 132, 238.

Stolen Harmony (Alfred Werker 1935) 183, 386, 394.

Stooge, The (1953) 465; 153, 308.

Stop the World I Want to Get Off (Philip Saville 1966) 348.

Stop, You're Killing Me (1953) 115; 178.

Stork Club, The (Hal Walker 1945) 60, 63, 117, 121, 225, 394, 461, 490.

Stormy Weather (1943) 457; 8, 68, 221, 405, 436, 488.

Story of Three Loves, The (1953) 331; 23, 64, 412, 415.

Story of Vernon and Irene Castle, The (1939) 373; 16, 33, 70, 84, 143, 409, 500.

Stowaway (1936) 435; 117, 149, 183, 394, 466.

Straight Place and Show/They're Off (1938) 57; 328, 359, 398.

Street Girl, The (1929) 419; 79, 280, 353.

Strictly Dishonourable (Norman Panama & Melvin Frank 1951) 209, 237, 272, 366, 399.

Strictly Dynamite (1934) 352; 2, 133, 145, 262, 480.

Strictly in the Groove (Vernon Keays 1942) 212, 356.

Strike Me Pink (1936) 465; 6, 13, 52, 62, 180, 328, 349.

Strike Up the Band (1942) 31; 139, 153, 163, 169, 237, 331, 377, 411, 425, 455.

Strip, The (Leslie Kardos 1951) 14, 68, 101, 157, 283, 362, 411, 455.

Striptease Lady. See Lady of Burlesque.

Student Prince, The (1954) 469; 39, 51, 267, 281, 295, 360, 362, 410, 455.

Student Tour (1934) 392; 53, 133, 138, 163, 186, 391.

Subterraneans, The (Ranald MacDougall 1960) 64, 163, 382.

Sultan's Daughter, The (1944) 128.

Summer Holiday (1948) 302; 37, 46, 113, 163, 181, 209, 314, 411, 425, 486, 487.

Summer Love (Charles Haas 1958) 174, 303.

Summer Magic (James Neilson 1963) 440.

Summer Stock/If You Feel like Singing (1950) 486; 45, 68, 72, 85, 113, 139, 169, 183, 190, 245, 253, 362, 367, 445, 487.

Sunbonnet Sue (1945) 344; 391, 458.

Sun Comes Up, The (1949) 469; 295, 298, 382.

Sunny (1930) 435; 197, 247, 330.

Sunny (Herbert Wilcox 1941) 41, 65, 197, 247, 346.

Sunny Side of the Street (1951) 385; 25, 257.

Sunny Side Up (1929) 57; 52, 117, 148, 150, 172, 214, 359.

Sun Valley Serenade (1941) 223; 24, 25, 102, 109, 177, 183, 215, 363, 487.

Susan Slept Here (Frank Tashlin 1954) 374, 395.

Suspense (1946) 474; 30.

Swanee River (1939) 263; 7, 68, 82, 234.

Sweater Girl (William Clemons 1942) 45, 233, 287, 377, 461.

Sweet Adeline (1935) 278; 83, 132, 197, 247, 391, 437.

Sweet and Low Down (1944) 315; 24, 25, 183, 205, 334, 353.

Sweet Charity (1969) 158; 110, 151, 299, 336.

Sweet Genevieve (1947) 128; 241, 372, 402.

Sweetheart of the Campus (Edward Dmytryk 1941) 217, 244.

Sweetheart of the Fleet (1942) 26; 109, 146.

Sweetheart of Sigma Chi (1933) 306; 186.

Sweetheart of Sigma Chi (Jack Bernhard 1946) 60, 224, 391, 461.

Sweethearts (1938) 478; 41, 138, 298.

Sweethearts of the U.S.A./Sweethearts on Parade (Lew Collins 1944) 327.

Sweethearts on Parade (1944). See Sweethearts of the U.S.A.

Sweethearts on Parade (1953) 136.

Sweetie (1929) 474; 105, 240, 353, 495.

Sweet Music (1935) 189; 83, 145, 213, 341, 450, 475, 503.

Sweet Rosie O'Grady (1943) 93; 183, 186, 316, 349, 360, 391, 487.

Swinger, The (1966) 443; 12, 382.

Swing Fever (1944) 493; 24, 52, 145, 164, 168, 221, 314, 455.

Swing High (1930) 429; 182.

Weekend at the Waldorf (1945) 276; 145, 231, 253, 409.

Weekend in Havana (1941) 264; 149, 183, 332, 334, 349, 363, 487.

Weekend Pass (1944) 506.

Wee Willie Winkie (John Ford 1937) 349, 466.

Welcome Stranger (1947) 352; 56, 90, 444, 479.

We're in the Army Now. See *Pack Up Your Troubles*.

We're in the Money (1935) 142; 38, 391, 503.

We're No Angels (1955) 95; 218.

We're Not Dressing (1934) 465; 90, 105, 139, 183, 328, 394.

West Point Story/Fine and Dandy (1950) 115; 59, 60, 112, 213, 301, 316, 347, 383, 461.

West Side Story (1961) 400, 500; 23, 34, 69, 72, 147, 177, 190, 254, 271, 339, 449, 463, 502.

What a Way to Go! (J. Lee Thompson 1964) 80, 245, 299, 308, 436, 477.

What Lola Wants. See *Damn Yankees*.

What Price Melody? See *Lord Byron of Broadway*.

What's Buzzin' Cousin? (1943) 26; 8, 24, 116, 329.

What's Cooking? (1942) 76; 10, 24, 116, 162, 228, 356, 358, 388.

When a Girl's Beautiful (1947) 319; 229, 368, 402.

When Johnny Comes Marching Home (1942) 259; 116, 162, 228, 235, 356, 423.

When Love Is Young (1937) 333; 2, 54, 322.

When My Baby Smiles at Me (1948) 264; 96, 183, 186, 206, 230, 345, 349, 353, 472.

When the Boys Meet the Girls (Alvin Ganzer 1965) 14, 161, 175, 176, 241, 284, 380.

When You're In Love (Robert Raskin 1937) 151, 247, 338, 349.

When You're Smiling (1950) 429; 24, 257.

Where Do We Go from Here? (1945) 389; 205, 279, 300, 436, 445, 491.

Where's Charley? (1952) 57; 41, 249, 287, 324.

Where the Boys Are (1960) 282; 161, 362, 455.

White Christmas (1954) 95; 6, 32, 69, 77, 90, 121, 177, 242, 481.

Who Done It? (Earle C. Kenton 1942) 116.

Who Killed Gail Preston? (Leon Barsha 1938) 211.

Whoopee (1930) 165; 31, 62, 180, 186, 349.

Why Bring That Up? (1929) 1; 54, 86, 404, 495.

Wild Blue Yonder, The/Thunder across the Pacific (1951) 136; 200.

Wild Gold (1934) 307; 40, 437, 472.

Wild in the Country (Philip Dunne 1961) 379.

Wine Women and Song (Herbert Brenon 1933) 84, 396, 464.

Wintertime (John Brahm, 1943) 24, 53, 215, 261, 353, 404.

With a Song in My Heart (1952) 264; 105, 143, 210, 327, 349, 436, 472, 489.

Witness for the Prosecution (Billy Wilder 1958) 119.

Wizard of Oz, The (Victor Fleming 1939) 13, 28, 41, 83, 105, 139, 143, 163, 169, 195, 199, 256, 278, 415.

Wolf Song, The (Victor Fleming 1929) 79, 480.

Woman Destroyed, A. See *Smash Up*.

Wonder Bar (1934) 19; 31, 114, 129, 234, 369, 374, 487.

Wonderful World of the Brothers Grimm, The (1963) 282; 463, 508.

Wonder Man (1945) 223; 152, 180, 213, 242, 316, 481.

Wonder of Women, The (Clarence Brown, 1929) 79.

Words and Music (1948) 465; 4, 6, 23,